PAGAN FAMILY VALUES

THE NEW AND ALTERNATIVE RELIGIONS SERIES
General Editors: Timothy Miller and Susan J. Palmer

Hare Krishna Transformed
Burke Rochford, Jr.

Transcendent in America:
Hindu-Inspired Meditation Movements as New Religion
Lola Williamson

Prophets and Protons: New Religious Movements and Science
in Late Twentieth-Century America
Benjamin E. Zeller

Digital Jesus: The Making of a New Christian Fundamentalist
Community on the Internet
Robert Glenn Howard

Saints under Siege:
The Texas State Raid on the Fundamentalist Latter Day Saints
Edited by Stuart A. Wright and James T. Richardson

Pagan Family Values: Childhood and the Religious Imagination
in Contemporary American Paganism
S. Zohreh Kermani

Pagan Family Values

*Childhood and the Religious Imagination
in Contemporary American Paganism*

S. Zohreh Kermani

NEW YORK UNIVERSITY PRESS
New York and London

NEW YORK UNIVERSITY PRESS
New York and London
www.nyupress.org

© 2013 by New York University
All rights reserved

References to Internet websites (URLs) were accurate at the time of writing.
Neither the author nor New York University Press is responsible for URLs that
may have expired or changed since the manuscript was prepared.

LIBRARY OF CONGRESS CATALOGING-IN-PUBLICATION DATA

Kermani, S. Zohreh.
Pagan family values : childhood and the religious imagination in contemporary American paganism / S. Zohreh Kermani.
pages cm. — (The new and alternative religions series)
Includes bibliographical references and index.
ISBN 978-0-8147-6974-4 (cl : alk. paper) — ISBN 978-1-4798-9460-4 (pbk. : alk. paper)
1. Neopaganism—United States. 2. Families—Religious life. I. Title.
BP605.N46K47 2013
299'.94—dc23   2012049432

A previous version of chapter 4 appeared as "Don't Eat the Incense: Children's Participation in Contemporary Pagan Practice," *The Pomegranate: The International Journal of Pagan Studies* 11, no. 2 (2009): 181–196. © Equinox Publishing Ltd 2009.

New York University Press books are printed on acid-free paper, and their binding materials are chosen for strength and durability. We strive to use environmentally responsible suppliers and materials to the greatest extent possible in publishing our books.

Manufactured in the United States of America
c 10 9 8 7 6 5 4 3 2 1
p 10 9 8 7 6 5 4 3 2 1

For my family

Contents

List of Figures	ix
Acknowledgments	xi
Introduction	1
1 Crafting History	25
2 Old Souls: Pagan Childhood	57
3 Parenting in Neverland	70
4 Don't Eat the Incense: Children in Ritual	89
5 A Room Full of FireFlies	114
6 My Dream Come True	153
Conclusion: Building Fairy Houses	181
Appendix A: "American Pagan Families and Family Values" Online Survey	189
Appendix B: "Second-Generation Pagans: Experiences and Opinions" Online Survey	193
Notes	197
Selected Bibliography	219
Index	223
About the Author	235

Figures

1. Little witches at a festival. Photo by Zohreh Kermani.   10
2. "Willow saying hello and good-bye to a September Monarch butterfly. . . . Maggie [Willow's twin sister] said the butterfly was blessing Willow." Photo and caption by Jess Gerrior.   16
3. Erin and Aisling's toddler-friendly circle. Photo by Zohreh Kermani.   92
4. "The ultimate fall ritual." Photo by Jess Gerrior.   108
5. Running the labyrinth. Photo by Zohreh Kermani.   111
6. Jess and Ryan hold Silverling Circle's talking stick. Photo by Zohreh Kermani.   123
7. A SpiralScout at a fall ritual. Photo by Jess Gerrior.   130
8. A FireFly in uniform. Photo by Jess Gerrior.   136
9. Exit signs at the Council of Magickal Arts festival. Photo by Lisa H. Dugger.   177
10. A SpiralScout places her fairy house in the woods. Photo by Zohreh Kermani.   182

Acknowledgments

An ethnographic project is entirely dependent on the goodwill and assistance of many people. I am profoundly grateful to the many Pagan families who provided me with access, information, and excellent conversation during my fieldwork. It seems an obvious point, but without the generous assistance of the Pagan communities in New Hampshire, Texas, Massachusetts, and Ohio and other Pagan families around the United States, this book would not exist. My deepest thanks go to the many families who warmly opened their homes and their lives to me during this project. Jess Gerrior of Silverling Circle has been an amazing resource and friend since my first awkward attempts at fieldwork. She welcomed me into her home, vouched for me when I seemed particularly suspicious, and has continued to provide photos, conversation, and support. I am grateful to her and to her wonderful children, Ryan, Maggie, and Willow. Erin and her daughter (who is called Aisling in this book) humored my many questions and invited me into their home to watch and participate in rituals, and I thank them for their kindness and hospitality. I am immensely grateful as well to the families of Silverling Circle, Spiral Bear Hearth, the Sea Dragons, the Sea Witches, and the First Church of Wicca for their unflagging kindness as I scribbled notes and asked too many (or not enough) questions. Atashih, Selene, Raven, and Deanna took me to my first Council of Magickal Arts gathering (and then my second, third, and fourth) and made me feel like family. Janet Callahan and Pete "Pathfinder" Davis provided full access to SpiralScouts International leader handbooks and other information and facilitated my earliest conversations with SpiralScouts leaders. I am also extremely grateful to the many anonymous and pseudonymous respondents to my surveys posted on WitchVox.com, eCauldron.com, and Beliefnet.com (and to the administrators of these websites, who allowed me to post these surveys). I hope that I have represented your words and your meanings accurately.

Many people at Harvard University offered challenging conversations, insightful questions, and encouragement for this project. The idea for this book initially arose during conversations with Robert A. Orsi, and his thoughtful comments, support, and friendship carried this idea forward. Ann Braude raised important questions throughout the writing of this manuscript that changed the ways I thought about Pagan children and adults, and her encouragement and insights are immensely appreciated. Stephen Mitchell offered conversation and commentary throughout the research and writing process. My work as a teaching fellow for his course on witchcraft and magic contributed to the historical grounding for my studies of contemporary Wiccan beliefs, and I am grateful for his consistently good humor and good coffee. Michael D. Jackson was kind enough to offer assistance at the eleventh hour, and this work benefitted significantly from his suggestions. Diana Eck also provided valuable information and discussions throughout the project, and I am grateful for her help.

I am indebted to numerous friends and colleagues at Harvard and elsewhere who offered comments and critiques on ideas for and drafts of this project. Atalia Omer, Alyssa Beall, and Rosemary Corbett have been wonderful conversation partners, and discussions of their fascinating research have benefited my own work. The members of the North American Religions Colloquium and the Ethnography of Religion Workshop at Harvard University provided helpful comments and suggestions on earlier versions of this work, and I am particularly grateful for comments and suggestions from Brandon Bayne, Lauren Brandt, David Charles, Heather Curtis, Curtis Evans,

Linford Fisher, Rachel Gordan, David Hall, David Hempton, Hillary Kaell, Jim Reed, John Seitz, Stephen Shoemaker, Josef Sorrett, Adrian Weimer, and Eliza Young Barstow. At Youngstown State University, Bruce Waller generously and graciously adjusted my teaching responsibilities to facilitate the completion of this manuscript. L. J. "Tess" Tessier got me started in the study of religion, and I continue to value her personal and professional friendship more than two decades later.

I am very grateful for the guidance from my editor at NYU Press, Jennifer Hammer, and to the two anonymous readers whose helpful suggestions improved the manuscript. Any remaining errors, of course, are mine. Generous financial assistance for the research and writing of this project was provided by Harvard University's William R. Hutchison American Religions Fellowship, the Center for the Study of World Religions Summer Research Grant, the Graduate Student Council Research Grant, and the Graduate School of Arts and Sciences Dissertation Completion Fellowship.

I am blessed with a rich network of family and friends whose support was instrumental in completing this book. My parents, Dr. Taghi T. Kermani and Shirl Kermani, have provided immeasurable support and unwavering love, faith, and encouragement. I thank my sisters, Venus Pallo and Joy Harkins, for their friendship and their sympathetic ears. Pati Carlson and Michael Sauvante have offered boundless love and support, and I am proud to be part of their family. I wish that I could have handed a copy of this book to Bob and Gery Carlson. I have also been fortunate to have an extended family that has offered emotional and practical support during every step of this project. I especially thank Tanya Alsberg, Jen Armstrong, Carolyn Berlin, Gretchen Brown, Christopher Byrne, Jasmyn Byrne, Rachael Byrne Riddick, Kathleen Dearing, Spencer Farkas, Maureen Frost, Elaine Habeger, Tina Mays Hyde, Scott Merisalo, Heather Moser, and Crissy Thompkins for their help and their friendship.

Finally, I am immensely grateful to my family, Devlyn Carlson and Hank Kermani-Carlson. My husband Dev's constant support and conversation have kept me (and the household) going for a long time now. He has eased my anxieties, provided keen intellectual insights, and done far more than his share of laundry. This book would not have been possible without him, and he has my wholehearted thanks and love. I began this project with a great appreciation for the children of others, but with no plans for my own. As this work nears completion, my son, Hank, is four, and every day with him is a delight. It is already hard to remember life without him, and I think this project was dedicated to him all along.

All children, except one, grow up.
—J. M. Barrie, *Peter Pan*, 1911

Introduction

Four-year-old Oliver is at his first SpiralScouts meeting, and he is obsessed with the apple that is just out of his reach. Last night, his mother, Carolyn, told him about SpiralScouts—that it was a scouting group kind of like the Boy Scouts, but for children whose families were Pagan. Oliver is not sure what a Pagan is, but he loves to talk about "growing his magic," and his mother is trying to raise him in a vaguely earth-based, religiously tolerant, "spiritual-but-not-religious" home. She told him that he would learn about magic at this meeting and that he would have fun, but Oliver has found that neither of these things happened, and now he is tired, bored, and hungry. He was confused by the adults who lit candles for no apparent reason at the beginning of the meeting and by the pledge that the older children repeated after the circle leader. When he was unsure about how to complete the first activity, a craft that required the scouts to gather in the circle leader's crowded dining room and cut coffee filters into snowflake shapes, the other circle leader took Oliver's coffee filter and safety scissors and made Oliver's snowflake himself. As the leader explained that the scouts were going to learn about nutrition, Oliver spotted a basket of apples on the counter and asked his mother for one. Already embarrassed by Oliver's earlier comments in front of the group ("You said this would be fun, but it's boring!"), his mother said no. As the other children looked at printed images of the food pyramid, Oliver's pleas for *just one apple* became increasingly desperate. The group took a snack break, but Oliver and his mother had forgotten to bring snacks. Despite Oliver's obvious desperation and his mother's obvious embarrassment, none of the adults or children offered the crying child juice or crackers, with most of the adults making a seemingly deliberate effort to avoid making eye contact with Oliver or his mother as his meltdown intensified. Carolyn took Oliver out of the room to try to calm him, but what had begun as a request for fruit had quickly become a tantrum of epic proportions. Oliver's mother ended up carrying the screaming, sobbing, shoeless child out of the house and into the car. Six years later, Oliver remembers that they never went back to retrieve his forgotten shoes.

Oliver's first (and last) visit to a SpiralScouts meeting was also my first attempt at fieldwork, but—unlike Oliver—I continued to visit other SpiralScouts groups in other states over the next four years. During these years, I puzzled over Oliver's experience, wondering what, if anything, this seemingly ordinary tantrum by a cranky four-year-old had to do with a study of the values and religious lives of Pagan families. Although the memory of this incident lingered, I decided not to include it in an earlier version of this book; it seemed too personal and too specific to shed light on larger understandings of Pagan childhood and the shared religious imaginations of Pagan adults and children. As the years went by, however, I found myself returning repeatedly to thoughts of Oliver's apple. Although the irony was apparent in the scene of a crying child begging for an apple while the adults around him ignore him in favor of a discussion of the food pyramid, there seemed to be a number of additional tensions and contradictions at play in Oliver's experience with SpiralScouts. Almost none of the other adults or children present at this meeting had spoken to Carolyn or Oliver, despite their obvious awkwardness and distress. The exception was Derek, a father of one of the other children, who attempted to engage Oliver in conversation by telling him, "I heard your mother say that you wanted to be a chef when you grow up. I have two words for you that will upset your mother: Magic Chef." When the four-year-old looked (understandably) confused, Derek began to explain the Magic Chef catalog to him, wistfully remarking, "You could easily spend forty thousand dollars there" (meaning, presumably, that an adult, not a preschooler, could spend this amount of money). Derek asked Oliver for his e-mail address, looked surprised when Oliver didn't have one, and advised him, "Get yourself a Hotmail address or something, and send me an e-mail and I'll e-mail you a bunch of recipes." In addition to Oliver's shoes and toy sword, Derek's e-mail address, written on the back of Oliver's copy of the food pyramid, was left behind during Oliver and his mother's loud—but carefully ignored—exit from their first and last SpiralScouts meeting.

This book examines the interactions between contemporary Pagan adults and children as they construct, inhabit, and negotiate understandings of childhood, adulthood, and the religious imagination. Although contemporary North American Pagan adults and children tend to emerge from a predominantly middle-class environment, Pagan adults' understandings of the religious and social worlds of childhood, relationships between parents and children, and memories and reconstructions of their own religious childhoods depart—sometimes radically—from those of mainstream Americans of majority religions. This book suggests that contemporary American Pagans draw on rich, diverse, mythologized understandings of their religion's history to construct a theoretical understanding of childhood as a realm of wonder, fantasy, and religious wisdom that adults frequently attempt to re-inhabit, through the experiences of their own children and through idealized presentations of themselves as "overgrown children" who retain contact with these magical childhood worlds. In many ways, Pagan adults construct a religious and relational tension in which they attempt to remain ideologically childlike while seeing chronological children as the bearers of an inherent religious wisdom. In many ways, Pagan adults displace Pagan children from the realm of childhood. The ways in which they do so both reflect and challenge mainstream patterns and understandings of parenting, childhood, and religious imaginations in the United States.

Pagans, Families, Values
Pagans

Pagans remain a numerical minority in the United States, although they maintain a significant and steadily increasing presence. This presence, however, is decidedly difficult to quantify. The American Religious Identification Survey (ARIS), a telephone poll of over 50,000

American households, identified 274,000 adult Wiccans and Pagans in 2001. Likewise, the Pluralism Project has estimated a Pagan presence in the United States of between 200,000 and 1,000,000.[1] Even some of the lower estimates of numbers of adherents would make Wicca the seventh-largest organized religion, or the tenth-largest religious grouping, in the United States.

Despite these numbers, there continues to be very little organizational structure among American Pagans. The sociologist Helen Berger interpreted the number of Pagan parents in the United States (more than 40% of those surveyed in her 2003 "Pagan census") to mean that the religion was on the verge of undergoing significant changes to accommodate the changing needs of new generations of Pagans.[2] Significantly, Berger observed the "routinization of spontaneity" in contemporary Paganism, which she had predicted a decade earlier. Berger distinguished this routinization from the classic Weberian model, noting that the lack of central doctrines and bureaucracy within contemporary Paganism altered the routinization process. She suggested that despite its unique trajectory, Paganism in the United States would seek greater legitimization and institutionalization as it adapted to successive generations. Although Berger's investigations of the religion as a whole provide a valuable contribution to the field of Pagan studies and the sociological study of new religions, the existence and extent of a routinized form of contemporary Paganism in the United States remains debatable. Pagans tend to eschew large-scale organization and deny routinization in their individual practice of the religion, which is often highly personalized. Longitudinal studies of Pagan children's religious practices, as these become available, may offer confirmation of the routinization Berger predicts, or they may indicate greater religious improvisation or attrition rates among second-generation Pagans. In either case, attention to the sociological and structural aspects of the religion provides a way to normalize contemporary Paganism within the study of religion, regardless of whether it actually reveals a trend toward routinization or organization among Pagans.

Berger notes that Weber explicitly excluded magical practitioners from his theory of routinization because of the apparent lack of magical "congregations." She argues that within contemporary Paganism, "it is not the magical qualities of charisma that are being routinized but the spontaneity and creativity of religious expression."[3] Like Weber, Émile Durkheim's work maintained a sense of the exceptionalism of magic among contemporary religions. Durkheim's assertion that "there is no Church of magic" reflects a similar understanding of magic as a private act rather than the "collective effervescence" that characterizes religion. Contemporary Paganism challenges this skepticism about the possibility of a magical community that is also a moral community of the sort that Durkheim considers "religious" and potentially offers a way to reconceptualize the possibility of a magical moral community. Rather than the solitary "magic society" Durkheim described, contemporary Paganism responds to the challenge of raising new generations by attempting to forge the "durable ties that make them members of a single moral body."[4] The moral and imaginative world of Pagan children is one area in which this potential becomes particularly evident. In a religion that lacks organizational and theological consistency, directing the religious and moral imaginations of children becomes one way of establishing a collective effort. The inclusion of children in contemporary Paganism has altered the religion in unforeseen ways, leading, for instance, to increased creativity in rituals and theology and a greater urgency to develop and explicate a clear moral framework.

Paganism's multiple and conflicting historiographies are the subject of chapter 1 of this book.[5] Briefly, the history of contemporary Paganism is usually linked to the "discovery" of Wicca by Gerald Gardner (1884–1964), a retired British civil servant and amateur anthropologist. Gardner's claims to have located and been initiated into a surviving pre-Christian coven of witches in the New Forest region of England in 1939 are an integral part of contemporary Pagan lore, although their veracity is questionable at best. Historians of the religion generally acknowledge that Gardner constructed the basic elements of modern Wicca with inspiration from Masonic and Rosicrucian sources as well as from Charles Leland and Margaret Murray's claims to have "discovered" surviving witch cults in the nineteenth century.[6] The beliefs and practices Gardner developed led to the modern form of Wicca that bears his name: a coven-based, initiatory practice emphasizing balance, duality, and the Goddess and God in equal partnership. Gardnerian Wicca was brought to the United States by Gardner's students, Raymond and Rosemary Buckland, in 1964, and many of its principles became the framework for contemporary American

Paganism. The historian Ronald Hutton contends that the history of contemporary Paganism has overemphasized Gardner's influence, but concedes that Gardner and his collaborators can nonetheless be considered the founders of modern Wicca.[7] Many contemporary Pagans seem to agree. More than one-third of the Pagans who explained the history of their religion to me specifically cited Gardner's influence, some commenting that he "brought the practices of paganism into the mainstream," "reconstructed" existing Pagan traditions, or "discovered" modern Wicca. Several respondents even offered lengthy and generally accurate accounts of Gardner's involvement in the early years of the religion.[8]

Contemporary Paganism is generally (although not always) understood by practitioners as an earth-based revival or a reconstruction of indigenous, prehistoric European religions. Pagan rituals are oriented around the "Wheel of the Year," a modern construction of the eight seasonal festivals of the Celtic year (the four solstices and equinoxes and four additional seasonal festivals, or Sabbats), with smaller rituals generally held at full moons (the Esbats). Like most aspects of Pagan belief and practice, views of the number and type of deities vary dramatically among covens and among individual Pagans (individuals who practice without a coven are sometimes called "Solitaries" or "Solitaires"). Many Pagans consider themselves polytheists or pantheists, although "traditional" forms of Wicca often worship a dualistic union of a female Goddess and a male God (usually with well-defined, culturally specific male and female attributes). Other versions (such as Dianic Wicca and Goddess feminism) maintain a relatively monotheistic belief in a single, supreme female Goddess. While American Pagans exhibit a stunning and confusing diversity of beliefs and practices, there are a number of beliefs that might be considered common to many (though, it bears repeating, not all) practitioners. These include recognition of the inherent sacredness of the natural world; an "ethic of freedom" that rejects the concepts of sin and salvation in favor of personal fulfillment (while minimizing harm to others); reverence for both male and female deities, as well as the divine within humans; and "creative performance of ritual." Many, if not most, Pagans can be said to share a belief in "a tolerant and pluralist society with maximum potential for individual choice and self-expression . . . [and] a concern for environmental issues."[9]

Given that American Pagans are adherents of a religion that self-consciously claims to sustain little internal consistency, in many ways, Pagans are remarkably homogeneous. Despite differing conceptions of divinity and religious practice, despite adamant contentions by many Pagans that their beliefs are more individually eclectic or more authentically reconstructionist or more esoteric than those of their neighbors, despite possessing only two explicit ethical codes (the Wiccan Rede and the Law of Return, discussed below), contemporary American Paganism—in all its varied paths and costumes—maintains a strikingly consistent moral world. In a Durkheimian sense, this collective moral world, which "abolishes the traditional Western distinction between religion and magic,"[10] might even be considered a "Church of magic," albeit a church that is unclaimed and unsupported by many of its members.

This book is grounded in an understanding of contemporary Paganism as a distinctly North American religion that assiduously maintains an oppositional identity among American religions at the same time that it strives for integration and normativity. The social, political, theological, and intellectual roots of contemporary North American Paganism are more firmly planted in nineteenth-century American alternative religions than in British Wicca or ancient and indigenous paganisms. Despite contemporary American Paganism's direct descent from the British Gardnerian variety, its introduction into the American milieu of the mid-1960s radically influenced its translation into an American religion; American Paganism in the twenty-first century bears only a cursory resemblance to its European antecedents. Much as Sarah Pike understood the Pagan festivals she studied as best contextualized within the American tradition of religious retreats, nineteenth-century evangelical camps, and Spiritualist conventions,[11] I contend that American Paganism is best understood as a distinctly, quintessentially American religion, one in a long line of alternative religions of dissent, opposition, and individual religious freedom that populate American religious history. These alternative religions have frequently been constructed by society and by traditional religious bodies as the "other"—dissenting, heretical, or dangerous. Perceptions of otherness and oppositional identities have also been internally constructed by alternative religions themselves as a way of garnering place and distinction in the competitive terrain of American religions. Laurence Moore's analysis of similar types of religious "outsiderhood" posits that this "language of dissent" has provided many American religious movements with a "characteristic way of inventing one's Americanness."[12] Like many of the religious movements Moore discusses, American Paganism maintains a complex and deeply ambivalent relationship with dominant American cultural paradigms, simultaneously resisting and craving routinization and inclusion. Despite its relatively consistent moral perspective and attempts at routinization, however, contemporary American Paganism maintains a highly individualized and oppositional ethos that resists full inclusion within American religions.

Family

I usually spend most of the time with my daddy. And he's the best. I love my daddy. Love him! He reads *Calvin and Hobbes* every night. One night we didn't read *Calvin and Hobbes*, and so the next night we read a month and a half, which is one month, and then half a month. I love Mommy. Deanna [Raven's little sister] is a very nice little girl. Also known as a pest. Is this thing on? I love Deanna. And here's Deanna, and then I'll tell you about me.
—Six-year-old Raven explaining her family, 2006

Trying to define family is horrendous.
—Atashih, Raven's father, 2006

At this point in the history of contemporary American Paganism, most Pagans are still late adolescent or adult converts to the religion, but the number of second-generation (and, less often, third-generation) Pagan children is growing. With the introduction of increasing numbers of second-generation children into the religion, many Pagans find it necessary to codify and clarify the religion's loose, individualized ethics into a coherent moral world for their children. This book considers the voices and experiences of these second-generation children and the kinds of moral and imaginative frameworks that are constructed in relationships between Pagan adults and children. Specifically, it considers the ways that contemporary American Paganism illuminates the religious imaginations and interactions of a particular segment of American adults and children as well as larger issues of childhood and religion in the United States. What are the experiences of the children who grow up within this decentralized, protean, and fantasy-laden new religion? What do Pagan views of childhood and children indicate about ways of being and religious imaginations? What about "children" as an ontological category makes this a reasonable site to reflect on the Pagan religious imagination? How does the category of "children" relate to the "real" children who inhabit these enchanted moral and religious worlds? Children are all too often overlooked in the study of religious phenomena, set apart from (or collapsed into the category of) adults, marginalized, or ignored. Pagan children's marginalization is exacerbated by their participation in a minority religion. Scholars of new religious movements tend to focus on mapping and understanding the beliefs and practices of adult practitioners. Children's experiences are often an afterthought, if they warrant attention at all. This project takes seriously the assertion that "looking at how children are raised in marginal spiritual groups will expand our ways of thinking about the social, psychological, moral, educational, and legal dimensions of family life."[13] As Robert Orsi has noted, children "are the very existence, duration, and durability of a particular religious world. . . . Children signal the vulnerability and contingency of a particular religious world and of religion itself, and in exchanges between adults and children about sacred matters the religious world is in play."[14] The relational sites within which Pagan children's religious imagination develops and Pagan childhood is constructed can illuminate the experiences and perspectives of both children and adults. In these interactions, tensions, fissures, and bonds between parents and children, the foundations of a Pagan religious imaginary are established.

Of course, this insight into the religious worlds of families and of adults and children in relationship is not limited to Paganism. The study of children's religious beliefs and experiences has the potential to illuminate the study of religions on a larger scale by documenting the beliefs and experiences of a neglected segment of the religious population, much as feminist methodologies have documented the importance of attention to women's voices. In the same way, the study of Pagan families can shed light on religious interactions and the interpersonal dimensions of childhood and religion in other American families. As I spent time with Pagan families at festivals, craft fairs, camp-outs,

Little witches at a festival. Photo by Zohreh Kermani.

and rituals, I learned that American Pagan families' lifestyles, for the most part, would not seem radically unfamiliar to many middle-class American Jewish or Christian families. Pagan parents and children eat dinner together, attend PTA meetings and soccer games, and participate in public and private holiday traditions. Contemporary Pagan family values may tilt slightly to the left of "average" Americans, but they emphasize fundamentally similar themes: family, responsibility, respect, integrity, patriotism. When I asked Pagan adults to describe their families in an online survey, many respondents made a point of describing their family as "standard," "traditional," or "normal." Several described their spouse's military service or their children's enrollment in public schools. One respondent wryly noted that his family included "myself, male, 35 . . . my wife, female (obviously), 33. 1 daughter who is 3. We are married and all live together and love each other, which makes us extremely weird . . . the only nuclear family we know."[15]

Interestingly, the tendency of American Pagans to gravitate slightly left of center is evident in some Pagans' descriptions of the factors that contribute to their family's "very American traditional life": selling organic produce and baked goods, living with multiple unrelated adult housemates, or embracing polyamorous relationships and lifestyles.[16] One survey respondent offered an example of this tension between "traditional" American values and the generally progressive and liberal values of American Pagan families: "We're pretty traditional: dad (43), mom (me—I'm 31), three kids (6, 4, 9 mos). We practice natural family planning (a la Catholicism, amusingly enough), extended breastfeeding, cosleeping, and attachment parenting."[17] In constructions and understandings of family—as in religion, parenting, education, and multiple areas of everyday life—Pagan ambivalence toward larger North American culture runs deep.

Values

Pagan practitioners and Pagan studies scholars generally agree that only two explicit moral codes form the basis for Wiccan ethics: the Wiccan Rede and the Law of Return (the latter is also known as the Threefold Law). In its most familiar form (and in typically rhyming, faux-archaic fashion), the Wiccan Rede states, "Eight words the Wiccan Rede fulfill: an it harm none, do what ye will." "Do what you will" is not generally interpreted by most Pagans as a license for self-centered hedonism, but rather as an exhortation to discover and fulfill one's personal destiny, providing it does not cause harm to others. It is usually understood to imply the need for individual accountability and responsibility. Many Pagan websites offer "exegeses" of the Wiccan Rede.[18]

The second moral tenet of Pagan (specifically Wiccan) morality, the Law of Return, is a variation on the concept "As ye sow, so shall ye reap" (again, the archaic structure is favored by many Wiccans). It suggests that every action, whether benevolent or harmful, returns to the actor three times over. Like the Wiccan Rede, its inclusion in contemporary Paganism probably comes most directly from Gardner's writings of the 1950s and 1960s. It is mentioned in 1971 as deriving from a line in a Gardnerian second-degree initiation ritual, "Learn, in witchcraft, you must ever give as you receive, but ever triple."[19] The law expands on the fundamental "harm none" premise of the rede, but it can be understood less as a moral code and more as a cosmological statement about the way the universe operates. Some Wiccans go so far as to equate the Law of Return with the Law of Gravity, contending that both operate impartially and universally. This interpretation tilts the Threefold Law's emphasis away from individual belief and toward the province of moral law.[20] Despite the brevity of these guidelines, Pagans recognize and model a range of moral and ethical behaviors in their daily lives. Children raised in Pagan households (or, often, in households with one Pagan parent) interpret, assimilate, and imitate adults' behaviors, with or without accompanying verbal instruction. Beyond these two basic codes, the moral landscape of contemporary Paganism remains virtually uncharted. This apparent lack of explicit moral guidance, in combination with ritual practices that are frequently unfamiliar to non-Pagans, has led many observers and critics to conclude that Paganism lacks a system of ethics—that it is fundamentally amoral, unethical, and hedonistic, and therefore easily dismissed. Many of the seemingly amoral and hedonistic conceptions of contemporary Paganism are likely the result of some of the more dubious personal practices of Aleister Crowley and Gerald Gardner as well as exaggerations of rituals based on re-imaginings of nature-based fertility rites.[21]

The phrase "Pagan family values," as used in this project, is an attempt to expand the concept of "family values" beyond the "traditional" values espoused by American religious and political conservatives. Since the use of the phrase by then Vice President Dan Quayle in 1992, it has come to be shorthand for support of "traditional" families—that is, nuclear families consisting of a heterosexual married couple and their biological, born-in-wedlock children. "Family values" is often used to reflect a political and social ideology that opposes same-sex marriage, legal abortion, feminism, and gender equality, among other issues. Pagan family values may not mirror these values, but the phrase is not an oxymoron.

Pagan family values expand on mainstream American values to include a redefinition and expansion of the "family," support for gender equality and civil rights, and a focus on adult sexuality that emphasizes personal responsibility over legislation. The values that Pagan parents teach to and model for their children include an ecological consciousness and respect for humans, animals, and the natural world (often envisioned as a "web" of connectedness). Self-reliance, independence, and personal religious choice are among the values prioritized within Pagan families. Despite intra-faith debates regarding the appropriate level of children's inclusion in the religion, most (although by no means all) Pagan parents make an effort to teach their children their religious beliefs, practices, and values, irrespective of whether they relate these values directly to their religion. When I asked Pagan parents directly about the values they felt compelled to teach their children, their answers were similar to those likely to be mentioned in almost any Jewish, Christian, or Muslim home: Pagans mentioned honesty, integrity, cleanliness, courtesy, responsibility, kindness, commitment, justice, and empathy. Certain values—respect (in general, but specifically respect for the earth and nature), tolerance, and the value of individuality, for instance—seemed to receive a disproportionately strong emphasis among Pagan parents. Over one-third of the respondents to an online survey on Pagan family values explicitly noted the importance of communicating to their children the need to respect the earth, nature, and other living things:

> I believe that children today need to learn to respect nature since as a society we are so separated from it [but] we still need it to survive. I teach my children the importance of recycling and cleaning up after yourselves at the park and not to litter. *(Wiccan mother of three)*

> That all life is sacred, and should be treated with respect. *(Pagan parent of two)*

> I want my children to have respect for others and for all life and the Earth Herself. *(Wiccan mother of three)*

Tolerance is a value that is frequently emphasized among Pagan parents, particularly in relation to respect for humans, animals, and the earth. The importance of religious tolerance in the lives of Pagan adults and children will be discussed in the following chapters, but its importance to the specific issue of Pagan family values cannot be overstated.

> I try to teach them to be good honest people. . . . I also try to teach them to respect others and what other people believe and to be tolerant of those beliefs. We are all individuals with our own paths, [and] we only have to answer for our own actions. (*Pagan mother of two*)

> Equality of all people, respect for all paths. We emphasize these especially. My oldest child attends a public school where she is in the racial/ethnic minority as well as religious, so this comes up frequently. (*Pagan mother of three*)

Some Pagan parents related the values they teach their children to explicitly Wiccan values:

> Love everyone. Love everything. Everything you do comes back to you 3x. If you do bad, you'll [receive] worse, but if you do good, the blessings will flow. (*Eclectic Pagan mother of two*)

> I guess the most common moral code among Wiccans is the Wiccan Rede. This states that you have free will to do as you like as long as it harms none. This can be interpreted in a number of ways. But, we discuss this often and how to apply it to our daily lives. We discuss how [our] actions will affect others. Not just humans but animals, plants, insects, and the Earth herself. This makes for good debate and offers a great opportunity to teach truthfulness, honor, kindness, etc. (*Wiccan mother of three and grandmother of one*)

In some cases, this emphasis on a specifically Pagan approach to values is accompanied by a rejection of "mainstream" values:

> My values are not those of mainstream society. Above all, I teach my children not to be sheep, but to be an individual, and use the brain they were given. Question, challenge, and decide for yourself what you believe and value. I also stress respect for the individual, and the planet.

And to stand up for themselves, and not allow others to make them feel bad for what and who they are. Amazingly, they have adopted my values, anyway. (*Pagan mother of four*)

Finally, a few Pagan parents rejected the question about values entirely, emphasizing the distinction between religion and a less formal type of morality:

Religion and moral values are not connected in our household. You don't teach through the threat of a bigger parent punishing you should you behave immorally. Morals are the product of acting in accordance with ideals. When we talk about deity, we assign it the qualities of our ideals. God is the mirror in which mankind reflects upon their own divinity. We see in God all the best things about ourselves. In order for God to embody these ideals, we first have to uphold the ideals to the best of our ability. Belief in the ideal has to come first. You don't take things that don't belong to you. Not because god said so, but because the consequences of doing it are going to involve corrective action on either your part, or by an outside party. (*Pagan parent of two*)

Moral values have nothing to do with religion. I teach my children that being ethical and moral has to do with standards that we set for ourselves for our honor and [conscience]. If a person needs a religion to define morality to them, then that person never had any to begin with. (*Wiccan father of three*)

Despite their varied responses to "mainstream" American values, Pagan parents, for the most part, strive to instill in their children fairly consistent values of tolerance, compassion, and responsibility that will remain with them as they grow to adulthood—regardless of the religion these children choose to practice as adults.

"Weren't *You* a Pagan When You Were a Kid?"

At one of the many SpiralScouts meetings I attended during research for this project, the children were given "officer" jobs as a way to increase the Scouts' sense of accountability toward the circle, the leaders, and

"Willow saying hello and good-bye to a September Monarch butterfly. . . . Maggie [Willow's twin sister] said the butterfly was blessing Willow." Photo and caption by Jess Gerrior.

the other scouts. Children volunteered or were selected by the leaders for the roles of "pledge officer," "snack officer," and "cleanup officer." As usual during the "business" part of many of these meetings, the children and leaders were seated in a circle on the floor while the Scouts' parents watched from chairs nearby. I sat on a folding chair next to Erin, scribbling field notes in my notebook, also as usual. After all the officer positions had been assigned, one of the scouts, a six-year-old named Ryan, exclaimed, "Wait, Z didn't get to be an officer!" I pointed to my notebook and said, "I can be the recording officer." Ryan looked doubtful for a moment, and then offered, "Well, you can be the hat and coat officer." For Ryan, my suggestion apparently seemed less practical than an (invented) office with the hefty responsibility of making sure scouts retrieved their personal belongings before leaving the meeting. Ryan was not alone in his uncertainty about my role in Silverling Circle or my status within the group. SpiralScouts children often seemed uncertain about how to understand my presence at their meetings, events, and homes. In Susan Ridgely's study of Catholic children's First Communion classes, she writes that her "in-between" status—not fully a "grown-up" as the children understood her, but clearly not one of the kids—became a key element in her relationship with the children she studied.[22] Like Ridgely, I found that the children often assumed that because I was clearly not a SpiralScouts parent or leader, I must be a larger, slightly awkward child—one who asked them too many questions about seemingly obvious things. For example, at another SpiralScouts meeting, the scouts made animal-shaped name tags and tried to guess which name tag each scout had made. When Jess asked, "Which kid seems most like a lion?" Ryan had pointed at me. Ryan's suggestion that I needed an officer position seemed to reflect this view.

Contemporary Paganism is particularly well suited to ethnographic research, and an ethnographic methodology has frequently been used as the most effective and appropriate means to approach this new religious movement. Paganism's fundamental and assiduously maintained decentralization produces radically individualized beliefs and practices within the larger tradition, providing rich material for ethnographic study. Ethnographic fieldwork for this project was conducted at several different sites. Between January 2006 and May 2007, I visited and interviewed families in New England, most of whom were affiliated with

SpiralScouts International, a Pagan children's scouting organization that is discussed in more detail in chapter 5. Silverling Circle, a large, active group of SpiralScouts families (equivalent to a troop in other scouting organizations), was initially the primary focus of my observations. Families belonging to Silverling Circle eventually branched off to form several new circles in the area (Silver Sapling Circle, the Seacoast Dragon Riders, and Spiral Bear Hearth), providing the opportunity to explore variations among developing SpiralScouts circles. Additional fieldwork was conducted with the (now defunct) First Church of Wicca (FCOW), which formed a SpiralScouts circle to meet the religious education needs of the church's children. I attended the FCOW's Sunday services and meetings of their SpiralScouts circle, the Duxbury Sea Witches.

In addition to these families in New England, I conducted participant observations and ethnographic interviews throughout 2006 and 2007 with the families of Spiral Winds Coven at the semi-annual Council of Magickal Arts festivals and in their homes. Fieldwork at these additional sites supplemented my analysis of the explicitly Pagan types of religious imaginations created and negotiated in SpiralScouts with a deeper understanding of the tensions that emerge in the religious and imaginative interactions and collaborations of adults and children in more quotidian contexts. In addition to unstructured conversations at meetings, festivals, events, camp-outs, and other sites, approximately ten Pagan children and twenty Pagan adults participated in formal ethnographic interviews, and approximately forty more children were present during my numerous participant observation experiences with SpiralScouts groups in 2006 and 2007. Most of the children interviewed and observed were in the three- to nine-year-old range (the SpiralScouts "FireFly" program level). Fieldwork was also conducted with half a dozen children between the ages of nine and fourteen.

Additional data on Pagan families were collected through an online survey of adult Pagans—the "American Pagan Families and Family Values" (APF&FV) survey (reproduced in appendix A)—which I developed in 2006 and posted (with permission from site administrators) to a number of websites frequented by Pagan adults, including the Witches' Voice (www.witchvox.com), Beliefnet (www.beliefnet.com), and the Cauldron: A Pagan Forum (www.ecauldron.com). The Internet has provided a vibrant site for researchers as well as for practitioners of contemporary Paganism, and scholars have explored the potential of the Internet as a "site" for virtual ethnography. The sociologist Douglas E. Cowan's study of Paganism on the Internet suggests that attention to online religious practices and communities can demonstrate "how new information spaces are being colonized by religion and its practitioners, how these spaces provide alternative, hitherto unavailable venues for the performance and instantiation of often marginalized religious identities, and how potential for the electronic evolution in religious traditions such as modern Paganism is supported by the very architecture and philosophy of the World Wide Web."[23] In this study, virtual methods, such as online surveys and e-mail conversations, supplemented traditional methods. Transcripts of in-person interviews, field notes, and written surveys were coded and categorized using the ATLAS.ti software program. During the course of fieldwork for this study, I attended four festivals hosted by the Council of Magickal Arts (CMA) in Texas as well as approximately forty events related to SpiralScouts or Pagan family activities. Attendance at these events provided a rich variety of general observations as well as the opportunity to interact informally with ten to twenty adults and children at each event.

In addition to these observations, informal interactions, and conversations, I conducted eleven formal, audio-recorded interviews with Pagan children and their parents (five of whom were interviewed at least twice) and twenty-two formal interviews with Pagan adults (eight of whom were interviewed multiple times). The APF&FV online survey yielded forty-four completed surveys in which Pagan adults wrote about their family's experiences related to their religious beliefs and practices. A second online survey targeting second-generation Pagan children—"Second-Generation Pagans: Experiences and Opinions" (reproduced in appendix B)—was completed by eight adolescents and young adults with parental supervision and consent. All fieldwork for this project, including in-person participant observations and the content and implementation of data collection through virtual sites, was approved by Harvard University's Institutional Review Board. The confidentiality of participants' identities was ensured in accordance with Harvard's Institutional Review Board and the American Anthropological Association's Code of Ethics. Surveys and requests for information on websites and online forums were posted with the approval of the site's owner or moderator. Throughout all of my encounters with Pagan parents and children at SpiralScouts meetings, Pagan festivals, and online forums, I identified myself as a non-Pagan (but "Pagan-friendly") academic and explained that my research focused on the experiences and values of Pagan families with children. In an effort to respect the privacy and agency of informants in this study, all children and adults were offered the opportunity to choose their own pseudonyms. Many chose to use their public magical names, some elected to let me choose a pseudonyms for them, and a few chose names for reasons known only to them. Names are a powerful thing among Pagans, and magical names, like names of deities, are not chosen, used, or shared lightly. With this in mind, when informants asked me to select their pseudonyms, I attempted to choose names that reflected the general meaning or tenor of their real names. In a few cases, adults whose public presence was a significant part of their life as a Pagan asked that I use their real names, and in these cases, I have complied with their wishes. Jess, the leader of SpiralScouts' Silverling Circle, was one of these people. Active in the local community and within the SpiralScouts organization, Jess sent me this response to my inquiry about her preferred pseudonym:

> As for use of my name—I used my full name when I coordinated Pagan Pride Day, and I include it in calendar listings and press releases for SpiralScouts, because using a pseudonym would mean admitting there is a danger of religious persecution, and I choose denial! . . . I understand and respect people's decision to protect their own names and those of their families—everyone has their reasons—but I do wish more people would use their real names in association with Pagan activities. Too often [pseudonyms] only perpetuate the public perception of Pagans as kooks, equivalent to hippies, communists, vegetarians, and other weirdos :).[24]

Jess was not alone in her desire to be recognized as a member of the Pagan community; similar sentiments were expressed by some of the children I spent time with for this study. One afternoon in 2006, I sat with the families of Spiral Winds coven in a shady gazebo at one of CMA's Samhain[25] festivals. I was accompanied by four children between the ages of five and eleven—Deanna, Raven, Cricket, and Stephen—and their parents. During a pause in our conversation, nine-year-old Cricket asked me, "Why do you ask us so many questions?" I told her that I was trying to learn what it was like to be a child growing up Wiccan, as they were, so that I could write about it. She asked, wide-eyed, "You're going to write about *us*? You mean we're going to be inside books?" She turned to Raven and exclaimed, "We're going to be inside books. She's going to write about what we say!" Stephen asked, "Can I be in a book?" and Raven shouted, "Me too!" I assured them that they would all be in the book, but not with their real names. Cricket's response was immediate and passionate: "No! I want them to know I'm a Pagan child!" Her mother smiled, but asked—despite her children's protests—that I use the children's magical names as pseudonyms. "They may think it's fine now . . . ," she added, her voice trailing off. The understood message seemed to be that as (potentially non-Pagan) teenagers and adults, they might not want their real names associated with their Pagan childhoods.

Some of the most significant challenges to an ethnographic study of Paganism involve the lack of an internally consistent, bounded community and the relative invisibility of the population, resulting from decentralization, stigmatization, and other factors. Many of the challenges specific to conducting ethnographic research in Pagan communities are exacerbated when children are involved. Parents may be particularly reluctant to publicize their beliefs for fear of repercussions from children's teachers, peers, or non-Pagan family members. Locating groups of Pagan children is difficult in the absence of Pagan schools, day cares, or youth organizations. The uniquely structured and participatory nature of SpiralScouts International alleviated some of the difficulties in accessing groups of Pagan families. Unlike festivals, open rituals, or other public sites where Pagans gather, SpiralScouts maintains membership records and contact lists. Families in SpiralScouts tend to be comfortably "out of the broom closet," as they put it, about their religious beliefs, at least to the extent that they participate in a fundamentally (although not exclusively) Pagan organization. SpiralScouts parents participate in meetings and activities, so parents and adult leaders were present for all discussions and interviews with minors. The methodological difficulties in locating groups of Pagan families that arose during research for this book reflect many of the difficulties encountered by Pagan families (and Pagan individuals) in attempting to locate a community for themselves. Many Pagan groups are ephemeral, coming together to celebrate Sabbats and festivals and often dissolving as members' interests or circumstances change. The sporadic nature of these gatherings does not provide an opportunity for extended contact for either researchers or practitioners. In many ways, this inability to immerse fully in Pagan culture contributes to the ambivalence within Pagan communities. Moreover, Pagan parents' emphasis on freedom of religious choice for their children means that some parents are reluctant to consider their children "Pagan" until (and unless) the children themselves decide to follow Pagan paths, making locating "Pagan children" even more difficult. This focus on volitional religion for children is an area fraught with ambivalence and tension for Pagan adults and children, reflecting parents' valorization of the personal religious quest at the expense of a religious tradition or heritage for their children.

Chapter 1 of this book examines the multiple and conflicting histories of contemporary Paganism and how these varied understandings both reflect and influence Pagans' understandings of their religion as well as differing ways of approaching and understanding Pagan religion, parenting, childhood, and daily life. Many individuals, families, and groups contributed to the information in this book, but three main groups of Pagan families are central to this story: the families of Silverling Circle in New Hampshire, the families of Dragon Moon/Spiral Winds Coven in Texas, and the First Church of Wicca in Massachusetts. The first chapter of this book introduces each of these groups.

Chapter 2 explores Pagan childhood as an idealized realm that is constructed, maintained, and, at times, exploited by Pagan adults. Pagans' appreciation for childhood as a protected temporal and ideological category that emerges from Romantic and New Age ideals of purity, magic, and innocence reflects adult Pagans' desires; whether these ideals also reflect Pagan children's experiences is a question considered more carefully in this chapter. The valorized and romanticized images of childhood that are constructed and maintained by Pagan adults often lead, unsurprisingly, to an overvaluation of "childlike" or "innocent" (or magical and inversely powerful) qualities in adults.

Chapter 3 examines the many ways Pagan adults conceptualize and present themselves as "childlike" adults in an attempt to both usurp and invert traditional understandings of power, responsibility, privilege, and spirituality. At the same time that adult Pagans position themselves as childlike and magical, however, they frequently suggest that real, chronological children may be unable to participate appropriately in religious ritual. These tensions and ambivalences between the varied religious, interpersonal, and social dynamics of Pagan adults and children, on the one hand, and larger, more firmly established social and religious institutions, on the other hand, are the subject of chapter 4 of this study. These interactions between Pagan adults and children and between Pagan children and other institutions are influenced by specific understandings of the role and nature of the category of the "child." That is, Pagan adults and Pagan children interact with many of the institutions discussed in this chapter—scouting organizations, public schools, and other religious traditions—based on specific understandings of what it means to be a "Pagan child" or a "Pagan adult."

Chapter 5 addresses some of the debates surrounding the inclusion of children in Pagan rituals and the appropriate level of religious instruction for younger generations in this new religious movement. Some Pagan parents respond to the religion's tendency toward the exclusion of children by developing innovative ways to include children in religious ritual and daily practice. This chapter suggests that rituals involving Pagan children can challenge scholars and practitioners to rethink understandings of what constitutes religious ritual, especially rituals involving children's participation, and to include the interactions and events of everyday life as well as the structured performance of formal rituals. Rituals such as Wiccanings, which welcome young children into the religion, reflect the tension within contemporary Paganism between the desire for legitimacy and the desire to differentiate Pagan welcoming ceremonies from similar practices in other traditions, such as Christian baptisms. Ceremonies and rituals such as blessings and coming-of-age rites are intended to welcome infants and teenagers into the religion, but—unsurprisingly—these rituals are also contested within the religion. The importance of religious choice for Pagan children is a core value within the religion and is one of the few principles that receives nearly unanimous support from adult Pagans. These Pagan life-cycle rituals and the ambivalence they elicit are discussed in chapter 6 of this book. Finally, the conclusion situates the collective religious imagination of contemporary American Paganism, as evidenced by Pagan understandings of childhood, within the context of North American religions.

1

Crafting History

Three Pagans, Five Opinions

Pagans sometimes joke that if you ask three Pagans a question, you'll get five answers. Even after half a century as an American religion, contemporary Paganism remains decentralized both in doctrine and in practice, and very little consensus exists among scholars or practitioners on more than the most fundamental aspects of the religion. Unsurprisingly, contemporary Paganism is also fraught with contentious and varied interpretations of its historical roots. In a striking convergence of popular and scholarly opinion, it is often the case that any three scholars' descriptions of the nature and origins of the religion will result in five answers—different from one another and from the first five as well. This dissension is as old as contemporary Paganism itself—but do the roots of this religion reach back millennia or decades? Is contemporary Paganism a nature religion, focused on reverence for the earth and oriented toward environmentalism, green living, and the cycles of the seasons?[1] Is it a mystery religion based in ancient—or modern—esoteric beliefs?[2] Is modern Paganism a continuation of Neolithic Goddess-worshipping matriarchies or a reconstruction of indigenous Celtic traditions?[3] Are contemporary Pagans the spiritual descendants of the women and men persecuted as witches in Europe or in Salem, or are they the intellectual descendants of nineteenth-century occult and magical societies?[4]

In different ways, each of these histories is the history of the religion. Lacking an "official" historical or mythological foundation, contemporary Pagans take full advantage of the freedom to build their own foundation. The decision by individuals or groups of Pagans to support a particular history determines the tenor of personal and local expressions of Paganism itself, and each of these histories evokes a different set of morals, goals, and values and a corresponding religious identity, imagination, and practice. This process of imaginative historicizing is a key component of the construction of contemporary adult Pagans' identities and imaginations. As such, this historicizing has a significant impact on the rhetoric and practice of Pagan parenting and child rearing and on Pagan children's experiences of their religion.

This chapter considers the multiple and varied historical, intellectual, and sociopolitical sources of contemporary American Paganism as they are understood by scholars of religion and by adult Pagans. The religion's antecedents in Romanticism, Spiritualism, reconstructions and fantasies of indigenous religions, and magical and occult societies offer valuable insights into the diverse expressions of contemporary Paganism. Likewise, the decision of an individual practitioner, coven, or tradition to emphasize a particular historical and mythological lineage to the exclusion of other options illuminates the dynamic and sometimes capricious process of Pagan self-identification. The choice of a relevant past shapes the religious, cultural, and personal practices that express these values. Simply put, the Pagan historical imagination shapes the Pagan religious imagination and has significant repercussions on the lives of Pagan adults and children.

The histories of Paganism that contemporary Pagans create, rehearse, and revise in their religious practices often differ from those identified by historians of the religion. These sometimes-dissonant accounts may be a source of anxiety for Pagans, but nearly as often, the opposite is true. Many Pagans see a creative tension in this ambivalence. Scholars and practitioners see the juxtaposition of these different registers of historical awareness as a hallmark of the religion's development within the American religious landscape. A large part of American Paganism's distinctiveness from its European precursors emerges from its introduction into the social and cultural milieu of the mid-1960s United States. Paganism's grounding in American culture and religion over the past fifty years has profoundly oriented Pagan thinking and shaped the values that Pagan parents instill in and expect of their children.

During fieldwork with Pagan families around the United States, I asked the people I met what they meant when they called themselves "Pagans" (or Wiccans, or heathens, or Green/Eclectic/FamTrad witches) and how they understood the history of their religion. I listened to late-night discussions over bottles of homemade mead, to songs families sang around campfires and while washing dishes, and to the stories that Pagan parents and children told one another. This chapter presents four perspectives on the complicated issue of Pagan identity in the contemporary United States: Paganism as a prehistoric indigenous religion; Paganism as an earth-based nature religion; Paganism as the heir to the esoteric and Mind Cure movements of the nineteenth century; and Paganism as an eclectic integration (some might say "appropriation") of beliefs and practices from globally and historically diverse non-Christian traditions. Two of these perspectives—nature-based "Green Wicca" and the quasi-esoteric "metaphysical Wicca"—are represented in this book by the radically different understandings of Pagan history held by two geographically proximal (but intellectually and spiritually distant) circles within SpiralScouts International. Even within one of the very few centralized, national Pagan organizations, these two groups (which have, presumably, somewhat similar goals for shaping Pagan children's experiences) vary considerably in their views of their religious histories.

It should be apparent that the four perspectives presented here do not exhaust the histories and mythologies of contemporary Paganism. Rather, they offer a glimpse into the radically divergent ways that superficially similar Pagan groups imagine and explain their histories and how they deploy these histories in the construction of religious worlds for themselves and their children.

"We Honor the Earth": Green/Eclectic Wicca

"SpiralScouts, circle up!" Jess calls, and the eleven scouts of Silverling Circle gather on the carpet in the circle leader's sunny, open living room on a beautiful New England afternoon. Their parents find seats on the couches and chairs around the room or sit with their children on the brown, tan, and green blankets laid out on the floor. The various colors represent the three age groups of the SpiralScouts program: FireFlies (three- to eight-year-olds), SpiralScouts (nine- to thirteen-year-olds), and PathFinders (adolescents from fourteen to eighteen years old).[5] Although SpiralScouts circles technically include scouts of all three age groups, PathFinders are rare; I met only three during the time I spent with SpiralScouts circles. There are a number of possible reasons why older Pagan scouts are elusive: most children's scouting groups tend to have higher attrition rates as adolescents follow other interests; the lack of peer support and involvement in Pagan scouting may discourage teenagers from continuing through the ranks; or there may simply be fewer second-generation teenage Pagans because Pagan children are increasingly encouraged to choose their own religious paths (a phenomenon discussed in more detail in chapter 6). At this meeting, as at most of the SpiralScouts meetings I observed, the majority of the scouts fall into the three- to eight-year-old FireFly range.

Jess brings out a stocky green pillar candle and five small round candles in different colors for the meeting's opening ritual and sets them on a large, round tray in the center of the floor. As she lights each smaller candle, she asks the scouts which element each color represents. "What does the red candle stand for?" she begins, and a first-grade FireFly with bright red, waist-length pigtails says, "Red is for fire." Jess smiles in agreement and reminds the scouts and parents that red is also the color of imagination; when they light this candle, they call both on the element of fire and on their imaginations. "What about blue? What's the blue candle for?" Several of the children here today are new to this group, and they listen curiously and fidget with the edges of the blanket. Some of the returning scouts, including Jess's six-year-old son, race to see who can answer Jess's question as quickly as possible, and three or four scouts shout at once: "Air! It's for *air*!" One of the older scouts says, "I thought it was for water." Jess says that blue is usually for water, emotions, and feelings, but it can remind us of air, too, acknowledging and validating the older scout's lone dissenting opinion. The yellow candle that Jess lights next is usually the one associated with air, but as she begins to light it, her son Ryan exclaims, "For the *sun*!" and Jess lets his answer stand. Paganism's freedom to improvise rituals and redefine common symbols extends to children as well as adults, and although adults frequently offer children relatively standard explanations for rituals and religious objects, they rarely insist on these explanations or on specific "right" answers. The oldest scout, Noah, says that the small green candle is for earth, and as Jess lights the white candle, four small scouts eagerly shout, "Spirit!" Jess says, "Right! And what about this big green candle?" A four-year-old who has been sitting on his father's lap suddenly yells, "For grass—no, *trees*!" at the same time that Ryan confidently offers, "That's for SpiralScouts!" Jess explains that other SpiralScouts groups all over the world might use different kinds and colors of small candles, but all SpiralScouts circles everywhere have a big green candle like this one—"Because we're all SpiralScouts, and because we honor the earth." That the scouts know (or can guess or improvise) the meanings of the candles' colors is impressive, considering that this opening ritual is not performed at the beginning of every meeting; in fact, this is the only time I saw this ritual performed in this way at this circle.

Silverling Circle is a SpiralScouts circle, the equivalent of a troop in more traditional scouting organizations. SpiralScouts International aligns itself with marginalized cultural groups (and deliberately distinguishes itself from better-known groups like the Boy Scouts of America) by welcoming children of minority religions as well as atheists and agnostics. At the same time, it follows "traditional" scouting models and tends to flourish in areas where scouting is popular, such as the American Midwest and South. SpiralScouts International (or S*SI, as their promotional material suggests the name be abbreviated) is a scouting organization rooted in Wiccan ethics and designed for children of earth-based and other minority religions. In a religion that continually negotiates its relationship with mainstream religions and society, SpiralScouts offers a model for the inclusion of children's experiences and perspectives at the same time that it reflects the adult architecture of these experiences. Like all SpiralScouts circles, Silverling Circle affirms an earth-centered spiritual worldview. Jess describes the circle's orientation as "Green and Eclectic Wicca," indicating a willingness to draw on values, beliefs, and practices from a variety of earth-based traditions while maintaining a thoroughly ecological (or "green") consciousness.

This emphasis on the sacredness of the earth and on ecological and environmental concerns is clear in all of Silverling Circle's activities. Silverling scouts plant trees, assist with ocean shore and river cleanups, participate in weekend-long campouts, and end many meetings with unstructured "outside time" that allows the scouts to roll down hills or climb trees. Green Wicca adheres to what many might consider the "traditional" view of Wicca as a nature religion with values rooted in nineteenth- and twentieth-century ecological, conservationist, and Romantic movements. Catherine Albanese has pointed out the multivalence of "nature religion" in the United States, noting that many groups that fall under this rubric maintain varying or even opposing ideals.[6] The historian Chas Clifton has attempted to circumscribe the bounds of American Paganism as a nature religion, suggesting that it can be seen as rooted in Cosmic Nature, Embodied/Erotic Nature, or Gaian Nature.[7] Cosmic Nature, Clifton proposes, includes metaphysical understandings of nature that emerge from Renaissance practices of "natural magic," whereas Embodied Nature is concerned with the sacralizing of sexuality and the human body. Silverling Circle's focus is most closely associated with Clifton's third designation, Gaian Nature, a phrase that emerges from Oberon (Tim) Zell-Ravenheart's 1970 article on "deep ecology."[8] Clifton describes adherents of this type of Paganism as "likely to speak of the spirit of nature and, as heirs of the Romantic Movement, to see humanity as suffering from its spiritual divorce from nature."[9] This assessment of contemporary Paganism as a primarily nature-based religion remains a popular way of understanding and practicing the religion. Graham Harvey's analysis of contemporary Paganism notes that despite the many other ways of perceiving it, "Paganism is a religion centrally concerned with celebrating Nature. Pagans are people who are listening to the living, speaking Earth."[10]

Proponents of the nature religion view of contemporary Paganism find that it integrates well with political and social activism. Starhawk's San Francisco–based Reclaiming Collective frequently organizes and participates in political protests and leads a course on "Earth Activist Training."[11] Other Pagan groups and individuals have found ways of expressing their spiritual and political views through association with organizations like Earth First![12] Regardless of whether they choose to ally their spirituality with organized politics, many nature-oriented Pagans find environmental activism an important part of their daily practices and values. As Jess observes, "Even things like recycling can be a ritual if you do it with the intention of healing the earth."[13] Jess's commitment to a green lifestyle is apparent in both her personal and professional choices; she has a degree in environmental education, has worked as a biology teacher, and currently coordinates a number of sustainability projects, both informally and professionally.

Silverling Circle regularly chooses activities that reflect the group's attentiveness to the earth-based and pantheistic elements of their tradition, and this focus informs the values that parents in this and other nature-based communities impart to their children. Silverling Circle's nature-based focus is evident in the books included in the group's lending library and the book list maintained on its website, which include dozens of wildlife and nature field guides as well as books on nature myths, earth-centered activities, natural health care, earth science, plant lore, and a three-part series on "Green Witchcraft."[14] Likewise, nearly all of Silverling's activities involve a focus on nature, the earth, or the seasons. Silverling scouts have spent meetings learning to navigate with compasses, gathering sap from maple trees, cleaning community parks, going on winter and summer hikes, and picking a variety of fruits and vegetables.

Individual families that share Silverling Circle's commitment to earth-based spirituality and nature-oriented religious practices often express these beliefs through seasonal rituals and crafts, environmental activities (from putting out food for birds and other wildlife in the winter to assisting in community park cleanups or collecting litter on beaches), and informal and formal attempts to "take care of the earth." One earth-based Pagan described her "earth-based spirituality" to me as "very much an integrative thing." She explained:

> I hate the idea of "primitive peoples," but the concept of how First Nations and aboriginal peoples don't have a word for religion, but having their spiritual experience be an outgrowth of their everyday activity—that's part of what this means to me. That's why I shit in a bucket.[15] That's why I grow my own food. That's why I buy food from my neighbors. Because those are outgrowths of my spiritual relationship with the earth.[16]

Although there is certainly a continuum of beliefs and practices among earth-based, eco-centered Pagans, most Pagans of this sort stress their "respect" or "reverence" for the earth. One Pagan mother explained her religious practices in a way that would likely be familiar to other earth-focused Pagans:

> I don't think I practice [my religion], I live it. When I garden I put fertilizer in the soil and am conscious to be thankful while I'm picking up my produce that the earth gave of herself to give this to myself and my family. Anyone who is around is aware that I hold in reverence what nature has given us. The children know that I water the flowers and plants and herbs and help them be healthy and that this is our way of thanking them. They do this themselves.[17]

The families of Silverling Circle and other green and earth-based Pagans emphasize this connection with and reverence for the earth in their formal and informal religious practices and in the interactions between adults and children. This emphasis is often manifested through rituals that mark the seasons or, as one seven-year-old Pagan child told me, a strong emphasis on the need to "reduce, reuse, recycle! But I don't know what 'reduce' means."

"The Oldest Faith": Paganism as Premodern Religion

Some nature-based Pagans understand their earth-focused beliefs and rituals as part of a more or less unbroken lineage that has existed for tens of thousands of years. Janet is a Pagan mother of two who follows a Celtic witchcraft path. She explains her understanding of the history of her religion this way:

> I believe Paganism is the oldest faith, reaching to the dawn of civilization when humans realized there were powers greater than themselves. Those powers became gods and goddesses. Paganism has been in America as long as people have been here—there are many basic beliefs of the Native Americans and Pagans that are held in common.[18]

Janet's explanation of the history of contemporary Paganism is a popular one. She suggests that Paganism, as practiced today, is the direct descendant of an ancient religion with roots that stretch back to

Paleolithic Goddess worship and animism. This approach to Paganism suggests that small pockets of Pagans resisted conversion to Christianity and other religions, covertly passing their polytheism and nature worship down through generations. For Pagans who hold this view, the phrase "contemporary Paganism" is a misnomer; the Paganism practiced today is less contemporary than continuous. It is a fundamentally pantheistic (or panentheistic), precolonial, nature-based tradition that perpetuates (or effectively reconstructs) the "Old Religion" and traces its lineage to pre-Christian (if not prehistoric) times. Some Pagans rhapsodize that the religion has "always been" and that humans' interactions with nature are (or should be) inherently reverential: "For as long as Nature has been, humans have been enchanted by It, taken care of It, loved It! [sic]."[19] They may insist that "there is no 'contemporary'—it is ageless. . . . [The] practice of witchcraft is as old as humanity," because prehistoric peoples worked "magic" through the forces of nature."[20]

Scholars of Pagan studies acknowledge the fundamental importance of such legitimating claims to antiquity for a religion that is both historically and personally recent for practitioners, many of whom discovered the religion in late adolescence or early adulthood. The author Margot Adler notably referred to this idealized connection with pre-Christian, agricultural, pacifistic, matriarchal people who lived in harmony with nature as the "Myth of Wicca" and noted that variations of this myth appear "in almost all the introductory books on the modern Craft, including works by Gardner, Doreen Valiente, Justine Glass, Patricia Crowther, Stewart Farrar, and Raymond Buckland."[21] This perspective gained popularity in Pagan self-historicizing in the 1970s and 1980s, especially among feminist and Goddess-oriented Pagans. It has since fallen out of favor as subsequent scholarship has challenged the methods and sources of these earlier scholars. Nonetheless, it remains an important part of the historical and mythological imaginings of many contemporary Pagans, and Gimbutas's "archaeomythology" is an apt metaphor for Paganism's "uncovering" of constructed histories. Strictly speaking, the "myth of matriarchal prehistory" predates the religion, albeit by decades instead of centuries. The historian Ronald Hutton has documented the process by which Matilda Joslyn Gage's *Woman, Church, and State* (1893) integrated the French historian Jules Michelet's theories of early Pagan "witches" with contemporary theories of matriarchal prehistory, linking both of these to the early modern European witch trials to create, nearly whole cloth, what would eventually become the "Myth of Wicca." The history of contemporary Paganism may not be millennia old, but the myth itself dates back over a century—not insignificant, although a much shorter span than might be hoped for by many contemporary Pagans seeking the authenticity and legitimacy of deep and ancient roots.

The nostalgia for an imagined utopian past inherent in this view of Paganism carries with it an underlying and abiding antimodernism that is evident in contemporary Pagan rhetoric and ideology. It is not uncommon to hear Pagans who assert that "Paganism is as old as the earth" pair this opinion with a dystopian view of the dangers of the modern world: "People have always believed in the powers of nature, until Science [sic] taught them not to."[22] This tendency to romanticize premodern thought and life (and the concomitant vilification of modernity) is itself part of the historical legacy of the nineteenth- and early twentieth-century founders of contemporary Paganism. Many of the major historical figures responsible for the current form of the religion shared a tendency toward political and ideological right-wing beliefs and an abiding antipathy toward modernity. These views are abundantly apparent in the writings of Aleister Crowley and Gerald Gardner, perhaps the most significant influences on the traditions of magic and witchcraft that would become the basis for contemporary Paganism. Others in their milieu shared these premodernist tendencies, including William Butler Yeats and other members and leaders of the Hermetic Order of the Golden Dawn. These early contributors to the movements that would inspire contemporary Paganism also espoused some of the less appealing sides of this right-wing ideology and spirituality: elitism, distrust of the masses, and an unfortunate tendency toward neo-fascist ideology and rhetoric.[23] The juxtaposition of this virulent premodernism and these figures' esoteric spiritual leanings established the foundations of ritual and ceremonial magic in combination with the (purportedly) pre-Christian and premodern beliefs on which Paganism would be built.

For Pagans who refer to Paganism as the "Old Religion" and take this myth as foundational, the focus of the religion is the transmission of religious practice that has remained suppressed but unbroken since

Paleolithic times. For Pagan parents who take this view, the desire to pass along the traditions of these "old ways" orients the way they shape their children's religious worlds. This is likely to include an emphasis on religious lineage, tradition (whether extant or invented), and practices that reflect or recreate premodern agricultural and seasonal festivals. The view of Paganism as an old religion (or as the "Old Religion") does not necessarily exclude other views of the religion's history, and many Pagans seem to have little difficulty maintaining modified versions of this perspective. A Pagan mother in New Hampshire explained her view of her religion this way:

> Contemporary Paganism is a new offshoot of an old religion. That's how I look at it. Like the Quakers. Their religion is very new, but they are an offshoot of Christianity which has been around for some time. The difference is that theirs was more continuous whereas ours seems to be more of a revival. I'm sure there were several groups or families in England that kept it alive continuously through the years. Even Gerald Gardner, one of the main people [responsible] for opening the door for this new wave of Paganism, claimed to have been initiated into the "old religion" by an already formed group of some kind. It came to America the same way everything does—with the constant influx of people—and spread from there. Still, contemporary Paganism is a whole new animal, and I think we have only ourselves and our communication to thank for it.[24]

"I Can, I Will, I Believe": The New Thought Inheritance

On a chilly Saturday afternoon, six children and three adults fill a suburban kitchen in Massachusetts for a meeting of the Sea Witches, a SpiralScouts circle that doubles as the religious education program for the First Church of Wicca. For today's craft activity, the scouts are making pentagrams from red, green, and brown raffia and floral wire. Sandy, an adult volunteer and mother of two of the scouts, shows the children how to wind the wire in a circle and wrap the raffia around and through it, covering the edges and forming the central five-pointed star of the pentagram. The instructions are complicated, and wrapping the fiber is tricky, so Sandy suggests that the scouts work in pairs.

Watching Sandy pull the raffia taut and wrap it around the wire, one of the younger scouts worries, "I can't do that craft. I know I can't!" Tim, the Sea Witches' adult leader, reassures her that she can, adding, "We don't say, 'I can't'! Say, 'I can, I will, I believe!'" Tim's nine-year-old daughter, Alana, joins in on the first "I can" and says it with him, and they turn it into a chant: "I can, I will, I believe! I can, I will, I believe! I can, I will, I believe!" rising in intensity as the other scouts wrestle with their complicated wreaths.

* * *

The New Age echoes of positive affirmation and visualization in this chant would not be out of place at many Pagan gatherings, but in the case of the First Church of Wicca, this affirmation is a direct and explicit reference to the tradition's roots in nineteenth-century metaphysical and Mind Cure movements. Practitioners rarely acknowledge contemporary Paganism's debt to these movements. The First Church of Wicca's description of its tradition as "metaphysical eclectic Wicca" suggests that this is not a coven of traditional Gardnerian Wiccans, as does the habit of the church's minister (whose parishioners call her "Rev. Dr. Kendra") of wearing black velvet robes, a crystal headband, and a clerical collar for all public appearances.[25] It is not altogether surprising, then, to learn that the first incarnation of this Wiccan church was as a New Thought center. Rooted in nineteenth-century Mind Cure movements, New Thought promoted holistic healing and the power of positive thinking, visualization, and affirmation to correct physical and mental ailments. It stressed a universal spirituality in service to a supreme divinity existing both beyond and within human beings. Remnants of New Thought are evident in many areas of contemporary American culture, including the pop psychology of self-help gurus like television's Dr. Phil, the popularity of quasi-metaphysical fiction like *The Celestine Prophecy* and *The Secret*, and many New Age and contemporary Pagan beliefs. A member of the First Church of Wicca remarks that the switch from New Thought to Wicca was straightforward: "It was a matter of going to the website one day and instead of seeing New Thought Spiritual Center, seeing 'The First Church of Wicca.'"[26]

Of course, the switch required considerably more effort and planning than this abrupt change suggests. Tim, Kendra's husband, explains, "We wanted a church within the New Thought Spiritual Center, so the whole idea was that it was going to be all around metaphysics and New Thought. So if you wanted crystals or crystal treatment, acupuncture, meditation, religion . . . well, that was the big question: what do you do about religion?"[27] The First Church of Wicca's solution was to incorporate the two: New Thought provides the nondenominational metaphysics of the group's tradition, and Wicca supplies the religious base. Rev. Kendra acknowledges that while the juxtaposition of metaphysics and Wicca may initially seem jarring, "You really cannot practice one without the other."[28] The church's tenets include belief in "the Spirit of Nature, represented by a God and Goddess" as well as "the Metaphysical trinity of Mind, Soul, and Body or Idea, Thought, and Manifestation."[29]

What the First Church of Wicca offers is an eclectic tradition that draws on contemporary Pagan philosophy and spirituality as well as on harmonial and metaphysical philosophies.[30] Sarah Pike has explained that contemporary Paganism and metaphysical movements share a significant body of history, beliefs, and practices:

> Characteristics of the New Age and Neopagan movements, such as salvation through the discovery and knowledge of a divine inner self and the continuity rather than separation of matter and spirit, have been present for centuries in the occult tradition. These new movements self-consciously updated and synthesized older streams of religious thought and practice.[31]

The roots of contemporary Paganism are evident in these earlier movements, specifically in their common views on the sacrality of the self, the correspondence between natural and supernatural worlds, and the power of the mind to influence health and prosperity.[32] Contemporary Paganism shares these earlier movements' dedication to social change and progressive liberal views on gender issues in a way that aligns its metaphysical and political roots and ideals. For example, Ann Braude has pointed out the relationship between Spiritualism and the emerging women's rights movement, noting that Spiritualism offered women a public platform, leadership roles, moral critiques of traditional forms of authority, and support for women's increasing agency. Likewise, Catherine Tumber has remarked on the "moral revolution of metaphysics" and the value of "New Thought's reconception of moral selfhood" on women's social equality. Nineteenth-century magical and occult groups—themselves precursors of contemporary Pagan beliefs and practices—emphasized the power of the individual will to effect change in one's environment. Like New Thought, magical groups such as the Hermetic Order of the Golden Dawn and the Ordo Templi Orientis welcomed women's membership and considered them spiritually (if not entirely socially) equal to men. Because these religious developments implicitly and explicitly challenged traditional religious beliefs and structures, they offered opportunities for innovation in terms of social and sexual roles as well as religious ones.[33]

Despite the similarities between nineteenth- and twenty-first-century manifestations of these ideals, however, "the New Thought movement's intellectual descendants among proponents of New Age spirituality do not know much about their own historical roots in American religious culture."[34] This point is true of many proponents of Pagan spirituality. Most Pagans are considerably more familiar with the historicized mythology of their religion than they are with its more recent history. The First Church of Wicca's explicit association with its metaphysical roots separates it from many of its contemporaries in this regard; the church frequently and explicitly locates itself in relation to its religious and spiritual forebears. When their town held a Fourth of July parade with the theme "American Ingenuity," the FCOW entered the parade with a float titled "Religious Freedom Is American Ingenuity." The float included a series of hand-painted signs commemorating significant events in the history of religious freedom in the United States. The signs began with the 1620 arrival of the Pilgrims and progressed to the ratification of the First Amendment in 1789, the United Nations Universal Declaration of Human Rights Article 18 in 1948, and the 1986 *Dettmer v. Landon* case, which legally recognized Wicca as a religion in the United States. Given the church's ongoing attempts to locate itself within its intellectual and spiritual lineage, it is unsurprising that the FCOW listed as the culminating event in this progression the founding of the First Church of Wicca itself.

The FCOW's attention to its New Thought roots affects its approach to the religious education of its children by highlighting the importance of positive affirmation and harmonial philosophy in daily life. In contrast to Pagan families and SpiralScouts circles that emphasize green, nature-based Paganism, the FCOW's SpiralScouts circle, the Sea Witches, prioritizes positive affirmations and metaphysics. Although Kendra's claim that she is the "only person I know of who brings metaphysics to the practice of Wicca"[35] may be disingenuous, the FCOW's emphasis on metaphysics is one of the group's distinguishing features. Kendra is quick to point out that her use of this word is deliberate, intended to imply "true metaphysics" rather than "crystals and all that stuff." The FCOW offers metaphysics classes in addition to classes on meditation and "Wicca 101," all of which are taught by Rev. Kendra.[36] During a group interview with Kendra, her husband, Tim, and one of their church's most active parishioners, Kendra explained her understanding of metaphysics:

> Metaphysics is the connection to the divine through meditation, through positive affirmation, through visualization. That's how you shape and mold and change your life. What people don't realize is that in witchcraft when we do our spells, the incantation is the metaphysics because of the way that it's worded. So we teach metaphysics even beyond Wicca; we teach it as a way of life. So whatever faith my children choose to be when they get older, [later] on in life, they will be metaphysical. The most important piece is the metaphysics. I've had several people from the church come to me and say, "You know, I always knew Wicca was my path, and it worked for me, but now I realize that if I walked away from Wicca tomorrow, it wouldn't matter because I'd still have metaphysics."[37]

Kendra and Tim are clear that the metaphysics they practice in their church and in their home with their eight-year-old daughter and their eleven-year-old son is a highly formalized and intentional practice. During this discussion, they explained to me—in unison—that their practice consists of "negative release statements, positive affirmations, visualization, meditation," a phrase they treat as a self-contained litany. They discuss the similarities between magic and prayer, noting that "magic is a form of prayer" that can be manifested through visualization and incantation. This integration of magic and prayer and the ubiquitous presence of metaphysics in their daily life are evident in the blessing that Kendra, Tim, and their children recite together before meals:

> The table round contains the earth and thus becomes the Mother.
> We share Her bounty in this hour and bless and love each other.
> So mote it be. It's a good life.
> I can, I will, I believe!
> Thank you, God and Goddess.

Like their activities at home, the church services conducted by the family have a distinct emphasis on metaphysical thought and positive affirmations. The group's church services typically begin with church members and visitors "sweeping away negativity" by making sweeping motions with a wooden broom while stating negative thoughts, emotions, or experiences so that they can be "spiritually present" in the ritual. Adults sweep away things like "work stress," "judgment and pain," and "tax burdens." The children, who sit on the floor in the middle of the circle made by the seated adults, sweep away the "last day of vacation," "going to school tomorrow," "the pain of getting my ears pierced," and, intriguingly from a nine-year-old, "guilt." Several children choose to pass when their turn comes, out of confusion or shyness. Kendra's sermons during these church services focus on topics such as "finding your spirituality," values, and "telling our parents we are Pagan." The sermons and the magic performed during these services have a strong emphasis on the power of positive thought and energy to change both internal and external circumstances. Kendra explains how this focus on New Thought principles manifests in the pastoral counseling she offers to her parishioners:

> I've even had parishioners come to me and say, "I can't stand coming to pastoral counseling because all you do is tell me to get over it." But the reality of it is, I say to them, "Yes, that stinks. So why aren't you looking for another job? Why aren't you spending the energy to look in the papers? Why don't you have the self-confidence? Why don't you believe in yourself?" I help them figure out their personal truths, and it always comes down to, "Well, I was always told my whole life by my parents that

I was stupid, and so I really don't think there's anything else I can do." OK, let's negate that. You're not stupid, you're smart. Let's give you a new positive affirmation that tells you you're smart, and let's get you on the road to finding another job, and while we're doing it, let's make a connection to the God and Goddess because they're your strength; they're with you the whole entire way. They know you can do it. And that's really what it's all about.[38]

The meetings of the Sea Witches also focus on the group's New Thought principles, often at the expense of a focus on more nature-based aspects of the religion. At one Sea Witches meeting, the scouts and Tim, the Sea Witches' adult leader, planned activities for their upcoming meetings. When one of the scouts suggested "jumping in leaves" as a fall activity, Kendra, who was listening to the group from the stairway, quickly interrupted: "No jumping in leaves—there might be ticks!" Likewise, when another scout suggested camping, Kendra reminded the scouts that no one in the group had "camping skills." Although the group participates in activities related to nature and, in particular, the changing seasons, it clearly prioritizes the internal over the external world—or, more precisely, the effect of the internal on the external world. As the scouts were running through the house at another Sea Witches meeting, several girls knocked from the wall a wooden broom used in the FCOW services. As Tim replaced the broom, one of the young scouts asked, "Can you really fly on that broom?" Tim joked, "I can't fly—I don't have a license." Before the scout could wander off, Tim added, "No, we can't really fly. But we can visualize it."

The Conversion of the First Church of Wicca

In 2004, the First Church of Wicca was established as a congregational church in the "metaphysical eclectic tradition of Wicca." This combination—Wiccan practice in a congregational setting—is, in fact, as anomalous within contemporary Paganism as it sounds. By the time I began attending services at the FCOW in June 2006 as part of the ethnographic fieldwork for this book, the church claimed a following of more than two hundred people, many of them families with young children. The FCOW's minister and "elder high priestess," Rev. Dr.

Kendra Vaughan Hovey, maintained that she personally ministered to "thousands of people worldwide."[39] In January 2009, the First Church of Wicca officially closed its doors via an e-mail to the church's members, supporters, and friends. The message from Rev. Dr. Kendra detailed the moral and ethical failings of Wicca and announced Hovey's plans to reopen a new church—a Christian church, in keeping with her new faith. This church promised to "focus on helping people heal from their experiences of inequity from past religions and religious institutions, using Jesus Christ and his teachings in the Bible as the foundation of how to have a meaningful relationship with God, as well as how to attain holistic health of mind, body, and soul."[40] In March 2009, the website for Hovey's new church, Living Waters Community of Hope, bore an "under construction" notice and the heading, "Quench Your Thirst for Truth."[41]

On a smaller scale, the conversion of a Wiccan priestess to Christianity would be interesting but not overly noteworthy. Contemporary Paganism values free will, personal choice, and the spiritual quest, and Pagans move freely into, out of, and around the religion. Spiritual seeking is often understood to mean moving from traditional religions to more esoteric or eclectic spiritualities, but most Pagans see the choice to leave Paganism as an acceptable one, understanding personal choice as more important than the growth or maintenance of religious community. In Hovey's case, however, her conversion resounded through certain Pagan blogs and websites, causing a flurry of discussion in online forums and blogs. In a religion that generally lacks central public figures and cohesive public communities, Hovey had attained some measure of celebrity through her active public advocacy of Wicca, her own strong personality, and her unusual interpretations of her religion—for example, her decision to wear a clerical collar for all public outings. Wearing the collar to the supermarket, she explained, let people know that she was clergy and available to help them—a duty, as "elder high priestess," that Hovey took seriously. She provided pastoral counseling for FCOW members on a sliding fee scale and Wiccan chaplaincy services to the local hospital; during one of our conversations, she acknowledged that hospital staff members were frequently surprised to see her walking the halls in her long black velvet robe, clerical collar, and pentacle headband. A member of local interfaith councils, Hovey wrote and published a book about Pagan wedding ceremonies, and at the time of her conversion, she had begun editing a collection of essays about Pagans' experiences "coming out of the broom closet."[42] In their most dramatically public move, the Hovey family (Kendra, her husband, and their two children) and the FCOW were the subjects of an hour-long episode of the TLC reality show *My Unique Family*.[43] Hovey welcomed this level of media exposure, and many accounts of the FCOW and the church's TLC appearance remarked on her tireless promotion of public understanding of Wicca.

Hovey's equally public conversion to Christianity came as a shock to many of the church's members and supporters. Although Hovey's conversion may have been unusually public (including her public baptism on a local beach during Labor Day weekend), it should not have been altogether surprising. The First Church of Wicca was an anomaly among Pagan groups from its inception, deliberately blending New Thought principles with contemporary Wiccan rituals; including children and families in its rituals, events, and complex membership process; and requiring members to tithe to the church, pay for Hovey's metaphysical classes, and dress in uniform robes during public appearances. The church's combination of New Thought, metaphysics, and eclectic Wicca, paired with a hierarchical religious leadership and a congregational worship model, offered an excellent example of the eclecticism of contemporary Paganism and the adaptability of the American religious landscape as it made room for Hovey's unusual variations on the religion.

Likewise, the closing of the First Church of Wicca highlights issues surrounding the central values of choice and spiritual seeking in contemporary American Paganism and in contemporary American religions. In its integration of the teachings of Jesus Christ and holistic healing methods, Hovey's version of Christianity seems to retain the integrative properties of individualized religions like contemporary Paganism at the same time that it recalls the FCOW's roots as a New Thought Spiritual Center. Her e-mail announcing the closing of the FCOW assured members that Hovey was "always available to help you with any questions, concerns, or thoughts that you may have about your Wiccan practice," despite what she had come to realize were the "serious failings of the Wiccan faith." Hovey writes, "A major problem with the faith is that there is no unity among the followers of the faith which makes it very challenging to define exactly what Wiccans do and do not believe in."[44] She adds that the religion lacks a unified code of ethics and suggests that this may lead to public misunderstandings of Pagan ethics, alleging, "Society would have no way of knowing, for example, if you are a Wiccan that practices the Great Rite or polyamory."[45] This comment is a nod to the fact that Hovey's departure from Wicca came on the heels of a controversial speech she presented at a Pagan Pride Day workshop purportedly on the topic of polyamory. Instead, Hovey delivered a diatribe about the moral dangers of polyamory, indicating her dissatisfaction with the uncodified and individualized nature of Pagan morality.[46]

Interestingly, many of the complaints Hovey registered against Wiccan morality are those that are generally lauded by contemporary Pagans, many of whom have left traditional religions that they saw as dogmatic and overly authoritative. For most Pagans, the necessity of finding or constructing one's own moral world is part of the appeal of contemporary Paganism, representing a welcome change from the rule-driven organized religions of their youth. Responses from Pagans in online forums to the FCOW's closing reflect a range of emotional and intellectual responses, from outrage to apathy, betrayal to support. A popular Pagan news blog hosted an online discussion about Hovey's conversion that metamorphosed into an extended discussion of contemporary Pagan ethics. Many of the comments from other Pagans in response to this post focused on Hovey's (mis)understanding of Pagan ethics and her criticism of the expectation that Pagans must make ethical and moral decisions for themselves. Commenters suggested that Hovey may not have fully understood the beliefs and practices of contemporary Paganism, leading her to fault the religion for aspects that other Pagan adherents consider the religion's strengths.[47]

It is unclear whether and to what extent former members of the First Church of Wicca followed Rev. Kendra to her new ministry. Some former members indicated their dissatisfaction with the church's closing or Hovey's actions; one longtime member of the FCOW reported that he and his wife began attending services at an Episcopal church. As of October 2009, Hovey's husband and one of her two children had chosen to accompany her on her "spiritual journey" to a holistic, metaphysical Christianity.[48] The church's closing and Hovey's conversion raise questions about the impact of adult Pagans' spiritual quests on Pagan children. Presumably, Hovey's conversion was a positive move for her, allowing her to begin to "heal the wounds" of her own childhood religious damage. But what was the effect of this conversion on Hovey's children, raised Wiccan from birth, who accepted their family's religious beliefs and traditions as fundamental truths, carried the collection bag at the FCOW's Sunday services, and proclaimed that they were witches on national television? Do they retain the opportunity to choose their own religious paths? Do they have the option to remain Wiccan when their mother has become a Christian minister? If they become—and remain—believing Christians, how will these children make sense of their first decade as Pagans?

In many ways, the religious options available to Hovey's children are an anecdotal example of the options available to all Pagan children, and this family's struggle with issues of religious tradition, moral behavior, and spiritual choice mirror those of many American Pagan families. At the same time that it highlights issues of religious family life, the demise of the First Church of Wicca also points to an inherent tension within contemporary Paganism. If religious choice and personal spirituality are prioritized while theological commitment and religious tradition are deemphasized, then religious community and social legitimacy are secondary to the capriciousness of the personal spiritual path. Put simply, the freedom of religious choice that created the First Church of Wicca ultimately ended it as well.

"We Steal from Anything": Eclectic Paganism

Yes, rampant thieves we are. I don't care where it came from.
—Daniel, father of two

Just in time for the Council of Magickal Arts festival, Spiral Winds coven has a new name and a new banner to mark its campsite. The purple banner is fringed with gold and painted with the coven's name and a large, enclosed spiral. Atashih and Freya, two of the four founding members of the coven, tell me that the proportions of the image are based on the golden mean. After the banner is installed at the edge of the campsite,

Atashih and his wife, Selene, and Freya and her husband, Gawain, the four children, and two potential students for their coven, Dolphin and Kale, gather around the campfire. Kale, the newest member of the coven, has just met Dolphin, and he remarks that he considered choosing Dolphin as a magical name, but he explains, "It didn't work with my birth number." Over dinner, the conversation turns to Chinese astrology. Freya remarks that her daughter Cricket is a snake, and Atashih is a horse. As I pull out my phone to look up the other children's signs on the Internet, Selene mentions that another friend calculated her daughters' natal charts and determined that her eldest daughter would be "an actress or a world leader" when she grew up. Conversations at the Spiral Winds campsite over the weekend include discussions of Kabbalah, Celtic mythology, the concept of *tattva*, elemental magic, eleven-year-old Stephen's newly invented "mallowmancy" (divining the future with melted marshmallows), and the spiritual aspects of a zombie apocalypse.

Not all Pagans understand their religion as primal, indigenous, and continuous or as directly rooted in nineteenth-century occult and spiritual movements. Some emphasize the contemporary aspects of their faith by drawing on a variety of alternative historical sources and religious practices. Conversations among the members of Spiral Winds often included extended debates about the potential for embracing another religion's practices or different cultural beliefs. During one of these discussions, Atashih argued for the universality of human practices and for the lack of historical distinctions between cultural traditions, while Freya disagreed: "I can practice an interpretation of a Navajo religion, but are Navajos going to call me a Navajo? No."

Eclectic Paganism may be the most popular form of practice in contemporary American Paganism. Pagan parents and families described an enormous variety of sources for their religious beliefs and practices in conversations, interviews, and written surveys. One mother described her kitchen altar for me, explaining that it included "various images of gods—Thor, Anubis, the Great Mother, Ganesha, crystals, a chalice with blessed water, seasonal decorations, usually some sort of flowers, offerings. . . . There are others scattered about the house—some Hindu gods, some Norse, occa[s]ional Christian saints, Egyptian. . . . I'm not sure what the kids have in their rooms—they are kind of messy, and since they are older, I don't feel I should intrude."[49] Another Pagan mother described a similar altar in her home: "The bottom shelf holds my Ganesha statue, my goddess statue (not sure which goddess yet), several crystals, a geode slab, a small pottery dish (decorated with spirals), and a few odds and ends that are important to me spiritually (a clay sheep my younger daughter made, a carved stone otter, a small box in the shape of a pumpkin)."[50] Pagan parents described religion within their families with the same diversity present in their home altars. One mother explained, "I simply refer to myself as Pagan because while I do worship a god and goddess [sic], I do not strictly adhere to any specific tradition. My husband is Native American so our child is . . . a pagan child one way or the other. Lady Moon, Mother Earth, and Father Sun are mentioned in her bedtime prayers."[51]

Many Pagans specifically use the word "eclectic" to describe their beliefs. Atashih described Spiral Winds coven as "very, very, very, highly eclectic Wicca." He said:

> Selene has this saying, and I agree with it: We steal from anything that doesn't run fast enough, and if it runs too fast, we make it up. . . . Eclectic Wicca is the best phrase for it. . . . Many Wiccans hit a point where they say there's nothing left in Wicca, and they turn to some mystery traditions, such as Kabbalah, Hinduism, Buddhism, something that has more of a rich mystery aspect to it. But my personal opinion is [that] the only way Wicca is going to develop any kind of mystical tradition is if it's developed.[52]

Other parents offer similar descriptions of the beliefs they share with their children:

> I consider myself an eclectic pagan. I am also a teacher, and have found "teaching moments" with my children at every opportunity. I would say they are also eclectic pagan, as we do not necessarily subscribe to any particular doctrine.[53]

> As a family we consider ourselves eclectic pagan. We don't follow one steady path. Instead we follow many. Norse, Celtic and Kitchen Witch all tied into one. Our children are considered eclectic pagan as well. I usually refer to myself as either Pagan, or a Kitchen Witch.[54]

> I refer to myself as pagan. I follow the Druid path with a Greek pantheon. So, eclectic can really best describe me.⁵⁵

> We're a Pagan family—we follow a nature-oriented, Goddess-centered belief system that pretty much falls in line with Reclaiming and Faery Wicca. I rarely use the term Wiccan, feeling that it should be reserved for initiates of specific traditions, while we're quite eclectic. I consider myself to be a Witch and priestess of Brighid who is currently studying Druidcraft (per Philip Carr-Gomm's book of that title) and Celtic traditional religion. My children are being raised Pagan, but they are free to question and explore, and decide for themselves when they're older what they believe.⁵⁶

One respondent to the online survey opted for slightly more colorful terminology when describing his family's beliefs: "Father (me) currently returned to Judaism. Was druid and hellenic recon[structionist]. Mother is vague pagan. One teen child, studying Jewish and vague Pagan."⁵⁷ Other Pagans responded to questions about their beliefs without specifically calling themselves "eclectic," but they described a rich combination of sources for these beliefs:

> I am Wiccan and a Witch. My husband is Roman Catholic. We have 3 daughters. The oldest, age 12, is also Wiccan and a Witch. My middle child, age 9, has not yet decided although she seems to be leaning towards Roman Catholicism with aspects of Wicca combined. . . . I believe that children should be exposed to many different belief systems and choose for themselves when they are old enough to make a commitment.⁵⁸

> I don't like the word "Religion." Instead I believe that we are all spiritual beings. I have felt comfortable the last few years with Pagan/Wiccan ways and have even found much help in [Buddhist] meditation. I just consider my daughter a spiritual being.⁵⁹

Parents frequently described their understandings of their children's religious beliefs with the same broad strokes, and many claimed that their children were too young to be considered adherents of any religion:

I consider myself to be a natural eclectic buddhist witch. My husband is an agnostic/semi-wiccan. My children are baptised United Methodists (at the insistence of extended family), but we consider them to be beings of light. They are too young to make that decision & we cannot force it on them [sic].[60]

I am a ecclectic celtic pagan my husband is a thiestic satanist. My oldest son is athiest, and our younger children are still to young to choose thier paths [sic].[61]

I'm a Solitary Ecclectic Pagan. My children are whatever they decide to be. My 13 year old has a tendency toward Athism and Budism, my 12 year old is more of a Druid than anything. My oldest son is a Scientist at heart so anything that supports his theories is good for him. My youngest three all are interested in what Mom does but they are still so young they don't understand that it has any "religious" connections [sic].[62]

The dizzying variety of cultural, geographic, religious, and historical periods covered by this small sample of Pagan voices leads critics of the religion to suggest that it is superficial, juvenile, or, at best, hopelessly solipsistic. Charges of dilettantism, appropriation, and egocentrism are frequently leveled against the religion's practitioners. In 1985, Robert Bellah's *Habits of the Heart* described a sort of super-individualized religious construction among Americans, culminating in "Sheilaism," Sheila Larson's infamous eponymous religion.[63] Sheilaism has frequently been cited as the quintessential example of self-absorbed, decontextualized, and individualistic religion. Among contemporary Pagans, however, the concept of such a radically individualized religion is not unusual—in fact, it may be the logical outgrowth of increasingly eclectic religious and spiritual beliefs. In a statement that echoed Sheila's comment twenty years earlier, a respondent to this study's online survey on Pagan values explained:

I do not have a name for my beliefs, [and] I do not subscribe to any single tradition. I also do not use the word Pagan to describe my beliefs (even though I technically belong under that umbrella); I suppose I feel it is too limiting. If I am ever asked about my religion, I will either explain my beliefs (if they seem interested), or I say I'm Becktarian (my name is Becky).[64]

Unlike Sheila Larson in Bellah's study, however, Becky's ultra-individualistic religion extends to her children. She describes her children's religious context:

> Kids: I have two, 10 & 7. Neither are being raised in any sort of religion and neither are being told what is the "correct" way. I do not consider a religion for my children[.] I feel that is a decision that should be made by them.[65]

One of the drawbacks of this highly individualized religion, as noted by Bellah and others, is its tendency to encourage or support individuals' lack of affiliation with larger religious communities. Becky is certainly not alone in her desire for a customized religious practice. Other Pagan parents echo this position, noting, for example, "My family is pagan. One of the reasons we don't have any more detailed definition is that it is a very personal path, and even Wicca has too much structure for us."[66] This propensity and willingness to adopt, adapt, and appropriate an enormous variety of religious beliefs and practices is a hallmark of many contemporary Pagan paths and is the core of eclectic Paganism.

"Take What You Like": Paganism as Postmodern Religion

Some Pagans go farther than the majority of eclectic Pagans in emphasizing the postmodern, deconstructed, and even surrealist aspects of this new and radically customizable spiritual path. One respondent to the online survey, who identified himself as a Chaote/Discordian Pagan, described the history of his religion this way:

> My opinion? It's not old at all. Gerald Gardner started up his brand of paganism back in the 50s to get naked chicks in his yard. As far as I've seen, it spread through the disenchanted and wacky folks pretty quickly. Already an outcast? Call yourself "Lady Faerie Moonbeam," wear a bedazzled bathrobe and tell anyone within hearing distance that you are descended from one of the Salem witches.[67]

Chaos Magic and Discordianism are among the most thoroughly postmodern of the Pagan paths. Discordianism has been referred to as a "religion disguised as a joke," a "joke disguised as a religion," and a "religion disguised as a joke disguised as a religion."[68] The central "text" of Discordianism (for better or worse) is the *Principia Discordia* (full text available at PrincipiaDiscordia.com). A typical explanation of Discordianism describes it as follows: "Even among Discordians, opinion is divided as to whether Discordianism is a complicated joke carefully disguised as a new religion or a new religion carefully disguised as a complicated joke. Both sides, however, tend to agree that the point is mostly irrelevant."[69] These paths are even more highly individualized and improvisational than other Pagan practices and are oriented toward surrealism, chaos, and irony. The *Principia Discordia; or, How I Found the Goddess and What I Did to Her When I Found Her*, the first (relatively) cohesive publication on Discordian philosophy, defines the Discordian Society by explaining, "The Discordian Society has no definition. I sometimes think of it as a disorganization of Eris Freaks.[70] It has been called a guerilla mind theatre. ... There are no rules anywhere. The Goddess Prevails."[71] Although there is some debate (within as well as outside Discordian circles) regarding its legitimacy as a distinct path of Paganism, J. Gordon Melton includes Discordianism in his *Encyclopedia of American Religions* under the category "Non-traditional Pagans."[72] Understandably, this view emphasizes an entirely different side of Paganism. In contrast to the elevation of a premodern past evident in the nostalgia for real or imagined prehistoric religions, this perspective highlights the religion's postmodern aspects.

Contemporary Paganism is often described by sociologists as a "quintessentially postmodern religion,"[73] and many of the defining characteristics of postmodernity—an emphasis on improvisation, eclecticism, irony, and bricolage, for example—are key components of contemporary Pagan beliefs and rituals. This postmodern orientation is perhaps most obvious in the fundamental decentralization of the religion, particularly its lack of central social and theological institutions, scripture, or membership base. (This decentralization is, in turn, at the root of many of the issues important to practicing Pagans, including the lack of a paid clergy and inadequate means of assessing numbers of adherents and demographics.)[74] For Pagans whose beliefs and practices emphasize the postmodern aspects of their religion, daily experience is often of more immediate concern than the religion's historiography. This perspective offers a pragmatic understanding of Paganism's spiritual and historical lineages, highlighting the integration of these sources by practitioners rather than the history of the religion itself. In fact, the uses of these sources in daily religious practice are, for many Pagans, the only aspects of their religion's history that matter.

Many contemporary Pagans emphasize a cultural and experiential break with the past, including an ultimately ahistorical perspective.[75] In response to questions about the religion's history, a Pagan mother of four writes:

> Personally, I'm not terribly concerned with how it has spread. Although, I have to admit that the Internet and the books that are available have been helpful. Those resources fall under the "take what you like and leave the rest" category for me, though.[76]

This resistance to employing (or even evaluating) a historical perspective can seem ironic in a religion that consistently endeavors to legitimize and root itself in prehistorical and pseudo-historical cultures, lending a kind of ahistorical historicism to contemporary Pagan practice. Contemporary Paganism's relationship to its own history (and the histories of the traditions and cultures from which it "borrows" freely) is deeply ambivalent and fraught with contradictions and complications. Nevertheless, many contemporary Pagans seem to have little difficulty developing innovative and powerful religious practices within this ambivalent space.

Parents who maintain these improvisational and eclectic approaches to their religion often express (or strive for) these spontaneous, absurd, and playful qualities in their approaches to their children's spiritual education as well. A Discordian father responded to my question about how having children had changed his religious practice by reporting, "It's made me believe the world is even more random then [sic] it was to me before. I don't do any rituals per se, so [my son] isn't involved . . . although I did give him a Discordian name, Rocket Sauce, The Unwashed and Prickly."[77]

The outcome of this individualized practice and the lack of structured affiliation for children remains debatable. Will the children raised in these radically individualized religious traditions, which can expand to encompass any combination of religious beliefs—no matter how culturally, historically, or theologically discordant—grow to adulthood with a strong and stable sense of religious tolerance or with a conflicted and unmoored sense of religious anxiety? Is "tolerance" a sufficient basis for religious belief? Longitudinal studies of second- and third-generation American Pagans would provide a rich area for future research on religious change, transmission, and continuity within this new religious movement.

Historicizing as Religious Practice

Pagan historicizing occupies an important place in the religious worlds of contemporary American Pagans. Pagans manipulate and interpret their histories to frame and understand their current circumstances and practices, and Pagan parents teach these methods of syncretizing and creative historicizing to their children.[78] In this process of imagining its histories, Paganism relentlessly self-historicizes in ways that are rendered transparent by the relative youth of the religion. This self-historicizing is common among new religions as they seek to carve a space for themselves in the American religious landscape by claiming legitimacy and authenticity through creative historiography. For example, Jan Shipps's analysis of Mormonism skillfully compares the relationship of Judaism and early Christianity to that of Christianity and Mormonism, observing that in both situations, the emerging religious form employed a strategy of reinterpreting scripture to accommodate its presence.[79] An excellent example of this interplay between Pagan self-historicizing and historical reflection on Paganism's sources can be found in the integration into contemporary Paganism of Rudyard Kipling's 1906 poem "A Tree Song." This poem appears in *The Paganism Reader*, a sourcebook of texts considered by its editors to be foundational to contemporary Paganism. The editors explain that over time, "Kipling's authorship has been forgotten and the poem regarded as an authentic relic of pre-Christian religion,"[80] and it appears in many modern Pagan rituals as the chant "Oak and Ash and Thorn." I have heard this chant sung at various Pagan gatherings around the country, but I have yet to hear Kipling's name mentioned by Pagans in connection with its use.

The emphasis in contemporary Paganism on the dynamic process of self-historicizing is particularly apparent in references to the "Burning Times," which portray contemporary Pagans as the cultural and spiritual descendants of the "witches" persecuted and executed during the early modern European witch hunts. Many Pagans find in this connection a valuable mythology of oppression and perseverance, and they consider it a defining part of their religious identity. Regardless of their own path within Paganism, nearly every adult Pagan I met during my fieldwork was familiar with the song that references this myth, which I have heard enthusiastically sung by participants across the United States. The song pits the witches, the archaic "healers and the teachers of the wisdom of the earth" who spend their evenings "chanting healing incantations, calling forth the wise ones, celebrating in dance and song," against the Christians, who "came to power through domination . . . bonded in their worship of a dead man on a cross." The subsequent verses present the mythology of Wicca through a creative reconstruction of religious history:

> The Pope declared an Inquisition
> It was a war against the women, whose power they feared
> In the holocaust against the nature people
> Nine million European women died.[81]

The fervor with which many contemporary Pagans embrace this mythology of victimization is puzzling considering the lack of historical evidence in support of any of the contentions of this myth: that all victims of the witch hunts were women; that the Inquisition targeted women only; or that any of the individuals accused and convicted in the hundreds of years of European witch trials (let alone those accused in the limited scope and relatively homogeneous religious landscape of colonial America) practiced anything akin to modern witchcraft or Paganism. Ronald Hutton's history of modern British witchcraft makes this clear: "Witchcraft could, at times, be a self-empowering fantasy for the dispossessed, but not a single person tried for witchcraft in Europe between 1400 and 1800 has been demonstrated to have adhered to a pagan religion."[82] Likewise, Diane Purkiss has critiqued the contemporary Pagan association with the witch trials and contemporary Pagan efforts to analogize the "Burning Times" and the Holocaust. She argues that contemporary Pagan mythologizing of this historical episode trivializes the Holocaust, distorts the specificity of each of these discrete historical periods, and glorifies the victimization and martyrdom of women in ways that contemporary Pagans almost certainly do not intend.[83] Purkiss acknowledges the need among Pagans to mythologize their history, noting that the power of this myth is that "it is a story with clear oppositions. . . . It legitimates identification of oppression with powerful institutions, and above all with Christianity," while casting witches—early modern, modern, or postmodern—as victims or "survivors."[84] Glenn Shuck suggests similar uses of this legend, but he highlights a rhetoric of resistance rather than victimization, noting, "The accounts assume greater importance as they reflect contemporary struggles against religious persecution and the oppression of women and give a powerful voice to these concerns," while evoking commonality with marginalized and persecuted people throughout history—albeit at the expense of historical accuracy.[85]

For many contemporary Pagans, the mythological and emotional valence of this account takes precedence over concerns about its historical accuracy. I once broached the topic of the dubious historicity of the song "The Burning Times" with the families of Spiral Winds coven, who had been singing it around the campfire. Atashih explained that even if the story was not true, it was "good mythology, anyway." He went on to note that no one knows how many witches were burned during the witch hunts, speculating that some suspected witches may have been killed by neighbors or that poor record keeping may have led to miscounted deaths. Freya had been staring silently into the fire, and now she spoke: "The answer is 'too many.'" Atashih agreed: "Two is too many." Eleven-year-old Stephen, who had been listening quietly in the shadows of the campfire, asked, "Too many what?" and his mother answered, "Too many people killed for religion."[86]

The contentious and varied perspectives of scholars and practitioners regarding the history of the religion suggest that no single historiography of contemporary Paganism can be considered foundational or primary among Pagan practitioners. Reviewing these points of contention, Ronald Hutton admits that it is "probable that the question of the origins of Wicca will never be completely resolved."[87] The issue of which history is seen as foundational gains importance not in terms of an accurate historical lineage but in terms of a mythological, intellectual, and moral one. The historical context in which Pagan practitioners or communities envision themselves affects their beliefs, practices, values, interactions with the larger community, and the imaginative and religious worlds in which their children are raised. Glenn Shuck notes that among contemporary Pagans, "While some hold to a thesis of historical continuity, it is by no means a necessary or foundational belief. For many contemporary Wiccans, history is more a laboratory of ideas than a mere chronicle of events."[88]

The sociologist Danièle Hervieu-Léger's analysis of religion as memory has important implications for understanding and interpreting these contemporary Pagan history-making practices.[89] Hervieu-Léger contends that the construction of genealogies is the fundamental characteristic of modern religions because the "chain of memory" necessary for the maintenance of community- and tradition-based religion has been severed with the emergence of modernity. This discontinuity with the past impels religious agents to continually produce genealogies in an attempt to rebuild the chain of memory. The imagined genealogy need not be historically verified or verifiable; the memory invoked "may be purely imaginary, so long as its recall is strong enough to allow identification to build and preserve the social bond in question."[90] These attempts to "reinvent the chain" create situations ripe for religious innovation. Hervieu-Léger refers to the "theoretically limitless possibilities for inventing, patching together and playing with systems of meaning that are capable of establishing tradition" as individuals and small groups attempt to re-establish the chains of memory or, failing that, to invent new ones.[91] Contemporary Pagan uses of history and dynamic historicizing offer evocative examples of this religious innovation at work in religious rituals, imagination, and daily life.

In an inversion of Hervieu-Léger's chain of memory, however, Paganism is as much about forgetting as it is about memory. Pagan individuals and Pagan communities make both deliberate and implicit choices to focus on certain aspects of their religion and to ignore others, to excise aspects of the religion's history that may be contradictory or unhelpful, and to emphasize historiographies that support their own religious, spiritual, and political values. In much the same way that they creatively historicize their religion, Pagans imaginatively remember and reconstruct their personal spiritual and religious histories. The result is a combination of memory and a kind of imaginative amnesia that, in the context of the daily lives of Pagan adults and children, shapes Pagan childhood, parenting, and religious imaginations.

2

Old Souls

Pagan Childhood

Be four years old as long as you can.
—Daniel, father of two, to his oldest son

Wise Children

This chapter examines Pagan perspectives on childhood and parenting and the ways that understandings of these idioms shape the religious and imaginative worlds of Pagan adults, children, and families. I suggest that contemporary Paganism maintains a complicated tension between the valorization of a sort of self-conscious, disingenuous naïveté among Pagan adults and an externally imposed perception of precocious wisdom among Pagan children. Put simply, contemporary Paganism seems to encourage a childlike immaturity in adults and, in some ways, an overly precocious maturity in children. Pagan adults seek to recapture the spontaneity of their lost childhoods (however oxymoronic that may be)—a spontaneity that is often lost as a result of their own disappointing or damaging childhood religious experiences. Likewise, adult Pagans attempt to prevent their own children from experiencing a similar spiritual disconnection by emphasizing, reinforcing, and, at times, inventing this connection themselves. Pagan understandings of the role and nature of the idealized concept of the "child" influence the spiritual imaginations and religious worlds of both Pagan adults and Pagan children.

When American Pagans talk about the historical roots of their religious worldviews, few of them mention the roles of Samuel Taylor Coleridge or John Keats, but the influence of these authors, and of Romanticism in general, runs deep. Scholars of contemporary Paganism acknowledge the religion's debt to the Romantics, which is evident in Paganism's reverence for nature as well as its critique of modernity and deep nostalgia for an idealized, premodern past. Ronald Hutton's history of contemporary Paganism, *Triumph of the Moon*, draws a direct line of descent from the nineteenth-century Romantic poets to modern Pagan views of nature, deities, and the sacredness of the natural world. Hutton is unequivocal about this connection, contending, "If [Paganism] is the child of any single phenomenon, then it is the belated offspring of the Romantic Movement."[1]

Romantic ideals of childhood innocence and purity were common tropes in sentimental Victorian views of children as creatures who inhabit a world of spirituality and fantasy. The troubling social, political, and personal ramifications of this glorification of childhood wonder and purity have been well defined by contemporary historians. Anne Higonnet suggests that understandings of children as "innocent" and "pure" present childhood purity as diametrically opposed to adult sexuality and risk constructing innocence as "alluringly opposite, enticingly off-limits."[2] Henry Jenkins notes that the myth of childhood innocence "empties" the child of its own political agency to better fulfill the symbolic demands made on this concept, and he suggests that childhood innocence is a cultural myth "inculcated and enforced" on children.[3] Likewise, James Kincaid observes that the distinct stage we call childhood is a "wonderfully hollow category" that exists within "an empty psychic and social space" ready to be filled with adult projections and fantasies: "A child is not, in itself, anything."[4] Finally, Susan Ridgely notes that this view of children as thoroughly innocent "implies (almost requires) that adults must protect them. And protection means, in part, that adults must speak for children because they are not informed enough to interpret the world around them." Ridgely emphasizes that this dynamic encourages adults to decode the significance of events in which children are the primary agents.[5] Paganism's understanding of childhood and children emerges from the Romantic premise of the innocent, spiritual, fantasy-steeped and wonder-filled child that informs these dilemmas of modern childhood.

Contemporary Paganism sees children as more spiritually "open" than adults, with a direct, unmediated access to the divine that adults lack.⁶ This spiritual "openness" and flexibility is often understood as the natural state of humans before we learn to deny fantasy and spirit in favor of rationality and the physical world. Children are seen as representatives of an undiluted, undenied, innate spiritual awareness. During one of our many conversations, Erin, an eclectic Pagan mother of a six-year-old, mentioned that she saw children's spirituality as different from that of adults "because they're more innocent and creative, and they're in tune. It's the adults that kind of wear that away, I think, and the teaching that wears it away."⁷ Erin is not alone in her assessment of children's increased spiritual capacities. Many Pagan adults use similar terms to explain children's spirituality (suggesting that children are "open" or "in tune," and that standard education makes children "unlearn" these spiritual proclivities). The sociologist Helen Berger received similar responses during her studies of Pagan families. She noted that many Wiccans believe that children can "more easily access the divine as they have not yet fully developed a rational, talking self."⁸ The idea that children's pure, untainted spirituality is gradually eroded and corrupted by contact with the adult world is a common theme among adult Pagans. Books with titles like *The Wise Child: A Spiritual Guide to Nurturing Your Child's Intuition*, *Child Astrology: A Guide to Nurturing Your Child's Gifts*, and *Your Magical Child* (the latter of which, presumably, includes implicit nurturing as well) are popular among Pagan parents, and references to children's natural propensity for the spiritual and supernatural occur frequently in everyday conversation.

At one Beltane festival, I sat with the families of Spiral Winds coven on a refreshingly cool early morning, wrapped in blankets and eating pancakes cooked over the campfire. Freya had responded to one of my many questions about the nature of children's spirituality by observing that children have "very deep thoughts that we don't understand." To illustrate this point, she told me a story about when her daughter Cricket was very young. As the family drove past a cemetery one day, Cricket said, "My friend Lucy is in there." Freya told her daughter that the site was a cemetery, but Cricket insisted that her friend was "in there." They stopped and went into the graveyard, and Cricket walked to a grave, marked "Lucy," of a child who had died young. Several of the adults murmured expressions of surprise or confirmation at this indication of Cricket's—what? Psychic powers? Spiritual connection? Evidence of reincarnation? Stroking Cricket's hair,

Freya added that there was more to this story: Cricket's middle name is Rose, for Freya's Aunt Rose, who had a childhood friend named Lucy. Freya observed that children have "this clarity, this closeness, that grown-ups tend to lose."[9] Eleven-year-old Stephen looked up from his pancakes to offer evidence of his own magical abilities: "I can wish for things and they come true.... But wanting something and wishing for it are a lot different." Atashih remarked, "That's because you were raised Pagan. Most kids are told that's not true"—that is, most children are not told by adults that they have the power to effect change through will (to paraphrase Aleister Crowley's definition of magic). Freya concluded this discussion by remarking, "There are a lot of distractions, the older you get; when we remove our own distractions, we can get back to that [childlike state]."

The belief in the heightened nature of children's spiritual sensitivities and the need for parents to encourage and indulge the childhood world of magic and enchantment is a common theme among Pagan parents. This is why a Pagan author can say, in a statement that is assumed to be self-evident to her adult Pagan audience, "Children are naturally magical people," with no need to elaborate on this truism. The tone of this statement suggests that this author and her readers know exactly what she means when she exhorts, "Encourage your children to be as magical as you know they already are."[10] Another writer in the same publication (a newsletter for Pagan families) boasts that all three of her daughters "instinctively" understand the "magical properties of many herbs and crystals." She explains the "lesson" she learned from her girls: "We don't really need to *teach* our children a magickal lifestyle. Our job is to make sure they don't forget the magick [sic]."[11] Adults regularly speak of children's enhanced "sensitivities," psychic powers, and inherent connection to the natural and supernatural worlds. Margie McArthur's *WiccaCraft for Families*, for example, notes matter-of-factly, "Children are more naturally attuned to a larger reality than adults." She reminds Pagan parents—who, it is assumed, know this already—that children "are naturally psychic" and can be taught to communicate telepathically with animals, acknowledging, "Some children know and do this instinctively."[12]

McArthur's caveat in this sentence—"some children"—is subtle enough to be overlooked, but the word "some" is fraught with a contentious position on the status of Pagan children. The implication seems to be that this instinctive knowledge is limited to or lost by certain children—although how and why this might occur or which children may be less attuned or less spiritually fortunate is not specified. Another author in this newsletter also seems to suggest that some children are more magical than others in an essay titled "The Enchantment of Youth." Encouraging parents to help their children resist "those unfortunate people" who refuse to recognize or promote "enchantment" (again, left undefined) in their lives, she explains that other children may attempt to strip more "magickal" children of their "enchantment and innocence."[13] Again, it seems that some privileged children inhabit a world of "enchantment," whereas some unfortunate children lack this quality and resent its presence in others (perhaps because these children have succumbed to the pressures of adult society and "forgotten" their inherent spirituality).

The belief in an innate childhood magic that is lost with the onset of adulthood reflects individual Pagan adults' nostalgia for the vanished "magic" of their own childhoods, whether this magic is recalled or re-created in adulthood. At the same time, it reflects a broader sense of the alienation and spiritual loss of modernity. Specifically, many Pagans see the emergence of Christianity in the West as the original catalyst for the disenchantment and demise of indigenous religions, in much the same way that exposure to Christianity (usually) or Judaism (occasionally) dampened their own sense of childhood enchantment.[14] Nostalgia for this lost spiritual innocence, on an individual level as well as on a cultural scale, fuels Pagan concepts of the precocious and vibrant spirituality of children. In both cases, adults look to children to remedy this loss and to serve as personal and cultural guides—and as metaphors—for spiritual renewal. The comments about children's spirituality that appear regularly in Pagan publications and conversations reflect adult views of children's spiritual capabilities, not children's sense of their own spiritual, psychic, or magical experiences. At best, these statements may not radically misrepresent children's experiences. At worst, they challenge the actual circumstances and lives of children whose desires and needs are overlooked in favor of a focus on their idyllic, idealized childhood.

Some Pagan mothers insist that their children's spiritual power is so strong that they were able to feel the child's soul enter their body during pregnancy. Kristin Madden's *Pagan Parenting* offers a lengthy discussion of children's prenatal energy and their ability to communicate from the womb. She believes that the "incoming spirit" of the fetus "settles" into the parental home in the first or second trimester, when the parents-to-be may be able to sense its energy and communicate with it. Madden maintains that at four months' gestation, her unborn son "was a huge and imposing mass of energy with a reddish tinge in our home." The fetus was also, Madden claims, "adamant that his name must be Karl and it must be spelled with a K. There was no questioning his insistence and the fact that it was obviously very important to him. That was the end of that."[15] In this scenario, the will of a sixteen-week-old fetus is already understood as taking precedence over the desires of his mother. Madden's capitulation to her unborn child exemplifies something that many Pagan adults suggest: children possess not only an innate spirituality but also a spiritual advantage over adults. Pagan writings and conversations are filled with discussions of the ways that adults can learn from children and the many ways that children function as spiritual guides for adults. The following instruction to parents is provided in *The New Wiccan Book of the Law*, a document considered "a compilation and modernization of other sets of Laws" (which is of unspecified origin but presumably archaic, making it authoritative for many Wiccans despite its "compilation" in the mid-1980s):

> Remember that your children are Goddess-spawned, and are free spirits. You do not own or control them. They are your brethren, come to visit for awhile, that they may share in the vision of your love and wisdom. Let each parent realize that we must teach and guide with love, yet the child shall also teach the parents, and aid them in their growth and development.[16]

The trope of child-as-teacher appears in countless Pagan texts. One Pagan author enthusiastically reminds parents, "The eyes of children offer views of wonder and enchantment in the everyday, which we can forget in our busy lives. . . . When we live the Wheel [celebrate the Pagan holidays throughout the year] with our children, we find that we are not so much teaching them as they are instructing us in the importance of the moment. Children's connection to the magical realm allows them to see and understand the world in ways adults have forgotten."[17] These descriptions—sometimes reverent, sometimes cloying—of innocent, magical children reflect the kinds of people adults imagine and need them to be.

One Pagan mother responded to my question about the religious composition of her family by describing herself as Wiccan, her husband as "agnostic/semi-Wiccan," and her children as "baptized United Methodists (at the insistence of extended family).... But we consider them to be beings of light."[18] At the same time, these understandings of children reflect the kinds of people adults believe they once were and the childlike spirit they (hope to) retain. Part of the process of becoming an adolescent or adult convert to Paganism involves recovering the wonder and spontaneity of the magical child within—who may bear little or no resemblance to the children these adults once were or to the children around them.

The Indigo Ideal

The spiritual advantage of children is most fully developed in the trope of the Indigo Child. Extremely popular in many New Age communities, the concept is discussed less often among Pagans, but the idea that some children display the advanced spiritual and psychic abilities that characterize Indigo Children receives equally enthusiastic support among Pagan adults. This is due in part to the significant overlap between the demographics, beliefs, and practices of the New Age and Pagan populations.[19] Pagan adults find the concept of Indigo Children relevant to their lives, either because they believe their child meets the criteria for this designation or because they believe they may have been "early" Indigo Children themselves—for example, according to Sarah Pike, "Neopagans often describe their child-selves as unusually gifted in imagination or intelligence."[20]

The group of children known as "Indigos" was identified by the San Diego parapsychologist Nancy Ann Tappe in the 1970s. Tappe believed that she had discovered a new class of children, recognizable by their indigo-colored auras, who represented the next step in human evolution. The authors Lee Carroll and Jan Tober brought this concept to a wider audience in their 1999 bestseller *The Indigo Children: The New Kids Have Arrived*. Carroll and Tober defined an Indigo Child as "one who displays a new and unusual set of psychological attributes and shows a pattern of behavior generally undocumented before. This pattern has common unique factors that suggest that those who interact with them (parents, in particular) change their treatment and upbringing of them in order to achieve balance."[21] Carroll and Tober provided a list of traits common to Indigos in an attempt to make them more easily recognizable to parents and other adults, with the expectation that these adults would attempt to encourage these traits and would adapt their expectations for these children accordingly. They suggest that Indigo Children tend to "come into the world with a feeling of royalty (and often act like it)"; have extremely high self-esteem and feel they "deserve to be here"; have difficulty with "absolute authority" and discipline, often refusing to obey authority figures or follow directions; be especially "sensitive" and "spiritually advanced"; frequently exhibit uncontrolled rage; and simply refuse to do certain things they find unpleasant—"for example, waiting in line is difficult for them."[22]

Of course, it is unlikely that anyone—spiritually advanced or not—enjoys waiting in line, and any parent of a toddler can attest to the banality of unpredictable emotions and stubbornness. Rhapsodic tone aside, this description suggests that Indigos are children brimming with entitlement and holding little patience for basic civility. In fact, some critics have pointed out that these children exhibit characteristics that are often diagnosed as Attention Deficit Hyperactivity Disorder (ADHD) or Oppositional Defiant Disorder (ODD), and much of the literature on Indigo Children suggests that they are often diagnosed with these disorders.[23] Even Tappe, the parapsychologist who initially "recognized" Indigos, admits that the impatience, anger, and resistance to authority that characterize these children can have radically negative repercussions if the children's "energies become twisted." Tappe reports, "These young children—every one of them I've seen thus far who kill their schoolmates or parents—have been Indigos."[24] In what seems a distressing lacuna, Tappe does not go on to provide parents and educators with information on how to avoid "twisting" their children's "energies" or how to prevent these children's less enlightened peers from doing so. Children with untwisted energies, one can assume, may be merely intolerable, not dangerous.

Proponents of Indigo Children, however, are quick to claim that these characteristics are misunderstood by the modern medical profession. They claim that Indigo Children are more advanced than other children, as are their even further evolved successors, the "Crystal Children." "Crystals" share the psychic and emotional sensitivities of Indigos but lack the ADHD-like symptoms (undoubtedly because their parents, the original Indigos, have no tolerance for these characteristics). Believers contend that Crystal Children are consistently misdiagnosed as autistic in the same way that Indigos have been diagnosed as ADHD. There seems to be some disagreement regarding the extent of the Indigo phenomenon; some authors seem to imply that only certain children have Indigo qualities, whereas others suggest that the entire generation of children born between 1995 and 2012 were "pure" Indigo Children, "born with a far stronger energy output and aura than their parents." Likewise, this generational theory of evolution suggests that all children born after 2012 "will be born with a fully developed Crystal aura,"[25] although some authors limit these qualities to only about 80% of this generation.[26]

In addition to their generally antisocial tendencies and hyperactivity, these children (whether Indigo or Crystal) are believed to have the ability to "see spirits, levitate, bilocate, communicate telepathically, bend time, and instantly manifest any spiritual or material need."[27] One author explains that these children "may seem like they cannot socialize, but, in fact, socialize very well with their *own kind*."[28] Those of their "own kind," of course, are others who are similarly "evolved." A typically effusive description of Indigos claims, "They have eyes that are wise, as if they have been here before. Their eyes are deep and display a hidden *guidance* for others in need. . . . [They] know they are here to change our world. They are here to show us love, peace, and harmony."[29] These believers suggest that Indigo Children are meant to be guides (albeit with "hidden guidance" available to those sufficiently spiritually developed to receive it) for ordinary, less-evolved adults and children. Many Pagan parents are already inclined to see their children as their spiritual guides based on their understandings of the spiritual advantages of childhood. The Indigo label provides additional confirmation of these beliefs for credulous parents while offering a convenient explanation for what might otherwise be seen as simply bad manners or an unfortunate sense of entitlement. A Pagan mother commenting on the popular religion website Beliefnet happily reports that her Indigo son "can spot a lie from 100 miles away" and helps his parents "to become better people every day by calling us on our BS."[30] Indigo Children's awareness of their "special" position can be equally disconcerting. An essay written by a fifteen-year-old self-proclaimed Indigo offering suggestions for "parenting the Indigo Children, from the Indigos' point of view" makes the point early and emphatically that adults can (and must) learn from these children. The author instructs parents, "Be ready to listen to us. We came here to teach, ultimately."[31] Comments such as these occur regularly on web discussion boards by self-proclaimed Indigo teenagers and those who have been told that they are Indigo by (presumably well-meaning) adults. Aside from the difficulty of taking these statements seriously (what fifteen-year-old doesn't believe they are smarter than their parents?), comments like these reflect a reframing of otherwise unacceptable social qualities into more desirable indicators of sensitivity, wisdom, and spiritual evolution.

The phenomenon and widespread acceptance of Indigo Children among New Age and Pagan parents offers a powerful example of many parents' aspirations and ideals for their children. Despite their problems with authority, uncontrollable tempers, and overbearing egos, Indigo Children are many Pagan parents' ideal offspring: sensitive, psychic, and strong willed. The traits common to Indigos are the same ones Pagan parents encourage and nurture in their children and highlight in their own childhoods: empathy, psychic sensitivities, nonconformist thinking, and resistance to authority. The Pagan author Lorna Tedder wryly observes, "Every Pagan woman I know who has a child under 10 or is planning to have another child believes she's birthing Indigo children," but she goes on to concede, "It's likely that many of them are."[32] Tedder herself is no exception to this trend. She comments that she thinks of her daughters as "chosen ones" regardless of whether she specifically calls them "Indigos," but she observes, "My older daughter has far more Indigo traits than her little sister." As if there were any doubt, she also acknowledges, "Based on my own genetics, my hypothetical [future] child would almost certainly have Indigo traits. I have almost all of the traits myself." Tedder thus not only includes herself in the group of "Holy Mothers" she mocks but also offers a perfect example of the projection of adult ideals onto children—abstract, hypothetical children as well as her own daughters (whose voices, unsurprisingly, are absent in her book). Like Tedder, many parents are quick to identify Indigo traits in their own children: some proclaim all their offspring Indigos, whereas others declare some of their children "more Indigo" than others.

Indigo characteristics are often those cultivated by Pagan adults themselves, so it is not surprising that parents of Indigos often believe they share these qualities with their children. Literature on the subject encourages parents to think of themselves as "Rainbows" or "Indigo

Pathfinders," and the tagline of a book aimed at an adult audience asks readers, "Are you a grown-up Indigo soul and don't know it?"[33] Parents post frequent proclamations of shared family Indigo traits on online community message boards.[34] In response to a question about Indigo adults, a participant in a Pagan discussion forum commented, "Isn't it amazing that we are just like our children. . . . It seems my family of 3 are indigo children."[35] Another mother confidently declared, "I have an Indigo daughter aged 8 and a Crystal Son [sic] aged 3. I am a rainbow adult."[36] What seems to ultimately be at stake here is less an assessment of children's psychic abilities than an assertion about the spiritual potential and identity of these children's parents. The concept of Indigo Children offers parents a way to talk about their own spiritual aspirations and their sense of alienation, difference, or distinction from the less-evolved masses. In the Indigo model, parental identity is largely shaped by parents' perceptions of the uniqueness of their offspring.

It is understandable, then, that parents often express considerably more enthusiasm and support for the Indigo label than do their children themselves. In an article for the *Houston Press*, the journalist Dylan Otto Krider interviewed several Indigo Children and their guardians. Krider reported that one of the children "says she knows she's an Indigo because 'my mother told me.' Jake found out he was an Indigo when his mother read a book on the subject."[37] The children Krider encountered repeatedly denied their parents' assessments of their special abilities, interjecting, for example, "You said that," in response to a parent's glowing report of a child's particularly insightful comments. Mental health and child development experts are often reluctant to support the Indigo theory; a research professor of psychiatry at SUNY, for instance, notes that the traits common to "Indigo Children" are so general that they "could describe most of the people most of the time." (This professor goes on to add, less charitably, "It's a sham diagnosis. . . . There's no science behind it. There are no studies.")[38] A specialist in the education of gifted and talented children suggests, "The indigo children movement is not about children, and it is not about the color indigo. It is about adults who style themselves as experts and who are making money on books, presentations, and videos."[39]

The long-term effect of this designation on children (and their parents) remains to be seen. What happens when a being of light has a tantrum in the grocery store, throws up in the car, refuses to do homework, bites another child, or is the source of any of the myriad other inconveniences and catastrophes of parenting? What happens to parent–child relationships when children fail to live up to their parents' expectations of them as guides and gurus? What becomes of Indigo Children who fail to save the world? Krider's article recounts the story of one mother, a "medical intuitive" who counsels Indigos, who believed that her son was among the earliest Indigo Children. When this son, as an adult, chose a career as an auto mechanic rather than as a spiritual leader or evolutionary icon, his mother became convinced that his "main purpose was simply to bring her grandchildren, who are the real teachers. She admits that her son and daughter-in-law, a fundamentalist Christian, don't agree that he's an Indigo."[40]

The certainty with which parents decide that their children have Indigo qualities, paired with the movement's lack of significant support within the medical and scientific communities, suggests that the Indigo phenomenon may be, at least in part, prompted and perpetuated by parents' ideals and aspirations for their children and themselves. The Indigo theory allows parents to identify as the planet's evolutionary leaders children who might otherwise be diagnosed with behavioral or emotional problems. At the same time, the Indigo label allows parents who have felt (or continue to feel) alienated from mainstream society to identify the genetic roots of these advanced abilities in themselves. The phenomenon of Indigo Children seems less a harbinger of an entire generation of super-evolved *Übermenschen* than a reflection of parents' struggles between spiritual narcissism and cultural significance. An unfortunate consequence of this struggle is its tendency to misjudge, overlook, or occlude the lives and experiences of real children.

Real Children and Inner Children

Contemporary Pagans frequently find the fact of children in the religion to be a point of contention. This is especially true when real Pagan children—the ones who whine, fidget, or sleep through rituals and who display varying levels of interest in their parents' theology and activities—are not necessarily identical to Pagan images of the spiritually evolved ideal child. Idealized views of Indigo Children as inherently spiritual and evolutionarily advanced can (and often do) coexist with real children in a community. The presence of children in a coven (or even in a family) does not necessarily ensure a realistic understanding of children's spirituality among the community's adults. In the same way that children are considered to have a spiritual advantage over adults, a paradoxical spiritual maturity is often assumed to accompany a deliberately childlike attitude. The particular qualities of childhood that are accentuated and valued by Pagan adults—the "childlike" traits of spontaneity, exuberance, playfulness, and connection to the natural and spiritual worlds—are also those that adults value in their own behavior. To many who practice it, contemporary Paganism is a playful and imaginative religion, as evidenced by its emphasis on costuming, theatrical and often lighthearted rituals, and Pagans' frequent uses of humor in organized rituals and daily life (qualities that have led Pagan studies scholars to refer to contemporary Paganism as a "ludic" religion).[41] The sociologist Lorne Dawson comments on this quality in Pagan ritual, observing that most rituals maintain "an attitude of irreverence and a ludic love of parody. They make few cognitive, moral, or even social demands on participants."[42] Some branches of contemporary Paganism highlight these playful qualities more than others; Discordians, for example, emphasize the surreal and absurd over all other aspects of their spirituality. Displaying attitudes that could have come directly from J. M. Barrie, many Pagan adults refer to themselves as "big kids" and vow to "never grow up" (facilitated, no doubt, by the scarcity of demands noted by Dawson). The playful, childlike, undemanding aspects of the religion appeal to many Pagan adults, while non-Pagan observers may find in these qualities sufficient basis to dismiss its religious sincerity and legitimacy. This particular debate is a recurrent point of contention in terms of contemporary Paganism's relationship to American religions and its place within a religiously pluralistic society, but it also points to an often overlooked issue: the place of real children in a world of childlike adults.

3

Parenting in Neverland

> When I was ten, I read fairy tales in secret and would have been ashamed if I had been found doing so. Now that I am fifty, I read them openly. When I became a man, I put away childish things, including the fear of childishness and the desire to be very grown up.
> —C. S. Lewis, "On Three Ways of Writing for Children," 1952

"There Are No Grownups Here"

The Council of Magickal Arts (CMA) holds a semiannual Pagan gathering on private land in central Texas. During my two years of fieldwork at this festival, I sometimes fulfilled my mandatory two hours of community service (required by CMA of all attendees at the festival) by volunteering at Fairy Mound (sometimes written "Faerie Mound"), an activity center and babysitting co-op for two- to six-year-old children. The name itself illustrates the deep connection in contemporary Paganism between children and the supernatural. Pagans often accept (seemingly as undisputed fact) that "children can see devas, fairies and nature spirits much easier than most adults." Some texts encourage adults to "prepare" their children for contact with these otherworldly beings so that they are not "frightened by a visit from a departed loved one or the appearance of a fairy."[1] Many adult Pagans claim to be able to see and interact with fairies (also "faeries" or the "Fey"). One author comments that she was able to see fairies as a child but had to reject teachings from her parents and society and relearn how to see these creatures as an adult.[2] Every mention of fairies in discussions with adult Pagans (a topic that arises in conversation far more often than would seem likely) leads to these matter-of-fact mentions of human interactions with supernatural beings. Whether adult Pagans "really believe" that they interact with fairies on a regular basis is less important to this discussion than the indication of the importance of retaining (or regaining) the childlike quality of conversing with fairy-folk as a sign of advanced spiritual growth.

Community service at Fairy Mound is not terribly demanding. The volunteers' duties largely consist of offering children water as they play in the hot Texas sun, ensuring that every child who leaves the fenced children's area is signed out and accompanied by a parent or guardian (ideally an adult, but children are regularly released into the care of slightly older siblings), and watching children play on the swings, the slides, and the castle playhouse. During my shift, I was joined by another adult volunteer, a middle-aged man named Mike in a tie-dyed T-shirt, and we stood in the shade of a scrubby tree, idly chatting about the heat and the festival. One of the children approached us, wanting to talk to a grown-up about some playground altercation. Mike feigned surprise and playfully asked the boy, "Why are you looking at me? I'm not a grown-up. The grown-ups I've known are always tired and unhappy. That's not me."

This resistance to being thought of as an "adult" arises often among Pagan adults, many of whom insist, like Mike, that they have no part in the sad, serious, conservative world of adults—that their place, instead, is in the magical world of childhood imagination, fantasy, and joy. But my fellow volunteer was charged with maintaining order and safety among the chronological children on the playground. If he was not a grown-up, if he situated himself in the world of the children he was meant to be attending, if the charge of adulthood is read as virtually an accusation, then one has to wonder: where in this religion do children learn to be adults? Because, despite messages like Mike's to the child on the playground, children clearly do grow up in contemporary Paganism. They rely on the adults in their lives to act as guardians and responsible (if not always authoritative) caretakers, and the adults, for the most part, attempt to meet these expectations—despite their protestations of not being "grown-ups." The Pagan parents I have met praise appropriate behavior, discipline children with time-outs when necessary, and explain consequences. With varying degrees of difficulty, Pagan children learn to share, to help with chores, to say "please" and "thank you," and (always!) to recycle. In most cases, children seem to model their behavior on the moral and social conduct they witness among adults rather than on the presence or absence of explicit ethical statements.

A fundamental tension in the study of Pagan families involves the presence of dissonant messages from adults to children regarding explicit and implicit moral codes as well as dissonance between these adults' ideals and behaviors. The dilemma that arises is something like this: is there room for Pagan children to act like children when the adults in their lives maintain a religious and ideological commitment to the denial of adulthood and to the glorification of childhood as a privileged spiritual state? More simply: Do adult idealizations of the spiritual, innocent, "Child" displace real children from the realm of childhood? Does parenting in Neverland leave any space for children?

This chapter examines the ways that Pagan adults remember and imagine their own religious childhoods and how these memories are shaped by the importance in contemporary Paganism of childlike spontaneity and the religious imagination. Does the religion's emphasis on childlike wonder encourage a disingenuous rejection of adulthood among Pagan adults? How do these adults position themselves as eternal children in the process of raising children of their own?

It's Never Too Late to Have a Happy Childhood

I was raised Southern Baptist. My experience of religion was pleasant but somewhat flat. I felt the movement of Spirit every so often in my family's church and when we had a well-educated pastor I enjoyed the sermons on an intellectual level, but most of the time there was just something missing. I felt much more spiritually uplifted running in the woods behind my home. I became interested in Wicca when my husband brought home some of Scott Cunningham's books just after our daughter was born. The first ritual I ever performed was the Ma'at ritual from Janet and Stuart Farrar's book *The Witches' Goddess*. Spirit moved in a big way, and I've never looked back.
—Patricia, Wiccan mother of one

If Pagans like to talk about their current religious beliefs, they love to talk about their religious backgrounds. Adult Pagans' recollections and reconstructions of their childhoods often take the form of narratives that illuminate the early origins of their Pagan tendencies in a "complex and dynamic" relationship between "Neopagans' current identities and their remembered childhood."[3] The landscape of childhood, for many Pagans, provides the backdrop for adult Pagan religious worlds rife with wonder, fantasy, and imagination and shapes Pagan religious beliefs and practices. First-generation adult Pagans recall childhoods characterized by communion with nature and the world of spirits, animals, and fairies. They often recall, as well, that these experiences were discouraged, if not demonized, by adults in their families and in their religious institutions. Adult Pagans very often "use the phrase 'shoved down my throat' to describe aggressive proselytizing by families and churches,"[4] and this seems to be true among Pagans of all kinds throughout the United States. Many Pagan parents told me that they felt their children's schools "shoved Christianity down their throats," and adults from different parts of the country recounted similar stories of feeling oppressed, bored, or misunderstood by their families' religious practices. Sarah Pike's ethnography of Pagan festival culture suggests that these adults seek to recover a sense of wonder, magic, and connection to the spiritual and natural world by recreating these qualities in their adult lives and in their practice of Paganism. I suggest that, beyond these re-creations of their own childhoods, Pagan adults also seek to redeem their lost magical childhoods by shaping their own children's religious worlds in such a way that these childhoods reflect (or surpass) the adults' own childhood experiences of unencumbered spirituality; they reconstruct the religious worlds they wish they had inhabited. In much the same way that reconstructing and retelling multiple histories imbues contemporary Paganism with relevant historical traditions, Pagans' retellings of their personal religious origin stories shape their own childhoods in ways that make their experiences more magical, more oppressive, or otherwise more relevant to their adult spiritual identities.

In an online survey of religious beliefs and values, I asked adult Pagans to tell me about their religious upbringings and their experiences of religion in childhood. Given the opportunity to write an unlimited amount of text in response to this question, the forty-four respondents to this survey provided significantly longer responses to this item than to any of the other survey questions. Adult Pagans are fiercely protective of these origin stories, and they tell and retell their stories of leaving the oppressive religions of their childhoods for the freedom of contemporary Paganism. As Sarah Pike notes, these accounts reinforce the dynamic relationship between the childhood self and the adult self:

> Childhood plays a dynamic role in Neopagan self-making; the childhood self is created through stories about the past. At the same time, childhood stories are used to constitute the adult self. Narrative both constructs a coherent self and heals wounds, and narratives of the self are not static; once told, they continue to be shaped by experience.[5]

There are a number of similarities in adult Pagans' accounts of leaving the religions of their childhood in favor of the more personally authentic spirituality of Paganism. In fact, these accounts seem to cluster into two broad categories. The first group involves stories that focus on the rejection of the teller's childhood and family religious beliefs (most often Christianity, but occasionally Judaism) due to conflicts with the social or theological teachings of the church. The second type of origin story focuses on Paganism as the culmination of a search for an authentic personal religion, emphasizing the spiritual search and, often, the teller's spiritual precocity as a child.

Adult Pagans raised in mainstream religions frequently recall feeling compelled to participate in their family's traditions, often against their will. A mother of two who describes herself as a "natural eclectic buddhist witch [sic]" succinctly describes her experience with the religion of her childhood: "My conflict with Christianity began at the age of 7."[6] Many Pagans recall the religious worlds of their childhoods as rife with boredom, confusion, shame, and fear. Another Pagan mother of two, raised Catholic, remembers:

My experiences were of being forced to attend services, and it was very strict. I particularly remember an instance where I attended service with my grandmother, and when it came time to receive communion (be forgiven for your sins), I was told that I could not receive it because I could not remember the words to the Act of Contrition. I thought that it was a mean God that would not forgive someone who couldn't remember the words.[7]

Conflicts with the church or with Judeo-Christian concepts of God are a common theme in many of these stories. Another Pagan mother wrote, "I was raised Jewish. I didn't like going to temple or going to hebrew school. I found it to be constricting. I didn't realize at the time that my objection was that there was no compassion in that God. There was also no Deity for me to connect with since the God of the Jews is typically seen as masculine, unless you study cabbalah very extensively."[8] Other adult Pagans remember conflicts stemming from the social aspects of the church: "Religion in my childhood was horrible. It was a forced event where I had to spend time with people who were on power trips looking for any way to keep the new girl from taking over their territory."[9] Another eclectic Pagan mother of a young daughter described her journey from Catholicism to Paganism as fueled by theological and social misgivings about the church:

I was brought up Catholic. I enjoyed my religion as a child and went to church every Sunday and went to confession a couple of times a year. We even went to holy day masses! I did not enjoy the inherent guilt in the Catholic church and did not agree on a lot of their policies. I always wanted a more direct connection to the divine. . . . I had been interested in witchcraft since I was 15 years old but was always afraid to research it because I thought I'd "go to hell." Finally, I bought a book and began reading (before I was married). After I was married, one of the priests in my Catholic Church gave a sermon about how women were the cause of all the sin and devastation and awfulness in the world. I was sickened and never set foot in a Catholic Sunday mass again.[10]

Some Pagans take an even more oppositional stance toward Christianity and Judaism, positioning themselves as both outside of and superior to the religions of their childhoods in language that conveys contempt for their religious foundations:

> My Perants [parents] are (were?!) Christian. Myself on the otherhand, hated going to church. I have always believed in magick, spells, Witchcraft. . . . Christianity was always like a child's story book. Full of tales of magnific[e]nt events and people. But even at the age of 7, it did not make sen[s]e to me [sic].[11]

The history offered by this respondent, a twenty-year-old stepfather of an eight-year-old boy, presents a more confrontational approach to Christianity than many of the other responses, but his critique of mainstream religion as a "child's story book" (in contrast, one assumes, to the more rational approach of spells and magic) is certainly not an isolated case. Adult Pagans frequently position themselves as self-appointed interlocutors of Christianity:

> I was raised Christian—mostly Baptist. But I asked too many questions. In searching for the answer I found paganism.[12]

> I was raised Methodist. Very Methodist. In fact, I was the president of the church youth group until I was impeached for asking questions.[13]

> I was [raised] Christian, we went to several different denominations growing up. From Southern Baptist, Assemblies of God to Lutheran. From the time I was little I questioned everything. I didn't like what the Christian answers to everything were.[14]

> I've always just had questions ever since I was little. I went along with my religion, but I guess faith is beyond me and just didn't make rational sense in my thoughts.[15]

> I was raised Presbyterian but have attended a variety of mainstream Christian churches. I started to fall away from the church at a young age (about 12) when I realized the church elders/preachers could not answer many of my questions and also due to the subordinate role of women.[16]

Many adult Pagans' stories of leaving the religions of their childhoods center on their initial contact with contemporary Paganism as a moment of familiarity or recognition. The "aha" moment marks many

Pagans' entrance into this new religion. They use phrases like "the more I learned the more it felt right to me," and they describe Paganism as the culmination of a "search to find something that would make me feel more complete."[17]

Some adult Pagans locate their propensity for religious seeking in their childhoods, often citing multireligious households or experiences with multiple religious traditions before arriving at Paganism. An example is the survey respondent who "spent 15 years as a Baptist and 11 as a Mormon before [she] found Paganism" or another who left Christian missionary work with the Word of Faith movement for Paganism.[18] Another Pagan parent described her experiences in a way that reflects many Pagans' narratives:

> I was raised by a Southern Baptist mother and an Episcopalian father. We attended every denomination in between, trying to find a happy medium, but it never happened. . . . I was always a seeker—in 3rd grade I read Edith Hamilton's *Mythology*, and set up altars to Athena and Artemis. When I was a teenager, I considered converting to Catholocism [*sic*] and pursuing a contemplative life. I always sought direct experience with the Divine, but I couldn't find it in church. A couple years after I got married, I was sitting in an Episcopalian mass, listening to the priest recite the liturgy, and it struck me that *I* could conduct the mass more effectively than he could! He was just mumbling the words . . . there was nothing behind them. God was definitely not there. I had to look elsewhere. I had always been drawn to the Goddess, but afraid to leave the religion I was raised with. I finally broke free and was able to be very honest with myself: I was not, could not be, a committed Christian. I did not hold with the tenets of that faith, I could not identify with that God. I needed my Mother. I came home to Paganism, to the Goddess, to my Bright Lady. I owned my own Witch self.[19]

Other adult Pagans extend their personal narratives of themselves as spiritual seekers or precocious religious savants to their families of origin, identifying family members or ancestors from whom they may have obtained their magical propensities. They mention grandparents who talked about psychic experiences or a Catholic grandmother who "remained grounded to the earth . . . and taught me to respect and love it."[20] They attribute Pagan tendencies and any traces of "traditional," "kitchen witch," or "hedge witch" practices to grandparents whose connection to "witchcraft" is assumed from their Anglo-Saxon or Native American heritage. In some cases, they even find spiritual kinship within their biological families:

> I was raised mostly Christian, but was always made aware of the other religions. When very young knew my mom was diffrent but not how she was diffrent. had my first vision at 7 and started to [doubt] christianity ... after the age of 16 (by this time my mom had told me she was a witch) and many yrs of rebelion and seeing the bs in the churches ... I started exploring other religions [especially] the pagan religions [sic].[21]

Finally, the spiritual narratives of some adult Pagans weave multiple themes into a coherent history of identity and self-discovery:

> Religion was always important in my family. I was baptized in my grandparents' parish. I received First Communion, confession, and confirmation all at the same church growing up. Church was family, you know? Church was community, church was ritual, church was celebration, church was safe space, church was growth, church was all of those things that it's supposed to be. . . . Somewhere in adolescence I started really questioning the church. Not the teachings of Jesus—forgiveness, compassion, do unto others, all that kind of stuff—that still rings very, very true, and I still hold those very dear. But I started to question the church, the patriarchy of it, the fact that women could not be priests, the fact that priests could not be married, all of those things that the church gets sort of a bad rap for, its attitudes about sexuality. And then I started thinking ... I had a lot of questions. When I got to college, as an undergrad, I had a couple of friends who had taken a course together in feminist spirituality, and that started this whole chain reaction of events. . . . Something opened up in my mind, and I started reading, and reading, and reading one book after another after another, and I checked out other religions besides Wicca. I checked out Taoism, I checked out Judaism, I checked out Hinduism . . . I remember that the more I read, the more things started to click. Like, hey, wait a minute—I've always thought that. That's always been what I'm about. And there's a name for it, and other people

are into this too, enough so that they're writing books about it. So . . . I don't think that I have ever left my spiritual core; I've just realized that I was practicing it in the wrong place.²²

One of the common motifs in many of these narratives of adult Pagans' spiritual development is their reliance on books to guide them toward and keep them on their paths. The single most unifying factor among Pagans may be this: Pagans read. Pagans may insist on intra-religious diversity and the exceptionality of individual belief and practice, but they share an immersion in and passion for literature. They read self-help books, graphic novels, fairy tales, and works of science fiction and fantasy. They read aloud to children, and they encourage children to read to themselves, to one another, and to adults. They read Robert Graves's *The White Goddess*, Joseph Campbell's *The Power of Myth*, Robert Anton Wilson's *Illuminatus Trilogy*, books of Greek, Roman, and Native American myths, Grimm's fairy tales, and *The Complete Calvin and Hobbes*. Literature is one of the most important catalysts for the religious imagination of Pagan adults and children and for constructions of Pagan religious childhood. There are frequent references in this book to the many types of literature referenced, shared, and enjoyed by Pagan adults and children because, inevitably, conversation with Pagans turns to what they are reading, what they have read, and what they think you should read next. Sarah Pike's ethnography describes the way adult Pagans talk about the literary narratives of their own childhoods:

> In their stories, Neopagans were children with an inordinate love of reading and a passion for books. In a way, Neopagans are manifesting in the "real" world what they remember of the fictional worlds of their childhood. . . . When I asked festival-goers how they came to be Neopagans, many of them recalled their childhood interest in fantasy fiction.²³

A Pagan father succinctly explained the importance of literature in his own spiritual narrative by noting, "My mom was a 'religious seeker' and took us to a lot of different churches, but never got involved with any. I think my early exposure to H. P. Lovecraft, Robert Anton Wilson, Douglas Adams and 'The Principia Discordia' permanently warped me."²⁴ Books, particularly mythology and fantasy literature, provide many Pagans with the impetus to learn about (or to learn more about) their own and other religions, and many American Pagans learn about their religion through books before they attempt to locate and practice with others. A Pagan father in Ohio whose family had recently begun attending services at the local Unitarian Universalist church explained his approach to learning about the UU tradition:

> After going [to the UU church] a couple times, I was like, "Where's the book?" Of course, I find out there is no book. I'm like, "Well, you have to have some literature somewhere!" And yes [laughs], there is quite a bit of literature. . . . Well, I don't have eighty dollars to spend on a collection of essays from the seventeenth century, although I would love to have it. I mean, if I'm going to spend eighty dollars on a book, it's going to be on *Dungeons and Dragons*.[25]

Many other Pagan adults mentioned the crucial role of books as they embarked on their new spiritual paths:

> I had a dear friend who after a year of practice finally had the courage to tell me she was a practicing Witch. I thought she was nuts and asked her for some reading material so I could understand better. I read one book and discovered this is what people like me are called.[26]

> I've considered myself Pagan since I was 15. I did a lot of reading and it interested me first as a novelty, then after studying [comparative] religions and being constantly irritated by Christians trying to [convert] me, I studied Paganism more intently and chose my path.[27]

> I was raised Catholic, sort of . . . I was never convinced of the teachings of the Church and always felt that my personal understanding of Deity was the right one, not what seemed to be the pettiness of the "God" of the Church. I became involved formally with Paganism about 20 years ago, but didn't have a name for it until I discovered books on Wicca about 13 years ago. That's when I knew there was a name for my beliefs.[28]

Pagans tend to have wide-ranging tastes in literature, but most maintain a passion for fantasy and children's literature—genres that keep them firmly rooted in the magical, spiritual, idealized world of childhood. Pagan adults and Pagan children talk about the fantasy literature they read as though these books are the sacred texts their religion lacks, and Pagans often "assume that there is a dynamic relationship between fiction and their own lives."[29] Little wonder, then, that so many adult Pagans take to heart those first words of J. M. Barrie's classic of children's literature: "All children, except one, grow up." Deep down, every adult Pagan is that one eternal child.

* * *

The author Judith Warner explains that the cultural attraction of the "inner child" has led to situations in which mental health professionals are confronted with adult patients who "were so wedded to their inner children that they were refusing to grow up. Even the shock of having children—real children, as opposed to inner ones—didn't necessarily lead patients to separate from their little selves."[30] This fascination with reclaiming the childlike is not restricted to Pagan (and New Age) adults, although many adults in these groups take the cultural infatuation with the inner child to extremes.

In much the same way that Paganism recasts childhood as a time of both spiritual wonder and spiritual gravitas, Pagan adults seem to experiment with a type of psychological paedomorphism. In the traditional biological understanding of paedomorphism, adults of a species retain juvenile physiological characteristics. In contrast to the biological understanding of this phenomenon, Pagan adults' retention of juvenile traits is deliberate and reflects a psychological decision rather than a biological delay. The psychologist Bruce Charlton has referred to this "prolonged youthfulness" as "psychological neoteny," suggesting that this quality provides advantages in a dynamic, rapidly changing world.[31] Charlton sees this phenomenon as a psychological response to cultural pressures (including, oddly, the "prolonged average duration of formal education"). Although Charlton's hypotheses—published in his own journal, *Medical Hypotheses*—seem to have minimal scientific grounding, the concept of chronological adults who "never actually become adults" is a familiar one in contemporary Paganism. Pagan adults are often happy to meet children at their level rather than attempting to impose adult parameters or guidance. In response to my question, "Can you give an example of a conversation or activity between you and your child/ren in which you attempted to teach them your religious and moral values?" one Pagan father provided the following text:

> CHILD: "What happens when we die?"
> ME: "They put you in a casket and bury you in the ground."
> CHILD: "Oh yeah, I saw that on TV . . . Do you think we become angels when we die?"
> ME: "I have no idea. I guess some people think that."
> CHILD: "I think we become robots."
> ME: "Really? What kind would you be?"
> CHILD: "One that shots lasers from it's hand's [sic]."
> ME: "That's cool."[32]

There are two issues here: first, the message delivered from this father to his child in response to a metaphysical question; and second, the message this respondent intended to convey about himself and his parenting dynamic through the medium of the survey. In terms of the first issue, the father does provide guidance, of a sort. He neither answers nor ignores his son's question, but he prioritizes his son's agency and imagination in determining an answer. A dynamic in which the parent asks for and validates the child's input rather than providing religious and metaphysical answers reflects childhood experiences that many adult Pagans wish they had experienced and the religious and intellectual freedom they plan for their children. In terms of the second issue, the presentation of this exchange as a conversation about "values" seems to demonstrate nothing so much as the value of the childlike and imaginative over the more traditional; this father clearly seems to situate his four-year-old child and himself as peers in this conversation.

One area in which this insistence on the childlike is particularly prevalent among Pagan adults is in the realm of magic. Many adult Pagans regularly use magic (or magick, as it is usually spelled by Pagans), and they encourage in their children an appreciation for the magical, the enchanted, and the supernatural. Many Pagans perform structured magic in the form of individual or group rituals or spells, but this is certainly not the only way that magic can manifest. Pagans see magic in the growth of plants, in specific thoughts and intentions maintained while cooking, cleaning, or folding laundry, and in spells cast for the return of a lost pet. They talk (often) about the magic of fairies and familiars and about magical worlds—Narnia, Faerie, Lothlorien—as if these places were as real as their own backyards. They talk to trees, to animals, and to the moon. They populate and inhabit magical realms in everyday life, and they encourage their children to join them there: "with the 8yr old [sic] we encourage his visions or dreams . . . always tell him no such thing as imaginary . . . just because everyone else doesn't see it dont mean it isnt real [sic]. We talk about dragons, unicorns and the other things most think of as not real as if they live with us every day."[33] When eight-year-old Raven, flying a dragon-shaped kite with her father, wistfully remarked, "I've never seen a real dragon," her father said, "I have. When you're older and you can meditate, I'll show you where."[34] Pagan families frequently incorporate magical concepts into their everyday religious experiences, weaving the imaginary and the fantastic into their religious practices (and vice versa):

> Recently I got tired of waiting to exit from a parking lot onto a busy street and performed a quick little charm for a break in traffic. It's one I use fairly often and I happened to mention it to Michelle at the time, which occasioned a quick (and somewhat heated) discussion on the ethical dimensions of using magic for personal gain.[35]

Pagans' understandings of magic vary considerably, and some of these understandings seem to reflect conflicting or ambivalent views of the relationship between magic and the physical world. Pagans often describe magic as similar to prayer; one self-proclaimed "Christian Witch" told me, to the surprise and delight of the other Pagan adults in the room with him, "Magic is prayer with balls."[36] Many note that the main difference between magic and prayer is that Christians use petitionary prayer to obtain assistance, whereas Pagans "invest their own energy into the change they want to make and ask only for guidance and support from their [deity]."[37] Despite what seems to be a common assumption among Pagan adults—that magic is similar to prayer but requires greater agency—understandings of magic often reflect an ambivalent relationship between magic and the ordinary world. In a statement that echoes Pagan adults' notions of childhood as a pure, innocent time before education and adulthood "wear away" children's greater spiritual proficiency, one Pagan mother remarked, "Magic is not 'supernatural' (if it happens in nature, and magic does, it cannot be outside nature)[;] it has just not been explained away by science yet."[38] Another mother agreed: "Quantum physics is now addressing concepts which we who practice magik [sic] have acknowledged for ages."[39] Many parents note that they are careful to distinguish between "Hollywood" magic and "real" magic with their children:

> I say things to her like, "Now you know that real magic isn't blue sparklies coming out of your fingertips or turning people into frogs or anything, right? Real magic is getting your energies and the energies around you and getting them to do something you tell them to. You can't see it, but you can feel it." But this doesn't stop either of us from wishing we could wave our wands and make the house clean itself while we go out and play. I also make sure she doesn't practice magic without me or her father to guide her. She's still a bit young to really understand the larger cause and effect concepts to magic [and] children tend to blend reality and play so easily. I am always reminding her that real magic is not a game. It's serious business.[40]

Pagan adults' insistence on constructing and inhabiting magical and fantastic worlds and encouraging their children's religious imaginations does not always guarantee that Pagan children will feel equally motivated to participate in these religious imaginaries. One Pagan mother, the author of two books on contemporary Paganism, described a conflict with her daughter over the issue of magic:

> I have tried talking with my daughter about magic—I made her an anti-nightmare amulet to put under her pillow—but she insists that magic isn't real, so didn't want it. She's in a very black-and-white stage of thinking right now, so to her, a word can only have one definition: magic is only the stuff you see in movies and books. So I've backed off for the time being on trying to explain it. I have tried to steer her away from negative statements like "I can't," trying to teach her how mindset can be a powerful thing, so she should instead say "This is hard." It's tricky,

because magical concepts are much more subtle and complex than a five-year-old can grasp, and I myself tend to be skeptical about a lot of magical stuff, so I don't want to teach her to be gullible or think she's more powerful than she is.[41]

Again and again, Pagans insist on their right to playful, childlike behaviors, their right to "celebrate foolishness,"[42] and their refusal to "grow up" at the same time that they insist on maintaining their authority in the parent–child dynamic. During one of my visits to a CMA festival with Spiral Winds coven, Atashih joked that I should let him answer the child version of my interview guide. Nevertheless, he was thoroughly annoyed when the "guardians" (basically, volunteer security guards) at the festival attempted to give his daughters the glow-in-the-dark wristbands worn by all attendees under the age of eighteen. Minors at the festival wear these red glowing bracelets to allow lost children to be found easily after dark. When a guardian remarked that the wristbands were intended to keep children safe, Atashih insisted, "They're my kids. I'm the one responsible for their safety." As we walked back to our campsite (in the dark, amid the bobbing lights of other children wearing glowing wristbands), Atashih grumbled that there were "too many rules," that he was the only "guardian" his children need. Atashih had explained to me on the way to the festival how his understanding of "guardianship" had changed since the births of his daughters. Despite his insistence on being a "big kid" who "lives for mythology" and "doesn't have to grow up," his role as a guardian and guide for his daughters is one that Atashih takes very seriously.

Not all Pagan parents claim to be "just big kids." In a complicated but implicitly understood dynamic, however, those who do make this claim seem to encourage children to look beyond the words that seemingly relinquish their adult authority. If Pagan children take these adult protestations of childlike status at face value, they should assume equal standing—intellectually, socially, or authoritatively—with their elders. But Pagan children seem utterly unperturbed by adults' verbal abnegations of authority as they model their behavior on the daily activities of their caretakers. When Mike, my co-volunteer at Fairy Mound, rejected the identity of a responsible adult in favor of deriding typical adult behaviors, his words themselves seemed to have little impact on the children's behavior or on their understanding of the relationship dynamics between adults and children. The boy at Fairy Mound recognized Mike's teasing tone, if not the significance of the words themselves, and he waited for the adult assistance he was certain was forthcoming. Unlike the old parenting chestnut "Do as I say, not as I do," the message many Pagan children internalize has a "do as I do, not as I say" flavor. The children mirror the moral behaviors of adults and disregard the discourse. What is the relative weight of these words and actions in a religious context? What is the effect of this adult insistence on refusing to grow up on the children who are literally growing up in these adults' presence? Are children's ordinary childhoods supplanted by adults' extended ones? How does this emphasis on the magic of childhood and the "inner children" of adults affect Paganism's real children?

The ironic answer would be that Pagan children, in turn, attempt to fulfill adult expectations of the wise, spiritually advanced Child—that they act mature beyond their years, that they shoulder adult responsibilities with aplomb. To some degree, this is true: some Pagan children do demonstrate a somber, exaggerated maturity, though whether this is due to adult expectations, encouragement from adults and peers to think for themselves, or simply personality traits is unclear. At one SpiralScouts campout, a six-year-old girl composed and sang a lullaby for her mother about death and rebirth, reassuring her mother that it was all right to go to sleep because "everything changes and is reborn." Persuaded to sing the song to a group of scouts and adults the following morning, she sang in a sweet, high, barely audible voice, smiling at her mother the whole time. With a similar mixture of gravitas and charm, a blond four-year-old in a hooded cloak and a purple foam wizard's hat solemnly explained to me at a CMA festival that a dead butterfly on the ground would return to the Goddess before it "came back alive" through reincarnation.

In some ways, it does seem that adult appropriations of the childlike displace real children from the realm of childhood. When Pagan adults claim childlike status, they draw on both historical and contemporary views of children and childhood as well as theological understandings of the spirituality of children and adults. Yet their messages, at times, seem ambiguous and sometimes jarring. How does someone like Mike, my fellow Fairy Mound volunteer, understand concepts like adult authority and guardianship? In Mike's case, perhaps, the concepts are purely academic. The children of Fairy Mound are in no real danger (aside from the ordinary Texas threats of sunburn and chiggers), so Mike is not required to behave in an "adult" capacity; his presence among the children is sufficiently reassuring. Mike could confidently take the opportunity to mock cultural expectations for adults while simultaneously offering the children a glimpse of one sort of acceptable adult behavior: the refusal of adulthood. Likewise, the ambivalence evident in Mike's disavowal of the burdens of maturity is rooted in Pagan notions of childhood and adulthood. The "Child"—the innocent, spiritual, natural child—is an integral part of Pagan ideology. The existence of this idealized child, however, can necessitate mixed messages to the somewhat grubby actual child awaiting a response from the adult at Fairy Mound.

Whether these children choose to remain Pagan as adults, whether they choose to raise their own children in Pagan traditions, the ambivalence of these messages about adulthood, responsibility, and authority accompany Pagan children into adulthood as fundamental truths imparted by their parents and other trusted adults. Ultimately, the long-term effects of this dichotomy of the child and the childlike remain unclear, in part because of the lack of longitudinal studies of second-generation Pagan children. Beyond this sociological lacuna, though, looms a larger issue. The understanding of Pagan children's innate spirituality is not necessarily dependent on specific children—or even real children—for its emotional, psychological, and theological significance. In the same way that Victorian ideals of children's innocence and purity failed to reflect the actual lives or dispositions of nineteenth-century children, the "children" described by Pagan adults in Paganism's paeans to children's spirituality are, for the most part, idealized conceptions of "children." In this sense, real children are optional.

The dissonance between ideology and action evident in Pagan views of childhood and adulthood offers insight into the study of the religious imagination of children and adults as this imagination is constructed in relationships between them. Children's agility in negotiating the incongruities of the religious imagination seems to suggest that religious fluency proceeds as much from ambivalence and fissures as from narrative and instruction. Many Pagan parents maintain an ideological ambivalence between the ideal children they emulate and the real children they raise, and the line between childlike behavior and adult responsibility is ambiguous and constantly renegotiated. Despite these conflicting messages, Pagan children rarely seem confused about the boundaries separating "children" from "adults." Pagan children play with other children and, more often than not, they treat the costumed, playful adults they encounter with bemused indulgence. This incongruity between parents' views of adulthood and children's expectations of adults is part of the relational dynamic within which contemporary children imagine, engineer, and construct their religious lives. As part of this dynamic, Pagan adults model a particular type of adulthood—one that resembles, but does not quite mirror, understandings of adulthood in the surrounding culture.

It may be that what Pagan adults model for Pagan children is not the same kind of adulthood performed by the majority of American parents. Instead, it may be something new: a sort of Pagan–American adulthood, one that emphasizes fantasy, "childlike" wonder, and a complex and ambivalent relationship with authority. The shaping of this new kind of adulthood is one of the ways that the study of Pagan values and understandings of childhood and adulthood can offer insight into the construction of intergenerational religious imaginations within Pagan families. At the same time, these dynamics between Pagan adults and Pagan children can illuminate, in Pagan contexts, the dilemmas of modern American family life. In the tension between the ideals of childhood and adulthood, between words, actions, and expectations, Pagan children develop a religious and social Pagan–American identity.

4

Don't Eat the Incense

Children in Ritual

Toddler Tools

Erin's daughter Aisling was not quite two years old when Erin began her solitary practice of Wicca. Raised in a vaguely Protestant home, Erin had been curious about other religions from an early age and had visited a number of different churches as a child, but she found these experiences unfulfilling. What she found in these churches, for the most part, she describes as "hypocrites, manipulators, judgmental people, many unloving ways, women haters, tricksters."[1] Erin tried several other spiritual paths, briefly deciding that she was an atheist before finally joining a Unitarian Universalist church, where she was introduced to contemporary Paganism. Her husband is not Wiccan; Erin says, "I don't even think he would call himself spiritual," although she acknowledges his "philosophical" leanings. When Erin's family moved to a new state, Erin found herself alone with two-year-old Aisling for long hours at a time. Erin had recently become interested in Paganism, and she realized that finding a local group to practice with would be difficult. Determined to pursue her new spiritual path, she drew on the many books she had read and began practicing Wicca at home with her young daughter. She soon found that ritual practice involving standard tools, such as candles or an athame (a ceremonial knife used to direct energy during ritual), was difficult to reconcile with a rambunctious toddler. Erin remembers,

"I didn't want her breaking or getting hurt with the other stuff, but I didn't want to not do anything, and I couldn't be awake late at night or go anywhere—I was too tired." More important, she wanted to share her new path with her daughter. With an imagination inspired by desperation, Erin created a set of what she calls "toddler tools": child-friendly ritual instruments that allowed her to cast a circle and perform rituals with her daughter.

Erin's toddler tools had been stored away since their move to New England, but Erin and Aisling, who was now in first grade, agreed to show me how they had used these tools when Aisling was much younger. To begin the process of creating sacred space, they carefully place a chain of colored construction paper on their living room carpet. The colors of the paper chain represent the colors of the directions and help them remember where each element belongs. A symbol for each element—earth, air, fire, water, and spirit—is set on an easel made of construction paper and Velcro. Five "candles" made from empty paper towel rolls on cardboard bases, with yellow construction paper "flames" attached with a circle of Velcro, represent the cardinal directions and the center. The paper "flames" allow Aisling to "light" and "extinguish" the candles, and she and her mother call and dismiss the Four Quarters by simply attaching or detaching the "flame." The seashells and rocks they use to mark water and earth are standard enough in Pagan circles, but Erin and Aisling replace the traditional incense (air) and candles (fire) with child-friendly potpourri and a wand fashioned from a branch of the magnolia tree that grew in their yard in Texas.

Beginning in the North, Erin and Aisling invite the Watchtowers of each direction to join them in their circle. Aisling draws a pentagram in the air with an athame of cardboard and tinfoil, repeating after Erin, "Spirit of the North, element of Earth. We invite you to our circle. Please bless us with your presence." The last piece of this invocation Aisling knows by heart, and she enthusiastically bids the guardian of the North, "Hail and welcome!" Erin walks slowly around the circle with her, marking the boundaries of their sacred space with the magnolia wand, and together they invite the spirits of the East, South, and West and invoke the Goddess and the God. In the center of the circle, the Lord and Lady— also made from construction paper and paper towel rolls—preside over a plastic offering plate and a "chalice" perfectly suited for the ritual milk and cookies, the toddler equivalent of cakes and ale. Erin says, "The circle is cast. Naught but love shall enter in, and naught but love shall emerge from within," and Aisling softly repeats the words after her.

Once the circle is cast, Erin and Aisling ground and center by pretending to be trees, visualizing their roots stretching into the earth. They have brought children's books with earth-centered themes into the circle: *The Ox-Cart Man* and *When the Root Children Wake Up*, two of their favorites.[2] Aisling sits on Erin's lap while they read the books together. Aisling rings a bell to mark the different parts of the ritual: casting the circle, meditating, reading, grounding, closing the circle. This breaks the ritual into clear segments—good for holding a small child's attention—and allows Aisling to actively participate during their ritual. After they finish the books, Erin and Aisling sing and march around the circle to raise energy. Instead of "traditional" or familiar Pagan chants, they sing children's songs about Mr. Sun and Mommy Moon or, when Aisling was younger, songs from the television show *Barney*. They ground and center, visualizing tree roots again, and then they eat their cookies and drink the milk. They dismiss the Lord and Lady and the Guardians of the Four Quarters, "extinguishing" the candles by removing the Velcro flames from the cardboard rolls, and Aisling takes a bit of the leftover cookies and milk to the backyard compost pile as an offering for the spirits of nature.

* * *

The ritual improvisation evident in Erin and Aisling's ritual "toddler tools" is common among Pagans, but it becomes especially necessary and significant when it arises in the relational spaces of the religious imaginations of parents and children. Erin and Aisling's ritual circle reflects two important elements of rituals performed within Pagan families: it offers a glimpse into the kind of ritual creativity imagined and practiced by Pagan families, and it illustrates how Pagan understandings of children and childhood shape the creation and experience of these rituals. At the same time, these modified, innovative, child-friendly ritual tools demonstrate a newly Pagan mother's attempt to rectify the disillusionment of her own childhood religious experiences by providing her daughter with a religious childhood utterly unlike her

Erin and Aisling's toddler-friendly circle. Photo by Zohreh Kermani.

own. When Erin remarks that she wants her daughter to learn about "all faiths" so that she is able to "better make up her own mind and not be manipulated into any particular religion," her comment reflects both her hopes for her daughter and her disappointment with the religions forced on her as a child.

This chapter examines Pagan parents' innovations to include children in public and private religious rituals and Pagan children's improvisations of their own rituals based on (and sometimes in response to) their early religious experiences. These examples suggest that understandings of ritual can be expanded—especially when children are involved—to include informal, ordinary experiences within the family as well as formal ceremonial practices.

Children's Ritual Experiences

As I watched Erin and Aisling reconstruct the ritual circles of Aisling's childhood, I was struck by the difference between their circle and the adult circles I had witnessed. For the most part, Pagan ritual is nothing if not theatrical, and many (though certainly not all) Pagans expend considerable energy to achieve an ideal ritual ambience. Pagan ritual may be somber or lighthearted, structured or improvised, but even the most free-flowing adult ritual attempts to establish and maintain a deliberate mood. In contrast, rituals that include children—especially rituals in which children are the central participants—tend to produce an environment that can range from hesitant to chaotic. When Erin and Aisling set up their toddler tools for me to observe, they were recreating an earlier ritual experience in an environment that was intended to explain these practices to an outsider rather than to establish sacred space. Nevertheless, my recordings of this event document the casual interactions that characterize many rituals with children. As Erin and Aisling set up and cast their ritual circle, they discussed the placement and meaning of objects and recalled these objects' uses in other rituals. Aisling asked Erin where to place objects ("Is this north?" "Isn't wind yellow?") and sought connections with both her mother and her own childhood through the objects they had created together ("Did I use this when I was a little kid?" "Did we do this when we first got this house?" "Mom, did we make these?"). For her part, Erin encouraged Aisling to recall the positions and meanings of the objects ("I think you know where these go" and "Can you say what each color is and what element it is?"), and she indulged her daughter's typical first-grade digressions from the business of circle casting ("Look at these shells! I'm a sea monster. I'm the weirdest sea monster. I'm a hat!"). Aisling was hesitant to explain the ritual and its tools to me, frequently arguing that she did not remember the process or the materials ("What is this? What do I say? You do it. I don't want to.") or, like many of the Pagan children who explained their families' rituals, beliefs, and holidays to me, sometimes offering information that was enthusiastic if not, technically, entirely correct ("What do we do for our ancestors for Samhain?" "Scare them away!"). Nevertheless, Aisling was happy to read stories and eat peanut butter and crackers with her mother in the center of the circle they (almost) cast. As Erin noted, "The circle is big enough just for the two of us, really."

American parents who follow contemporary Pagan paths often find themselves faced with the dilemma of whether and how to include their children in their religious practices. Private rituals like Erin and

Aisling's circle fulfill parents' desires to guide their children on their spiritual path and reflect the difficulties in maintaining a religious practice despite the challenges of parenting small children. The task of teaching the principles and values of this new religion to children is sometimes complicated by deep (and, often, quite vocal) ambivalence or opposition on the part of some Pagan adults regarding the acceptable range of children's participation in the religion. Although many Pagan parents strive to find ways to include their children in their practice, others argue that Paganism is—and should continue to be—a religion of adults, albeit (paradoxically) predominantly "childlike" adults. Many ritual practices and tools intended for adult practitioners may be undesirable for children, involving long periods of quiet meditation, precise actions, incomprehensible invocations, and "adult" themes. Some parents feel that "traditional" elements of Pagan ritual (often, those borrowed from British Traditional Wicca), such as athames, rituals performed "skyclad" (ritually nude), and less popular (but still occasionally practiced) elements like the Great Rite or scourging, may be inappropriate for children.[3] Moreover, the presence of children can be distracting for their caretakers and other participants. Atashih, a Wiccan high priest and father of two daughters, understands Wicca as a mystery religion requiring intensive study, and most rituals his coven performs are mythologically oriented and difficult for children to understand. Within his family, he adapts some rituals to be child-friendly by emphasizing storytelling, dancing, singing, and active ways of raising energy. Within his coven, however, rituals are primarily for adults. He admits, "It's distracting when [children] are running out of the circle and I'm having to stop and say, 'Raven, don't eat the incense.'"[4]

Some parents respond to their own ambivalence about children's participation by choosing to exclude children from religious rituals or allowing them to be present as spectators rather than as active participants. The sociologist Helen Berger has addressed this tension within the Pagan community over the inclusion of children in rituals. Berger notes that some Pagans (often, childless adults) are concerned about children's effect on the religion itself—that Paganism as they know it might somehow become "diluted" if children participate. The source of this anxiety is not entirely clear. It may be that some Pagans view their religion as a mystery tradition with a core body of esoteric wisdom that cannot (and should not) be taught to children. Berger quotes a Pagan author who worries that "by bringing people on to the magickal path, as opposed to them finding the path themselves, we run the risk of finding ourselves dealing with an increasingly apathetic magickal community,"[5] although the effect of this apathy on other (presumably more engaged) participants is left unspecified.

Other adult Pagans find children's attendance distracting or draining to the "energy" of the circle. They claim that children are inappropriately noisy and unpredictable and that young children may not understand the boundaries of the circle, potentially creating "energy leaks" by leaving the circle before the energy is ritually released. The issue of children moving in and out of circle is one that family-oriented groups are forced to address. Once a circle has been cast, most Pagans believe that any movement through its boundaries breaks the flow of energy that has been raised unless a "doorway" is cut through the "wall" of the circle, usually with a ritual athame. At a weekly service at the First Church of Wicca, where children were welcome at all religious services, the high priest leaped to cut a doorway in the circle to allow a mother to retrieve a wandering toddler. When the mother and child returned to the circle, he cut another doorway to allow them to re-enter. No one mentioned the energy "leak" caused by the child, but several hands reached out to grab the boy before he could make a second escape through the circle's boundary. Despite this apparent concern for the ritual sanctity of the circle, the FCOW's stated position was that animals and children younger than thirteen could move freely in and out of a circle. The idea that the energy of "kids and dogs" is less disruptive and that they can travel between ritual and mundane spaces without disturbing the flow is common among many family-oriented groups. Kendra explained, "Children and animals live in their spiritual being and not their physical being; they are always protected."[6] Thus, even though the FCOW's explicit ideological stance, like that of many adult Pagans, was that children's spirituality is different from and purer than that of adults, the adults in the circle congratulated themselves and one another for "catching" the child before he could leave the circle a second time.

In contrast, most SpiralScouts circles, which are specifically designed for children, seem far less concerned with the ritual integrity of the circle and assume that children may need to leave a circle unexpectedly. This is likely one of the reasons that SpiralScouts groups rarely go through all of the steps to cast a formal circle. The way that different groups address this issue varies according to the group's composition and its philosophy on children and the sanctity of ritual space. However, the reluctance among some Pagans to include children in religious practices and the tendency to react to their presence in ways that contradict ideologies illustrate the pervasive emphasis within Paganism on the idealized child, often to the exclusion of real children.

Some Pagans hesitate to include children in rituals for fear of damaging the children involved, not the religion. They advocate for children's participation "as long as the energy used will not harm the child," debating the appropriateness of including children in "dark energy" rituals, like those for Samhain (as opposed to the "light"—albeit more "adult"—energy of rituals for Beltane, which emphasize fertility and sexuality).[7] Other adults argue against the inclusion of children based on their understanding of children's inalienable right to choose their own religious paths rather than having these beliefs and practices imposed on them (or "shoved down their throats"), even by their own parents. Pagan parents often express reluctance to "indoctrinate" their children with their beliefs or to "force" them to attend rituals. For many parents, freedom of choice—even for very young children—trumps children's participation in their family's traditions. This emphasis on personal choice in religious participation, combined with parents' reluctance to impose their beliefs on their children, may be indicative of one of the very few universal values among North American Pagans: a passionate commitment to religious freedom.

Because of the enduring impact of their own childhood religious experiences, many Pagan parents go to great lengths to ensure that their children's participation will be voluntary. For parents of very young children, there is often a fine line between what might be considered indoctrination and simply guiding a child's spiritual path. One mother of a four-year-old explained how her spiritual practice had changed since having a child: "I practice less now that I have a child so as not to force my beliefs on her. When I go to rituals I make sure she can at least sit in circle, but I don't force her to participate."[8] This mother's concern for her preschooler's freedom of religious practice eclipses her own spiritual endeavors—either a testament to maternal sacrifice or a statement about the relative importance of religious practice for American Pagan adults and children. Another Pagan parent of a four-year-old remarked, "Pagans in general do not [believe] in proselytization. I believe that forcing your children to believe the same [as] you do, spiritual or otherwise, is a form of proselytization. My daughter is being raised to make her own choice of spiritual path."[9] Half a dozen other survey respondents used the same language of reluctance to "force" their children's religious practice or expressed fear of "indoctrinating" them. The distinction these parents make is interesting: what Pagan parents call proselytization or force is considered by parents of other religious traditions to be appropriate childhood religious education. This fear of indoctrinating one's own children—even accidentally, by casual exposure to ritual settings—haunts many Pagan parents. Anxiety about this issue can loom so large that parents may be reluctant even to express their religious and spiritual beliefs within their family.

Some parents manage this anxiety by providing children with information about a wide variety of religious traditions and allowing them to choose their own path. Other parents may choose to practice alone or with other adults, understanding their parental role as the responsibility to neutrally answer their children's questions as they arise, without imposing judgments about their truth. In the book *Raising Witches*, the Pagan author Ashleen O'Gaea encourages this style of "regency parenting" for Pagan families. O'Gaea suggests that if parents are to achieve the goal of allowing their children to "self-actualize"—a goal she assumes all Pagan parents share—then "we [parents] have to deliberately give up the power we have over our children when they are born."[10] O'Gaea acknowledges one reason why parents might hesitate to include their children in their practice: "Knowing that it is everyone's inherent right to choose their own faith, some of us don't teach children about Wicca so as not to compromise their freedom."[11] Again, the presumption in O'Gaea's advice is telling; she assumes that Pagan parents recognize children's "inherent right" to volitional religion. At the same time, O'Gaea advocates including children in rituals with the children's consent and includes numerous ways to adapt rituals to make them more interesting for children (presumably, to ensure children's continuing consent for these practices).

This point is especially important to many parents who feel that rituals and religious practice should be tailored to children's interests in an attempt to increase children's engagement in and benefit from the practice. In an essay published on the popular Pagan website The Witches' Voice, a Pagan priest and father notes that the disadvantage of including children in religious rituals is that "a very young child might be at such a stage in their development that they will not be able to understand what is going on enough to get anything of value from it."[12] The assumption here (as with other Pagans who elect not to impose their religious views on their children) is that religion and religious practice should be comprehensible, beneficial, and compelling to children. Religious practice that does not meet these criteria is likely to be rejected by children—rightfully, these parents suggest. In *Pagan Parenting: Spiritual, Magical, and Emotional Development of the Child*, the Pagan parent and homeschooler Kristin Madden explains the importance of creating rituals for younger children that are "fun and freeform." She writes, "To force them to sit through a long, involved adult ritual will teach them nothing and will bore them to whining. No one wins in a situation like that. But in an age-appropriate ritual, they learn a great deal about the ceremony, the value of ritual, and about themselves."[13] This emphasis on choice and the importance of finding and following one's own spiritual path is a cornerstone of many Pagans' beliefs and echoes, in many ways, Pagan adults' rejections of their families of origin.

"The Circle Is Important": Public Rituals

Although many Pagan parents are reluctant to impose their religious beliefs on their children, others find that sharing these beliefs is a significant part of their family's daily activities. These parents make an effort to provide religious education for their children and to include them in rituals and other practices to varying degrees. The benefits to their families from this shared practice of Paganism outweigh the difficulties and complications involved. Jess, the leader of Silverling Circle, plans and conducts large, child-centered community rituals through SpiralScouts International, but practicing her religion with her children was not always easy. Jess remembers bringing four-month-old Ryan in a baby sling to a public ritual. When Ryan began crying, Jess took him out of the circle to quiet him. When they returned to the circle and Ryan resumed crying, she felt obligated to leave the ritual early with him. She recalls:

> I felt so much frustration in that moment because I wanted to be able to participate in a spiritual practice. I wanted my children, desperately, to be able to practice with me. There was no way I was going to exclude them from something as beautiful and as meaningful as this. But at the same time, by the last time we had to leave the circle and people cut open a doorway in the circle, there were literally—I could hear around me, just, sighs. . . . And I thought, you know, I'm being disrespectful by bringing him back into the circle. . . . I don't want to disrupt the circle and disrupt the energy of everybody else, but at the same time, how am I going to bring him along this path with me? This isn't the right kind of thing for him. And I think that kick-started something. I could have decided, OK, I'm just going to leave my kids home when I go to ritual . . . or I can figure out something else.[14]

Jess's commitments to both her new religious path and her young son are evident as she recalls this event, as is her desperation at feeling that these commitments were irreconcilable. Like Jess, some Pagan parents contend that parenting deepens and enriches their spiritual beliefs. These parents feel compelled to find ways to include their children in traditionally adult-oriented religious practices. By adapting ritual practices to accommodate and interest children, parents begin the process of establishing traditions of family religious practice. At the same time, this shared religious practice can enhance adult Pagans' sense of the authenticity and legitimacy of their religion. By sharing and adapting these practices with children and by attempting to encapsulate their religious values into information accessible to children, contemporary Paganism becomes a religious tradition rather than an individual spiritual quest.

The inclusion of children in rituals contributes to Paganism's already improvisational and mutable quality. Adapting rituals and ritual elements to maximize children's understanding and participation is one of the most effective ways of engaging them in the religion. The creation of child-friendly rituals is facilitated by the participatory, sensory aspect of most Pagan rituals, Paganism's cultural and spiritual endorsement of spontaneity and creativity, and the widespread belief in children's innate, advanced spiritual capabilities. Further, the fact that many rituals in American Paganism are created and improvised by participants (rather than recited or read verbatim) allows for greater flexibility when including children in the practice. As with Erin's set of toddler-friendly ritual materials, Pagan parents develop child-friendly ritual themes, materials, and structures, or they construct specifically child-centered rituals. Helen Berger has observed some commonalities among these types of rituals:

> Those rituals created with the inclusion of children in mind are shorter and worded in language that children can read or at least easily understand. Elements such as music, dance, and pageantry, which appear in all Neopagan rituals, are easily adapted for children. Children's rituals are less formal, but to help develop a sense of tradition, they are also more consistent. The goal for children is different than that for adult initiates. Parents want their children to become comfortable with rituals and with basic principles of paganism.[15]

For the most part, the rituals I have observed in which children are significant actors have not borne out Berger's assertion that children's rituals are "more consistent" than are adult rituals; rather, I have found children's rituals to exhibit a more casual and spontaneous quality than found in adult rituals. In part, however, this spontaneity in ritual structure may arise from that fact that—as Berger observes—the goal of ritual differs for adults and children. Likewise, the experience of ritual itself may be vastly different for different age groups. Pagan rituals offer sensory and kinetic experiences; children's (and adults') experiences in ritual may involve smelling incense, touching ritual tools, hearing invocations and chants, watching performances and ritual actions, tasting cakes and ale (or milk and cookies), and dancing or performing other activities. These sensory experiences enhance both children's and adults' understanding and retention of ritual themes and events.

For parents in many parts of the United States, solitary rituals involving only immediate family members are often the only possibility for practice. Pagan groups are rare in much of the country, and those that exist may be geographically distant or closed to children. Further, Pagan adults may fear persecution or harassment if they participate in public rituals. For some families in areas with a stronger Pagan presence, however, public and group rituals may be more satisfying than solitary practices. At the First Church of Wicca, all church services and Sabbat rituals are family-friendly, and children's attendance and participation are encouraged. Rev. Dr. Kendra, the church's minister and high priestess, explains that by including and welcoming children into the church, "We're teaching them a faith, we're teaching them respect, we're teaching them personal pride and self-respect."[16] Children have been an important part of the FCOW since its inception, and they participate fully in its religious rituals. At services for the new and waxing moons, the children sit on mats on the floor in the center of the adults' circle, directly in front of the altar. Between each part of the service, Rev. Kendra asks, "Will someone please ring the bell?" and the children—usually with some confusion over whose turn it is—ring a small brass bell on the altar. The children also participate in ritual activities, perform with the Bards (the church's musicians), and carry the offertory bag around the circle at each service, undoubtedly encouraging more generous donations than might be gained by simply passing the collection plate. Rev. Kendra explains her approach to including children in services:

> I'm very conscious to make sure that they're in a loving, nurturing environment. I'm also very conscious to make sure that when I set up ritual, it's something they can participate in—that it's not over their head, that it's not below their feet, that they fit in, that they feel like a part of the group. I'm also very conscious to make sure they understand—which they do, just from the nature of the atmosphere—that this is not playtime. This is serious ritual time. We've had very few, if any, circumstances where the children have gotten out of control. . . . If there's people who come to the church and say, "Hey, I can't get good concentration and I can't worship because of the children," well, guess what? This isn't the right church for you.[17]

The FCOW is clearly committed to including its children in ritual and religious practice. It is interesting, however, that it does not offer specifically child-centered rituals or significantly adapt its services for children. During fieldwork with this group, I observed only one specifically child-centered ritual at the FCOW, a group Wiccaning (discussed in chapter 6). The congregation also sings songs written by the minister's children; the two I heard were on the subjects of dragons and witches. For the most part, although children are welcome at regular weekly services (although not at metaphysical classes, which are considered beyond children's level of understanding and patience; the FCOW offers child care during these adult classes), these events are not altered or adapted for children's comprehension or participation. In this respect, the FCOW might be considered a family-oriented, though not child-centered, group. Like other Pagan families, the parents in the FCOW maintain that their children are free to choose their own spiritual path as adults. The church's objective is to provide its children with a foundation in Wiccan values and beliefs.

In contrast, SpiralScouts International offers a model for a specifically child-centered organization that provides children with Wiccan-oriented activities rooted in Wiccan values. It differs from an organization like the FCOW in that its membership is not exclusively Pagan, and it is designed to accommodate families of other minority religions or of no religious affiliation. SpiralScouts rituals illustrate many of the ways that Pagan themes, practices, and ritual structures can be adapted to maximize children's participation. Child-friendly adaptations to relatively "conventional" Pagan rituals are apparent in the following example of a public Yule ritual conducted by Silverling Circle, a SpiralScouts group in New Hampshire.

* * *

On a sunny afternoon in early December, the scouts, leaders, and parents of Silverling Circle and non-Pagan members of the local community visiting this Yule festival gather in a large, open room at a Unitarian Universalist church. The SpiralScouts parents and children form a circle in the center of the room, joined by a few of the braver visitors. Other onlookers sit in folding chairs around the room's perimeter. This is a community festival, and although active participation in this ritual is encouraged, passive spectators are accepted. Jess, the leader of Silverling Circle, hands small jingle bells to all the children in the circle and instructs them to hold the bells to their hearts and then to place the bells at the center of the circle. She does not explain the significance of this activity; it seems to be a way to involve the children early in the ritual and to make them feel that their "energy" is in the circle. Jess motions for someone standing near the door to dim the lights, and then she begins to read: "It is dark. The nights are long. . . . Less and less and less light, until the day becomes so short, the night so long, that we wonder if the light, with its warmth, will ever return. Every day we miss the sun more."[18] She continues, "So it is at Solstice," reassuring the group that the sun "is not gone" but is "waiting to be reborn." Jess and another adult in the circle, intended to represent the spirits of the East and the West, encourage the sun, "Wake up, wake up! . . . You have work to do! Plants to grow! People to warm!" Jess begins singing, and the group joins in: "Sing, break into song, for within you is the light!" While the circle sings, Jess hands pine branches to all the children and motions for them to begin casting the circle by walking clockwise within it, pine boughs raised above their heads. On their way around the circle, several children drop their branches, entangle their branches with those of the child next to them, or have to be reminded which way is clockwise. This casual disorder and informality are common to many child-centered rituals and are ubiquitous in SpiralScouts rituals. Most adults at these activities seem to take a "children will be children" approach to ritual structure, and neither the adults nor the children in this circle seem bothered by the confusion.

Jess's two-year-old twin daughters sit quietly outside the circle, one resting her head on her father's shoulder, the other watching her mother and older brother participate in the ritual from her seat on the floor. The toddlers are already familiar with ritual etiquette and SpiralScouts activities, and they attempt (with varying degrees of success) to sit quietly despite their lack of active participation in the ritual. Several non-Pagan visitors in the room seem less clear about the etiquette requiring respectful silence during a religious service—or, more likely, they fail to recognize the performance they are watching as a religious service at all, perhaps interpreting the events as a theatrical performance. One visitor, sitting on a folding chair just outside the circle of participants, repeatedly and loudly asks her neighbor (who, unfortunately, happens to be me), "What are they doing? What do Pagans do, anyway? Do they believe in God?" Although none of the adults present specifically addresses this disruption (and my only response is to shake my head and attempt to answer her questions after the ritual is over), the conversations adjacent to (and, it seems at some points, competing with) the solstice ritual draw exasperated sighs from a few other onlookers. In contrast, the disorder inside the circle perpetrated by the participating children seems easily accepted by both participants and onlookers as a normal by-product of children's ritual participation.

While the adult leaders invoke the elements and the Goddess and God, the parents and children in the circle stand quietly together. Most of the younger children hold their parents' hands, and the older children tolerate parents' arms resting on their shoulders. Finally, Jess announces, "Out of the dark comes light. Blessed be the Yule!" At this, the children enter the circle and dramatically reveal the "sun"—a large piece of yellow satin material stretched over a hula-hoop frame. Eight of the scouts in the circle pick up the "sun" and hold it flat as one of the leaders places bay leaves in the center of the satin fabric. As the children carry the sun around the circle, Jess tells the participants:

> As people connected to the Earth our Mother, we feel the light reborn within us today. As the children carry the sun around the circle, you are invited to take your bay leaf—your ray of light—to the sun. Bay or laurel is an herb associated with the Sun and Solstice—with the element of fire, with the deities Apollo, Ceres, Delphi, Eros, and Faunus, and with the properties of wisdom, protection, and purification. As you add your leaf of bay, say something about what makes you shine. What is your special gift? What are you thankful for? What is your sun? Name it as we go around the circle.

As the children pause in front of each person in the circle (with the sun wavering ever so slightly as all eight children attempt to carry it), each person takes a leaf and names his or her "light." All the adults in the circle respond to the prompt, saying that their "sun" is their family, love, or "hope for positive change in the world." A few of the children in the circle take a leaf but refuse to speak. Some children respond: an eleven-year-old boy, one of the oldest children in the group, says, "My sun is my family and me being alive." A six-year-old girl with waist-length red braids agrees: "I take the warmth of my family also." Jess's son Ryan smiles at his mother and says, "My sun is my mom and dad."

Some of the children enthusiastically offer responses, but many of the children—especially those new to the circle—seem worried about responding with the "correct" words or actions and quietly refuse to speak or to perform in the ritual. Again, adults or other children rarely remark on these lapses; choosing to "pass" is an acceptable response. Despite its cultural acceptability, however, this behavior raises questions—at least to those of us outside the circle—about the level of adult and child involvement in these activities. Are SpiralScouts activities designed for and beneficial to the children, who, more often than not, refuse to speak during rituals, or to the adults, who take every opportunity to participate? Is children's physical presence in ritual sufficient to instill basic religious and ritual foundations, so that children's lack of explicit participation does not diminish the experience for them? Or are children merely spectators at these "child-centered" events that are actually intended for and performed by their adult caretakers?

Most Pagan rituals within SpiralScouts circles share many of the elements present in Silverling Circle's Yule ritual: active participation by children and adults, an opportunity for each person to speak or perform some action in the ritual, and a shorter, simpler ritual structure than might be found in adult-oriented rituals. These rituals also share a sense of unpredictability and chaos instantly familiar to anyone who has spent time with groups of small children. Pagan children in SpiralScouts rituals freeze up when it is their turn to speak, drop ritual tools and props, and have to be threatened with time-outs or removal from the group. They also do surprisingly well at following directions, remembering elemental correspondences, and listening quietly while the leaders explain activities to them. Berger's observation that the goals for children's rituals differ from those of adult rituals is true in SpiralScouts circles, where the ideal ritual is not necessarily the one that is perfectly executed but the one that helps children understand the uses of ritual and the importance of the circle. Jess stresses this point to the children of Silverling Circle, reminding them, "The circle is important. We're all part of it. When we are in a circle, we are reminded of how we are all connected. Boys, girls, men, women—we all work together."

Pagan children learn important aspects of their religion through these rituals, but they also learn other things that are just as valuable in the eyes of many Pagans: how to improvise ritual words and actions; the joys of spontaneity, imagination, performance, and community activity; and the importance of interpersonal values, such as cooperation and responsibility to others.

"We Live with the Gods": Everyday Rituals

Most discussions of children's participation in Pagan ritual focus on adult adaptations of standard Sabbat rituals for children. Several sources exist for child-friendly ritual adaptations, such as the popular and widely used book *Circle Round*, which I saw used at family rituals and SpiralScouts events from California to New Hampshire.[19] Many Pagans have reminded me, however, that ritual—especially with children—is rarely limited to these formal, structured occasions. Pagan families regularly find ways to ritualize the seemingly mundane activities of their daily lives. Many families use blessings, prayers, or affirmations throughout the day as a way of ritualizing meals, bedtime, chores, or working in the garden.

When I asked Pagan parents to send me photos of their children "participating in ritual," I expected pictures from family Samhain activities or solstice celebrations. Instead, I received a dizzying array of photos: children making crafts at SpiralScouts meetings, having their faces painted as butterflies and tigers at community events, baking cookies for Yule, marching down Main Street as part of a small town's harvest festival, and jumping in leaves, an image that Jess, Silverling Circle's leader, described as the "ultimate fall ritual." Clearly, for many Pagan families, "ritual" is not limited to specifically religious or spiritual activities that take place within a circle. Rather, ritual activities are those that take on ritual and spiritual significance, that "re-enchant" daily life. This re-enchantment may arise from the time or the company in which these activities are performed, the theological, interpersonal, or spiritual meaning given to the activity by the participants, or the significance of the activity itself. Many families find that bedtime and mealtime offer excellent opportunities to reinforce religious practice in daily life. Jess keeps a small, spiral-bound notebook of daily blessings for her three children to use at mealtime, bedtime, bath time, the first day of school, and other significant events. Her family collects prayers from various religious traditions, books, and poems to say together on these occasions. She explains:

> Really, any part of the day can be a little ritual, if you make it that way. Washing your face can be a ritual—cleansing, and a metaphor of putting on your nice face. . . . Mealtime certainly is a ritual. Story time even can be a ritual, especially if it's a story with a lesson. But even just the simple act of everybody sitting in close together—that's a little ritual, too. My definition of ritual has changed since having kids. Rituals are those repeated things that have meaning. It makes it different from habit and different from just a routine; it has meaning and significance, some kind of symbolism to it. But it doesn't necessarily have to be calling the Quarters, casting the circle, all that kind of stuff. It can be much more simple than that. . . . Even things like recycling can be a ritual if you do it with the intention of healing the earth.[20]

Pagan families see this expansion of the definition of "ritual" less as an integration of the separate realms of the spiritual and secular than as a means of reinforcing the magical properties of the everyday. This is an important distinction to Pagan parents, many of whom remark that their religious beliefs and practices are an integral part of their family's daily lives. In response to a question about her religious practice, one mother writes, "I don't think I practice, I live it. . . . [Our] belief encompasses us daily. Today for instance, we collected eggs from hens at the farm and said thank you to all the hens."[21] Another mother offers an urban take on everyday life as ritual practice: "When we go to a shopping center I have my oldest [child] manifest a parking space for me. She is very good at it. Also, when we are at a bank of elevators they guess which will open first."[22] Yet another parent—the mother of four adult Pagan children—says simply, "We live with the Gods."[23] This sense of daily spirituality and magical presence is an important part of the ritual creativity and imagination present in the daily lives of Pagan children and adults. Pagan child-rearing practices aim to awaken and instill in children a kind of everyday, imaginative religion, encouraging them to inhabit and express a collectively constructed religious imaginary.

"The ultimate fall ritual." Photo by Jess Gerrior.

Pagan families live their everyday lives in these enchanted worlds, and this is the context in which Pagan children become fluent ritual improvisers.

The importance of ritual in everyday life is emphasized in Pagan households, so it is little wonder that Pagan children become adept at creating their own rituals and incorporating imaginative elements into their daily lives. Children raised among these practices (which often begin with a Wiccaning ceremony in infancy or a blessing ceremony before they are even born) find ways to include these themes in their daily lives and their play. Wiccan children sing Pagan chants to entertain themselves during car rides; "Hoof and Horn" was a favorite for a pair of eight-year-old girls whose parents led a teaching coven in Texas.[24] These two girls and four of their siblings and friends conducted an impromptu funeral for several baby pond fish, carving pentagrams into sticks and stacking them on piled dead leaves to make headstones, while a four-year-old with a chocolate mustache gravely informed me that everything that dies goes back to the Goddess. Even very young children attempt to mirror ritual practices they have observed or experienced.

* * *

At the semi-annual Council of Magickal Arts festival in Texas, there is a community labyrinth built into a section of the land. The children sharing my campsite were fascinated by this area, and they visited it often over the course the weekend. Children at the CMA festival are generally respectful of this space and of others within it, although they seem to find running the labyrinth path preferable to quiet, meditative walking. Signs at the entrance to this part of the Spirit Haven land, where the CMA festivals are held, inform visitors that they are "entering sacred space," and another sign near the outer gate of the labyrinth sets the tone for activities there, asking visitors to "declare your intention to travel to the heart." The "heart" to which the path leads is represented by the "heart rock," a huge piece of rose quartz in the center of the labyrinth.

Left to their own devices, the children create spontaneous rituals in the center of the labyrinth. Eight-year-old Raven told me about a ritual three of the children performed in the labyrinth. Raven cast a makeshift circle around herself and her friends, using a stick as a wand to draw an invoking pentagram in the air, exactly as her father had shown her the day before. Each child held a black rock in her hand and thought about a person or animal they knew who had died (or "gone to the Goddess") or who was otherwise no longer present. They placed the stones in a pool of water in the center of the labyrinth, and then spent several minutes "saving" bugs from the water by scooping them out with their hands and gently placing them on the grass. An adult observer would likely have missed this element, perhaps seeing it as an abrupt shift from ritual imitation and creation to another kind of play. All three girls, however, included the saving of the insects in their accounts of the impromptu ritual, and it was clear from their accounts that this marked an important conclusion to their ritual activity.

I walked the labyrinth path one afternoon with eight-year-old Raven and Cricket, five-year-old Deanna, and Cricket's mother, Freya. The entrance to the Outer Gate instructs visitors to "state your intent," and Cricket—taking the instruction literally and pragmatically—solemnly declared, "My intent is to go in there, and then to come back out"—an "intent" that was far more concrete and attainable than the lofty academic intentions I was pondering at the same moment. Once inside the gate, the girls ran the labyrinth path as Freya and I followed. The circular path of the labyrinth winds back and forth on itself, so the girls and I passed each other at every turn, and Cricket high-fived me every time her path met mine. While the girls seem to have no trouble running the path, laughing, making eye contact, and passing out high-fives, I found myself having difficulty following the circular path at all, at one point losing the path completely and inadvertently stepping over several lines of the labyrinth to get back on the right track. Once in the center, Freya helped the children carefully light sticks of incense, and the girls sat quietly near the heart rock for several minutes.

Another adult entered the second gate of the labyrinth behind us, and he sat on a bench a short distance from us, waiting to walk the path. As the girls lit incense and candles, Freya came over to them and quietly said, "I think this man is waiting because he needs to walk the labyrinth alone today," gently encouraging the children to begin walking the path out. Her comment was a way of reminding the girls of a number of different concepts at once: the need to be empathetic and aware of those around them, to respect the different needs of other people, to trust their intuition, and to remember that spirituality can be practiced alone or in community. The older girls followed Freya out of the circle, but Deanna was not ready to leave. She walked to the center of the circle, knelt down, and put both hands on the pink heart rock. With more gravitas than one would expect from a five-year-old in a foam wizard hat, she whispered, "It makes it hard to breathe."

Running the labyrinth. Photo by Zohreh Kermani.

Somewhat alarmed at being the only adult present—Did she have heat exhaustion? A bee sting? Would I remember how to perform CPR?—I asked her, "What makes it hard to breathe?" She answered, "When I touch the rock, because it's so powerful. It makes my tummy hurt." I reminded her that we could leave the circle, but she kept both hands on the rock; she wanted to stay. She suddenly stood up, clasped her hands together with her index fingers pointing to the sky, and said, "I'm costing [casting] spells here. I'm magic! I have to close my eyes and do this to cost spells." Deanna had watched her parents cast circles with their coven and in smaller family rituals, and her actions mirrored many of those she had witnessed among adults—although the stomachache in response to the power of the heart rock was entirely her own addition. She looked around the center of the labyrinth and exclaimed, "This place is magic. This whole campground is magic!" She knelt by the heart rock again, closed her eyes, pointed her joined index fingers at the rock, and began mumbling an incantation of her own invention. She finished by informing the rock, "We need opportunity. We need help. OK? Now you have to leave the spell in your head." As she looked up from the rock, she suddenly announced, "This is a scary place. It's creepy. There might be a snake in the grass." I asked her again if she was ready to leave, and she shook her head no. The adult who had been sitting on the benches had begun to slowly walk the path into the center; as the only other adult present, I felt that I needed to encourage Deanna to leave the center so that the adult who was waiting could enter. While watching her "cost spells" here and witnessing her reluctance to leave this area—a place that clearly had a powerful effect on her body, mind, and spirit—it eventually dawned on me that she had as much right to this space as the adult visitor. As I slowed down to walk at her pace, the waiting man in the tie-dyed sarong passed us on the labyrinth path and smiled at Deanna, announcing, "She has good energy."

Winding our way out of the labyrinth, I realized that my perception of the other adult—that he was impatiently waiting his turn, that Deanna's presence would be disruptive to his meditation—was a reflection of my own understandings of child and adult spirituality. The spiritual world of the other adult visitor included Deanna's presence, however marginal to his own experience (and, in fact, my presence was likely more off-putting to him, even if he somehow missed seeing my stumbling approach into the circle). For her part, Deanna's spiritual experience of the labyrinth was remarkably reflective of—but thoroughly different from—the experiences of the adults around her. The range of emotions and responses to the labyrinth, the heart rock, and her own "spells" that Deanna experienced during our visit to the center draws a complex and multilayered picture of children's participation in ritual and other spiritual practices. The combination of Deanna's focus on her own improvised ritual and her sensory experiences of the labyrinth, my anxiety at her ad hoc adult liaison to the labyrinth and the other visitors, and our tie-dyed companion's perceptions of children's spirituality, Deanna's "energy," and the shared religious space of adults and children illustrates many of the ambivalences, tensions, and idiosyncrasies of the religious worlds of Pagan adults and children.

The spontaneous rituals created by Pagan children make it clear that these children understand at least the spirit (if not the full theological message) of the rituals in which they participate. It is also apparent that Pagan children integrate messages from their parents and other adults regarding the magical, spiritual, and ritual aspects of daily life. These improvisations can be empowering for Pagan children, helping them to develop confidence in their ritual improvisational skills and in their place within their religious worlds. These improvisations also illustrate the ritual fluency and religious imagination of Pagan children as they take the foundations of ritual from adults and add imaginative, fantastic, child-centered elements. It is difficult to imagine an adult coven—no matter how explicit its emphasis on compassion, karma, or the interconnectedness of all life—closing a ritual meditation on death by scooping flies from the elemental water bowl. For Pagan children, however, this connection is intuitive and obvious.

The relationship between adult expectations of children's ritual participation and children's own spiritual experiences is complex, dynamic, and often fraught with ambivalence. Adults consciously shape the boundaries of children's religious worlds, unconsciously encourage or discourage religious activities and experiences, and interpret children's actions and experiences in ways that reinforce both Pagan values and adults' own ideals of childhood. For their part, Pagan children navigate the religious worlds offered to them by adults at the same time that they construct their own ritual experiences, which may have little or no need of adult presence at all. The same pair of young friends who sang "Hoof and Horn" during car rides also sang this song as they wandered through dusty festival grounds during a weekend-long festival, drawing appreciative and wistful smiles from passing adults. Pagan adults see in children the religious childhoods they lacked, childhoods filled with spontaneity, spiritual expression, and the sacredness of daily life. These adults shape children's religious experiences in ways that reflect adult understandings and ideals of childhood, encourage children's ritual improvisations, and construct the frameworks of Pagan children's religious worlds.

5

A Room Full of FireFlies

"You Get to Choose"

Erin is holding what looks like a magnolia branch wrapped with ribbon, but her six-year-old daughter Aisling knows that it's really a magic wand. Erin and Aisling use this wand to create sacred space for the rituals they have performed together since Aisling was two years old, and Erin has spent most of this chilly November afternoon telling me about these rituals. Aisling reluctantly joined our conversation once I managed to convince her that I wasn't asking trick questions ("Why do you ask so many questions?" she asked me suspiciously. "Weren't *you* a Pagan when you were a kid?"). Bored now, Aisling wanders over to the piano and violin resting in the corner of the room. She shuffles through the holiday sheet music stacked on the piano, reading the titles aloud: "Silent Night," "Jingle Bells," "Deck the Halls." Erin tells me that their SpiralScouts circle is planning to go "Pagan caroling" the following month at local community centers and nursing homes using rewritten, Pagan-themed lyrics to familiar Christmas carols. (There are many versions of these songs, which are mostly spread through word of mouth and the Internet; as of 2007, the Silverling Circle SpiralScouts group had an archived document on their e-mail group with the words to seventeen "Yule carols," including titles such as "Gods Bless Ye Merry Pagan-folk," "Hark, the NeoPagans Sing," and both "The Twelve Days of Yuletide" and "The Thirteen Days of Solstice.")

Aisling sits down on the piano bench, picks up the child-sized violin lying on top of the piano, and begins sight-reading and playing a scratchy but determined version of "The Holly and the Ivy." Erin helpfully suggests, "What if you stand up?" Aisling shakes her head and mumbles "No." Erin says kindly, "Well, OK, you're learning." She lowers her voice and—somewhat apologetically—explains, "She just got the music for these yesterday." Aisling suddenly stops playing, points an accusatory finger at the sheet music in front of her, and asks me, "Does that look like the right word to you?" Erin and I lean in over her shoulders and Erin smiles: "'Choir' is not one of the words Pagans use, it's true." Aisling considers the lyrics before her and suggests, "I could somehow change the word to 'power.'" Erin nods in agreement—"power" is a much more common word in Pagan parlance than "choir"—but she reminds Aisling, "This is just for the music—we have the words on another sheet." As Aisling turns her attention to the piano, she and her mother have this conversation:

> ERIN: What do you think is the difference between Christians and Pagans?
> AISLING: Wait, are we Pagans or Christians?
> ERIN: We've been practicing Paganism.
> AISLING: Yeah, because I think the Christians are the ones who sacrifice.

Erin hesitates here, and I remember an earlier conversation in which she had mentioned Aisling's belief that "only Christians sacrifice." After reading a historical children's book from the library that mentioned the Crusades, Aisling announced in the car one day, "Only Christians do sacrifices." Erin describes her response to Aisling at the time: "You know, today it's usually put by Christians in the other light: the Pagans are the ones that do the sacrifices. But I was reading her history, and I thought, 'Wow, how did I get her to believe this?' Because I didn't mean to! I just kind of explained about how it's not OK to kill people. But in this one story the pope said, 'Whoever goes on this crusade and kills all these other people can be forgiven of all their past transgressions and the other murders they committed.' So my goal . . . I wanted her to be exposed to every world religion . . . not to convert her over, but to study, and so that she would be prepared and then she could choose."

ERIN: Well...

AISLING: Because I think [Christians] are like, "Everybody should do this the same way we do." But, Mom? Well, why is Mara [Aisling's friend] Mormon?

ERIN: Mormon? Because that's just what her family believes.

AISLING: Yeah, well, I feel like they were making me Mormon at their house.

ERIN: Oh. Well, you get to choose what you are.

AISLING: Well, I didn't get to choose what I wanted to be there.

ERIN: Maybe not at their house; you respect what they are at their house. But you get to be, inside you and at your house, whatever you want to be.

AISLING: I think if they were making me Mormon in their house, Mara should be Pagan here.

ERIN: I don't think it works that way, honey.

* * *

This chapter examines contemporary Paganism's contentious and ambivalent relationship with American cultural and religious values and norms. Specifically, it considers Paganism's troubled relationship with majority religions in the United States as well as with two institutions of larger North American society, children's scouting and public education, through SpiralScouts International, a Pagan children's scouting organization, and through the phenomenon of Pagan homeschooling and unschooling. This contentious and ambivalent relationship is not unique to contemporary Paganism; in fact, it is a relatively common dynamic between new or alternative religions and larger, well-established traditions.

Historically, new religions in the United States have occupied a marginalized position in the religious landscape, and public perception often views these movements as heretical, dangerous, or simply incomprehensibly "other"—a view that can prove especially damaging and disruptive to children within these religions. Alternative religions most often enter the public arena through external constructions of difference or otherness, but it is often the case that the religious group itself internally constructs this sense of otherness or opposition. Laurence Moore's discussion of "religious outsiders" in the United States observes that alternative religious movements frequently employ a "language of dissent" to establish their "outsiderhood" against a posited established culture. Moore offers the example of Joseph Smith's masterful self-promotion of Mormonism, which established an expectation of recognition and credibility for the religion on par with religions bearing significantly lengthier records. (Clearly, Aisling was not alone in wondering about the relationship of Mormonism to her own religion.) Moore explains that early Mormons employed a "rhetoric of deviance" to establish themselves as separate and radically different from the surrounding religious majority, highlighting their minimal differences (rather than their many similarities) to the larger culture. Joseph Smith's foundational use of this rhetoric to invent a cohesive Mormon people out of a perceived or constructed sense of opposition marks the religion as quintessentially American. Moore describes the paradoxical relationship between this alternative religion and other contemporary American religions: "In defining themselves as being apart from the mainstream, Mormons were in fact laying their claim to it. By declaring themselves outsiders, they were moving to the center."[1] These assertions of difference and marginalization, Moore points out, were not based on concrete, significant differences between Mormons and the surrounding culture; in terms of family and gender relations, most Mormon values were not unlike those of the majority culture. This is not to say that genuine differences did not exist between Mormons and their contemporaries—Moore details the "peculiarities of the Mormon faith" that set them at odds against the larger culture—but, for the most part, these theological and ideological differences did not entirely alienate early Mormons:

> Mormonism's enemies tried hard to validate a claim that Mormons were morally and ethically peculiar. Mormons, they charged, lied, stole, swore, and fornicated. No doubt they did, just like many other antebellum Americans. . . . Nevertheless, any case for Mormon difference that rests on a purported Mormon rejection of middle-class standards of virtue is bound to fail.[2]

Contemporary Paganism has more in common with early Mormon protestations of difference than might first be imagined. Much like nineteenth-century Mormonism, contemporary Paganism has invented itself (and continues to re-invent itself) both in accordance with and in opposition to mainstream majority culture. Unlike Mormons, however, Pagans lack a foundational religious leader, body of scripture, or cohesive set of beliefs and practices—features that have helped to establish Mormonism and other new religions as legitimate religious alternatives. The lack of these elements, in combination with Paganism's acceptance of other religious paths and emphasis on religious choice rather than religious commitment for its children, are contributing factors to the religion's ongoing struggle for public acceptance and credibility. In conjunction with these factors, the many real or perceived differences between Pagans and other Americans in attitudes toward childhood, parenting, education, religious ritual, and sexuality tend to increase public anxieties regarding Pagan difference.

* * *

There is no Church of magic.
—Émile Durkheim

In many ways, contemporary Paganism's emphasis on improvisation, individual expression, and eclecticism mark the religion as preeminently American, descendant and heir to earlier alternative, dissenting, and occult religions. However, contemporary Pagans often fail to see themselves as part of this "familiar American path," constructing identities of opposition and dissent in an effort to mark their beliefs and practices as radically innovative. In this respect, Pagans follow a long line of American religions that have maintained a "carefully nurtured sense of separate identity"[3] while also maintaining a creative tension between the historical and mythological aspects of their religion. These factors are crucial to contemporary American Pagans' understandings of their religion.

American Pagans often disagree about their relationship to mainstream American religions (as they do about most aspects of their religion), but they tend to share a commitment to individual religious expression and the value of dissent. These socially, politically, and spiritually neoliberal tendencies are a recurrent theme in American Paganism and help to distinguish it from its European ancestry. Ronald

Hutton's history of British Paganism demonstrates how the increasingly conservative rhetoric of mid-nineteenth-century European Romanticism led to similarly conservative and reactionary uses of the figure of the Goddess as an essentialized, oppressive female icon in the works of early twentieth-century Romantic and occult writers. As an "enemy of female emancipation," the Goddess was often presented as Virgin, Mother, or Earth, but "She never seemed to stand for Woman as company director, Woman as brain surgeon, Woman as politician."[4] These views underwent significant changes almost immediately upon their introduction to the United States as British Paganism encountered the radical cultural and political upheaval of North America in the mid-1960s. The Bucklands introduced changes to the tradition that reflected the more liberal climate of the United States. Most important, they broke with Gardnerian tradition and declared self-initiation valid, paving the way for the highly individualized and solitary forms of American Paganism.[5]

One of the most significant influences on the development of American Paganism was second-wave feminism, which took the "old conservative idea of an essential female nature and simply reversed the sympathies," valorizing images of women that had been denigrated by earlier writers and prioritizing them in radical feminist rhetoric.[6] The impact of American feminism and the American counterculture of the 1960s on American Paganism cannot be overstated. These movements profoundly altered the political and social rhetoric of contemporary Paganism from its right-wing British conservative roots to its predominantly liberal American form. The rigid hierarchies of the Gardnerian initiation system were supplanted by self-initiation or democratic operation of covens, social activism was foregrounded, and women's roles were elevated. Hutton's explanation of the significance of this new version of Paganism is worth quoting at length:

> It would be simple to conclude that pagan witchcraft left Britain for the United States as a quietist religion, seeking a private but secure place within a wider society, and returned transformed into an evangelical one, seeking to alter the world. Though possessed of some truth, it would indeed be too simple. . . . American feminist witchcraft usually recognized the need for pluralism in belief. When Starhawk came to project

her blueprint image of an ideal society in the 21st century, in one of her novels, it was a San Francisco in which all citizens had not been converted to Paganism, but followed many different spiritual paths in harmony with each other. The point was that all of them also embraced a common culture of tolerance, egalitarianism, decision-making by consensus, pacifism, and self-sustaining, non-pollutant economics with a reverence for nature. Embedded in this . . . however, was a different assumption: that it was impossible to be a pagan witch without believing in all these things.[7]

The direct connection between these values and Paganism was an innovation of North American Paganism, and it shaped the way most American Pagans understand their religion. Contemporary Paganism in the United States is decentralized and intensely personalized, and different traditions may have very little in common with one another. The values that Hutton cites—tolerance, egalitarianism, pacifism, and consensus—constitute the core values of many strains of American Paganism. Lacking unified beliefs, practices, and organizations, these values may be the common thread in a distinctly American contemporary Paganism. Moreover, these values, combined with distinctly Pagan perspectives on childhood, adulthood, and the relationship between the two, influence Pagan family values, parenting, and the religious worlds of Pagan children.

To Serve the Wise Ones: Organizing Pagan Childhood

In October 2006, the SpiralScouts circles in New Hampshire hosted their first "Celebrate Samhain" event at the local Unitarian Universalist church. Samhain is one of the major festivals (or "Sabbats") of the Pagan "Wheel of the Year," corresponding to Halloween and marking the start of the Pagan (Celtic) year. The Celebrate Samhain event is hosted annually by the SpiralScouts circles that make up the Granite Tribe (all SpiralScouts circles in New Hampshire) and members of the New Hampshire Pagan community. Donations are requested from attendees: "Because community service and involvement is a significant part of the SpiralScouts mission, an admission donation of a winter clothing or non-perishable food item is requested."[8] The event features workshops on storytelling and "Samhain in the Celtic Tradition"; vendors selling jewelry, artwork, and books; a community drum circle; Tarot readings; and children's crafts. The event's community exposure and the beautiful fall weather draw interested local families as well as registered scouts to the next SpiralScouts meeting at Jess's house, and the parents and children crowd onto the living room chairs and floor as Jess discusses the success of the event. In addition to collecting almost two hundred pounds of food for the local food bank and funding for local SpiralScouts groups, the Celebrate Samhain event drew nearly five hundred people from the local community, many of whom were previously unfamiliar with both SpiralScouts and Paganism. At this SpiralScouts meeting, Jess passes around a thank-you card from the local Baptist church, which runs the food bank. The handwritten card thanks the Granite Tribe SpiralScouts for the large donation, adding, "It's good to know what SpiralScouts do," and concludes (unironically, one assumes), "May God bless your SpiralScouts."

Jess passes around a stack of business-card size cards, small enough to be tucked into a parent's wallet, that are printed with her contact information and the text of the FireFly Promise. The promise is short enough that even the three-year-old scouts can follow along with prompting from their parents, and a few of the older FireFlies, the seven-year-olds, know it by heart. The scouts and parents read aloud together:

> I promise to serve the Wise Ones,
> To honor and respect Mother Earth,
> To be helpful and understanding toward all people,
> And always keep love in my heart.[9]

The first line of the promise has recently been the subject of a heated discussion on the SpiralScouts e-mail group. Sparked by one parent's question—who are the Wise Ones?—the SpiralScouts leaders, parents, and administrators have contributed opinions and insight on the meaning of this line over the past several months. One circle leader suggests that the Wise Ones are "any beings to whom you turn for wisdom. This could be one God, the God and Godess [sic], Parents, Relatives that have passed on and you look to for guidance." Another parent agrees with this response and compares the concept of the Wise Ones to the concept of Akela in Cub Scout troops. Other parents agree that the Wise Ones might be ancestors. One mother, who makes a point of noting that she is a practicing Christian but adds, "We are all One," comments, "Also remember that we are the Wise Ones too—someday we will be the ancestors that our families are trying to honor."[10] One leader offers ideas from the children in her circle: the Wise Ones might be the God and Goddess, the trees, or angels. (Interestingly, despite the common belief among many contemporary Pagans that "Wicca" literally means "wise ones," the interpretation that this phrase refers to Wicca itself is absent from this discussion.) This circle leader encourages other leaders to ask the scouts to describe their understandings of the Wise Ones.

On this November morning, after Silverling Circle has read the FireFly Promise together, Jess poses the question, "Who are the Wise Ones in the Promise?" She suggests that they might be the spirits of nature, or ancestors—people, animals, or trees—who will "share their wisdom with us if we ask." But, she hastens to add, this is only one possibility. She proposes that they go around the circle so that each person can share their idea of the Wise Ones, "or you can say you don't know." Silverling Circle usually uses a "talking stick" when they speak in turn around the circle, allowing the person who holds the stick to speak without interruption. Silverling's talking stick is a long, smooth branch of wood decorated with stones, paint, feathers, and other natural materials and found objects. Every week a different scout is allowed to take the stick home with them to add a symbol or decoration representing their family's recent activities: yarn for learning to knit, a painted "7" for a scout's seventh birthday, and so forth. The stick serves as an artifact of the circle's activities and membership, and the scouts enjoy studying it and recalling each family's additions. The room is crowded today, though, and passing a four-foot-long piece of wood seems hazardous, so Jess suggests that the group pass around a small lavender-filled pillow instead, and she hands the pillow to the parent next to her.

The first two parents to speak both suggest that the Wise Ones are probably ancestors or elders. The next four children in the circle, two four-year-old boys and two six-year-old girls, gingerly take the lavender pillow from the person next to them, hold it briefly, and then mumble

Jess and Ryan hold Silverling Circle's talking stick. Photo by Zohreh Kermani.

"I don't know" and pass the pillow along. Next to these younger children are nine-year-old Henry and his sister, who, at eleven years old, is the oldest child at most of Silverling Circle's meetings. Henry is a slight, quiet boy with shaggy hair in his eyes and a sweet, thoughtful expression. He takes the pillow from the girl next to him and holds it, staring at the pillow and saying nothing. Eventually, one of the adults gently reminds him that he can pass, and he hands the pillow to his older sister, who—perhaps to make up time for Henry's extended pause—immediately says, "I don't know," and passes the pillow to Jamie. This is six-year-old Jamie's first visit to this circle, and he is here today with both of his parents and his baby sister Jasmine. Jamie glances at his mother for reassurance and whispers, "I think the Wise Ones are the ancient people." His mother proposes that the Wise Ones might be "people you're seeking information from," and Paul, Ian's dad, agrees that they are "those who have gone before us." I am sitting on the floor on Paul's left, and when he hands me the pillow, I offer that the phrase makes me think of ancestors and old redwood trees. Jess's six-year-old son, Ryan, is beside me, wearing a Superman cape over his SpiralScouts uniform today—a compromise with his mother, who vetoed the pirate hat and vest he had originally chosen to go with his uniform. Ryan says confidently, "I think they're our ancestors," and hands the pillow back to his mother. Jess explains that most people think the Wise Ones are "usually people, but they can be anything in our world we can get wisdom from," like stars, oceans, mountains, or trees.

The responses from each participant in this circle illustrate a recurrent pattern at SpiralScouts meetings and at many other Pagan rituals involving children. Repeatedly in interactive rituals, discussions, and activities, adults enthusiastically offer their opinions, suggestions, and contributions. Children, in contrast, tend to be remarkably reticent in these circumstances. Whether at SpiralScouts meetings when the talking stick is passed or at seasonal events where the main ritual is performed by everyone present, when children are invited to either contribute to the discussion or "pass," they overwhelmingly choose silence over speech. In this instance, only two of the eleven children present chose to offer their opinions on the subject. There are a number of possible explanations for this pattern: children may feel wary of giving the "wrong" answer, may not understand the question, may feel shy about speaking in front of the group, or may simply not be interested in contributing. In these interactions at SpiralScouts meetings, children who are new to the group or who have little knowledge of their family's religious beliefs wait for adults to model appropriate behavior. As children watch parents model responses in ritual, they gain a better understanding of the social and spiritual aspects of their religion. Of course, it may also be that these events and interactions are not entirely designed for children. Rather, SpiralScouts may offer an example of an organization for Pagan children that serves the needs of Pagan adults' "inner children" as much as it meets the needs of the chronological children themselves.

Shaping Pagan Childhood

The current incarnation of SpiralScouts International, founded in 2001, operates as an independent organization, but the organization originated in 1999 as a subsidiary youth program within the Aquarian Tabernacle Church in Washington State. The ATC (or the "Tab") was founded in 1979 by Pete "Pathfinder" Davis, the organization's "archpriest," as a "formal church organization." The ATC gained 501(c)(3) status in 1991 as a Wiccan church. The Tab's exhaustive chronicle of its history (as presented on its website) explains that the intention behind the founding of the ATC was "to establish a quiet place in the countryside outside of Seattle where Wiccans and Pagans could gather for worship without being hassled by ignorant neighbors or suspicious authorities who did not understand their benevolent nature worship practices."[11] The church offers this dense and somewhat breathless description of its vision and orientation:

> The Aquarian Tabernacle Church is a positive, life-affirming spirituality, a non-dualist, non-racist, non-sexist, non-exclusivist, bi-polar, ecologically oriented faith dedicated to the preservation of Holy Mother Earth, the revival of the worship of the Old Gods in a modern context, the achievement of the fullest of human potentials and the creation of a peaceful world of love, freedom, health and prosperity for all sentient beings.[12]

This description suggests that the ATC's orientation is an eclectic mix of British "traditional" Wicca, earth-centered nature spirituality, and indigenous reconstruction combined with a smattering of New Age beliefs and a New Thought inheritance (in its emphasis on the achievement of human potential). The ATC's vision, history, and traditions—largely written by Davis himself—are recorded in prolix detail on the church's website. The church is a hierarchical organization comprising a core group of about forty people, the "archpriesthood," and an advisory council. The ATC maintains that it is "not about [Pete Pathfinder Davis] personally, but has become something much larger,"[13] but much of the organization's history and public presence is dominated by Davis's influence and personality. The ATC's website presents a detailed chronology of Davis's life, with this note from the "WebCrafter":

> The following chronology describes much of Pete's life and accomplishments, and he expressed his concern over it looking like a "Pete Davis Dog and Pony Show." It is my contention that without the energy and vision of this one man, the ATC might never have been started in the first place, and certainly would not have grown to the size it is now, nor have accomplished even half as much. The members and clergy of the ATC should look upon this chronology as an example of what a serious minded Pagan can accomplish if he or she puts aside his or her own self-imposed limitations, stops talking about it and just does what is right.[14]

The suggestion that Davis's creation of the ATC is simply a matter of one person doing "what is right" warrants further analysis. Certainly, the ATC, with its twenty-five-year history, stands as one of the oldest and most highly structured American Pagan organizations, and Davis has testified in several lawsuits aimed at expanding the rights of Wiccan prisoners and U.S. veterans. Despite these efforts to promote and legitimize the religion, however, the public presence of the ATC remains minimal, even among Wiccans, the vast majority of whom have no familiarity with Davis, the ATC, or SpiralScouts International.[15]

Likewise, Davis's personality and vision dominate the SpiralScouts literature and history; ultimately, though, few SpiralScouts families ever encounter Davis, the ATC, or SpiralScouts Headquarters and administrators. S*SI calls itself a "brown and serve" organization that can be adapted to a variety of different contexts and needs, and this quality is evident in the differing orientations, activities, and cultures of individual local groups. SpiralScouts itself, despite its encouraging growth over the past eight years, is relatively unknown by many Pagan families. When I asked Pagan families around the United States about their involvement with or knowledge of S*SI, some parents responded that they were unfamiliar with the organization but that they found the idea intriguing. Many Pagan parents replied that they had heard of SpiralScouts but were unaware of a circle in their area. Other parents related disappointing experiences with their local SpiralScouts circle or with S*SI's headquarters, with many noting that they had e-mailed for information on local circles but had received no response. Some explained that their children disliked the meetings they attended or that it was "too complicated" for younger children. One parent explained—somewhat apologetically—that although she was interested in SpiralScouts, her children "are not really joiners. They have not had an interest in Spiral scouts [sic]. My son said that it was to[o] wanna be mainstream [sic]. which I took as an interesting comment. I never did too much research into it, because I never wanted to push them into anything. (that will always backfire on you) [sic]."[16] This mother's fear of "pushing" her children into SpiralScouts points to another concern many Pagan parents express about this or any "Pagan children's organization": the possibility that their children will be "indoctrinated," even if that "indoctrination" involves little more than seasonal crafts and discussions of religious values that align with their own.

SpiralScouts' informational material states that it is a scouting program for boys and girls of minority faiths that is "adaptable to any non-hostile religious or non-religious community."[17] Theoretically, this adaptability stems from SpiralScouts' vision of itself as a nature-based scouting organization rooted in "Pagan family values" rather than a specifically Pagan religious education program. S*SI's official stance on religion states:

> SpiralScouts does not discriminate on the basis of religion, gender, sexual preference, ethnicity, race, age, etc. Children and families can be of any religion or no religion at all. . . . While Pagan in origin, [SpiralScouts] does not teach religion per se. Rather, it teaches a way of viewing the world so that children may cultivate their beliefs on their own.[18]

SpiralScouts' approach to religion was explained by Janet, the program director of S*SI at the time, in a message posted to the central SpiralScouts e-mail group: "The amount of religion inherent in any Circle or Hearth[19] is up to the parents and leaders. . . . And every non-religious badge has a way it could be earned without ever touching religion." Acknowledging the diversity of spiritual leanings among Pagan families, Janet offered, "The Circle I co-lead has Wiccans, Druids, Native Americans, and just spiritual people in it. I know that some Circles have Christian, Jewish, Quaker, and atheist children. None of these has been a problem."[20]

This diversity of approaches to religion was evident at a planning meeting I attended for a new SpiralScouts circle in New Hampshire. Heading the list of discussion topics for the afternoon was how—if at all—this circle should "handle religion" at meetings. Jessie, one of the circle's coleaders, remarked that she felt the circle should "try to maintain an earth-based spiritual ethic," although ideally they would avoid focusing on any specific religious path. Her coleader Will asserted that it was important to "expose children to different religions," and the other parents murmured their assent. Dion's mother suggested that the group should stress the importance of tolerance and respect for all religions, and Jessie agreed: "That is one of the most important lessons we can teach here." Will added that he would like to teach the scouts "that all the earth-based religions are alike," and he suggested that teaching a variety of different mythologies would present children with a range of religious possibilities. Noah's father agreed: "We have no problem with that." He added that their family attended Unitarian Universalist church services and considered themselves "Wiccan–Unitarian." Over the course of the meeting, Noah's mother offered that she was raised in what she now believes was a variant of contemporary Paganism, although it predated the arrival of Wicca in the United States, and her parents maintained a code of secrecy around their religious beliefs. As a young adult, she converted to Christianity and raised her older children (now all adults themselves) Episcopalian. She and Noah's father were handfasted by a Lakota Shaman, in a juxtaposition of traditions that would be noteworthy even without the family's other religious influences.[21] Now that Noah, their youngest son, was ten years old, his family had returned to Wicca—technically, Wiccan–Unitarianism, although they incorporated aspects of their Medieval Reconstructionist interests into their spiritual beliefs.[22] In general, the parents and leaders of this circle agreed that it was crucial to keep this new group "well-rounded." With at least five distinct religious traditions represented among the four families present at this meeting, this seemed an attainable goal. At the end of the meeting, Dion's mother remarked that she was happy to have found this circle; it gets lonely, she explained, being the only family they know who celebrates Yule. Jessie empathized: "You want your kids to think, 'This is what my community does,' not just, 'This is what my family does.'" Dion's mother nodded in agreement and explained that her family sought out this new SpiralScouts circle because "we wanted him to see that there's a community of people celebrating the old way." She did not clarify whether this might include the old Episcopalian, Wiccan, or Lakota ways, but Jessie generously assured her that the leaders had a similar goal for this circle: "We want to be welcoming."[23]

S*SI's literature supports this aim in its stated intention to support "families practicing alternative and minority religions . . . in transmitting the ethics, morals, and values these parents seek to instill in their children."[24] Some Pagan parents take a positive view of this moral education within the context of scouting activities, either recalling their own positive experiences with traditional scouting as children or lamenting the absence of an inclusive scouting organization like SpiralScouts in their own childhoods. For many families, however, the distinction between a Pagan children's scouting organization and an organization of Pagan children is minimal, and within the word "instill" looms the specter of potential religious indoctrination. The widespread opposition to the juxtaposition of scouting and contemporary Paganism illustrates the fundamental ambivalence within the religion toward its inclusion in dominant American culture. Contemporary Pagans seem to crave legitimation and normativity, and members of Pagan communities frequently create or plan Pagan scouting organizations, seminaries, schools, churches, and large-scale Pagan conglomerates with varying degrees of success.[25] At the same time, many American Pagans disdain organized activities, structured hierarchies, and the conformity evident in charters and uniforms. SpiralScouts draws skepticism from parents wary of placing their children in proximity to the terms "organization," "uniform," or "family values." Some parents suspect that despite its stated inclusivity toward all religions, SpiralScouts is fundamentally a Wiccan organization that will attempt to instill Wiccan religious values in their children—values that, given contemporary Paganism's emphasis on individual expression, are likely to run counter to their own spiritual practices or interpretations. Parents express concerns that S*SI's emergence from the ATC, a Wiccan church, is a sign

A SpiralScout at a fall ritual. Photo by Jess Gerrior.

that the organization is nothing more than a "church group hidden in a scout framework," as one concerned parent put it. Hoping to start a SpiralScouts circle in a highly conservative part of the Bible Belt, the mother who presented this concern worried that interested local parents, who hailed from at least ten different minority religions, might be apprehensive about the religious framework of the group. She claimed that SpiralScouts' emphasis on Wiccan principles and beliefs in the guise of "minority faith" beliefs was alienating to those who might find it overly specific.

The phrase in question that the parent found troubling was "harm none," a shortened version of the Wiccan Rede. Despite a response from the SpiralScouts program director confirming that this phrase is used nowhere in the SpiralScouts literature, the e-mail discussion quickly devolved into a debate between the parent and the SpiralScouts representative. The central issue of this exchange was less about the role of religion in the organization than about SpiralScouts' policies and procedures regarding access by non-chartered prospective leaders to information contained in the SpiralScouts leader handbook. As the discussion escalated and became increasingly confrontational, several other list members attempted to mollify the parties involved. Jess, the leader of Silverling Circle, offered her perspective on the organization and a suggestion for the original poster:

> As Co-Leaders we are all building SpiralScouts together, forming a new and positive community for the next generation. . . . Please open yourself to this suggestion: Take some very slow, long, deep breaths and focus on the word: intent. What change are you making in this moment? What is the story you are writing? How do your words affect others, and are you willing to cast off whatever blockades that keep you from *constructive*, *connective* communication?[26]

Interpersonal difficulties and tensions such as these seem to occur with some regularity within Pagan organizations. In many cases, these issues arise from ordinary personality conflicts exacerbated by the wide variety of approaches to personal spiritual practice. These discussions also reflect the ambivalence with which many Pagans regard inclusion in structured organizations. American Pagans continually negotiate the tension between individual will and self-determination, on the one hand, and the desire for inclusion and community, on the other. This tension becomes even more fraught and urgent for Pagans with children as they attempt to negotiate these desires in their children's public and private lives as well as in their own.

This fundamental conflict between contemporary Pagan quests for legitimacy and exceptionality is demonstrated within SpiralScouts

International itself. The organization maintains a somewhat schizophrenic desire to both model itself on and distinguish itself from traditional scouting organizations such as the Boy Scouts of America. SpiralScouts is not the first minority-faith scouting group; it follows in the footsteps of organizations such as the International Forum of Jewish Scouts, the National Islamic Committee on Scouting, and the Islamic Council on Scouting.[27] Like these groups, SpiralScouts was established as an alternative to traditionally single-gender and Christian-oriented scouting programs. S*SI's official handbook makes it clear that the organization was envisioned and founded in direct opposition to the "refusal of the Boy Scouts of America to allow recognition of a Wiccan religious badge," despite efforts by the Covenant of the Goddess to establish such a badge and the BSA's approval of "religious merit badges" for other faiths.[28] In fact, the BSA does not offer religious "merit badges," although it does offer Boy Scouts the opportunity to earn a "religious emblem," which is conferred by a religious leader of their faith. The Boy Scouts of America allows these emblems to be worn on official uniforms, but it does not create or administer them. It is true, however, that the BSA website does not list an approved Wiccan badge among its many available religious emblems.[29] Most Pagan parents are unaware of the significance of this specific issue as the impetus for the formation of S*SI, but some are familiar with the 2006 news coverage of the dismissal of two Wiccan brothers from a Louisiana Boy Scout troop. In the 2006 event, the twelve- and fifteen-year-old brothers were asked to leave the troop after admitting they were Wiccan during a discussion of religious diversity at the Boy Scout camp they were attending. The boys' family told a reporter that the scout leader "told them that if Cody had lied about his faith, the boys could have remained with no problem." The boys' mother expressed plans to begin the process of chartering a SpiralScouts circle in their region. This incident seems not to have been picked up by national newspapers, but the original article from the Louisiana local paper was widely circulated on Pagan parenting and SpiralScouts e-mail groups.[30] Many Pagans also maintain a negative perception of traditional scouting organizations based on lawsuits alleging that the BSA's exclusion and dismissal of gay and atheist scouts is discriminatory (for instance, the well-publicized "girls, godless, and gays" lawsuits).[31] The BSA has acknowledged and defended these allegations, invoking its constitutional right as a private membership group to dictate its membership standards. The BSA National Council's legal website asserts:

> That Boy Scouts also has traditional values, like requiring youth to do their "duty to God" and be "morally straight" is nothing to be ashamed of and should not be controversial. No court case has ever held that the Boy Scouts discriminates unlawfully, and it is unfortunate here that anyone would characterized [sic] Boy Scouts' constitutionally protected right to hold traditional values as "discriminatory." That is just name-calling.[32]

The BSA has continued to assert its right to hold what the organization calls "traditional values," and it has come under attack from Pagans as well as agnostic, atheist, and humanist groups for its insistence that scouts pledge to "do my duty to God" as part of the Scout Oath.[33] The BSA has maintained that this phrase is crucial to the oath and cannot be modified: "The Scout Oath and Law have served as the foundation of Scouting for 94 years. It would be a disservice to over five million youth and adult members of Scouting to allow members to pick and choose among the elements of the Oath or Law."[34] Because of this stance, in 2005 the BSA reached an agreement with the American Civil Liberties Union requiring troops to maintain private sponsors and to end relationships with public schools and governmental agencies. The ACLU directive held that the BSA's requirement of the Scout Oath posed a constitutional conflict with public sponsorship.

As a result of these sorts of disputes and lawsuits as well as personal and word-of-mouth conflicts with Boy Scouts troops, administration, or principles, many Pagan parents regard the organization warily, at best. Parents refer to "Bible-thumping" Boy Scout leaders, remark that they feel uncomfortable with information on the BSA website, or simply assume that, based on their knowledge of the organization, the prospect of their sons as Boy Scouts is absurd. Pagan children, these parents believe—and hope—are far too independent, self-aware, and enlightened to be Boy Scouts. Again, Pagan perceptions and ideals of childhood are at play here, as parents see children—particularly *their* children—as possessing a purer spirituality and a stronger will than either adults or their more mainstream, docile peers. In addition to these understandings of childhood, some Pagan parents bring to their encounters with SpiralScouts International their own disappointing childhood experiences of scouting and the hope of sparing their children the same. Others remember positive experiences of childhood scouting and hope to replicate these for their children. Still other parents felt the lack of a supportive, welcoming activity in their childhoods, and they wish that SpiralScouts had been available to them as children. In essence, SpiralScouts fulfills deep psychological needs for parents who want their children's childhoods to be as satisfying as their own, completely different from their own, or as idyllic as they believe Pagan childhood should be.

Part of SpiralScouts' appeal stems from this discomfort among Pagan parents with traditional scouting groups. SpiralScouts manages to distinguish itself from the Boy Scouts at the same time that it draws from and adapts much of the BSA's model of local, regional, and national hierarchical structure, activities, and uniforms. Children in SpiralScouts are strongly encouraged to wear uniforms, although the organization is clear that these are not required. SpiralScouts' everyday activity uniform seems innocuous enough to be acceptable in public settings as a generic children's activity uniform: khaki pants, dark green polo or oxford shirt, and the SpiralScouts neck cord, made of three thick cords (chocolate brown, tan, and forest green) braided together and held in place with a large sliding wooden bead. Most children at regular SpiralScouts meetings wear at least the green shirt and neck cord; the latter seems to be the bare minimum for the uniform, and many scouts arrive at meetings wearing their neck cord and ordinary clothing. Scouts generally reserve the full uniform for more formal events, such as badge ceremonies or public events like the Yule festival or the Celebrate Samhain event. In many ways, S*SI has established itself in opposition to the BSA. When I asked Jess about the relationship between the two organizations, she described her experiences with both groups:

> SpiralScouts is something completely different. It's not the antithesis of Boy Scouts or Girl Scouts. It's not trying to be the opposite. It's not against it in any way. It's just really its own separate thing. So if I had been in Boy Scouts or Girls Scouts [as a child], I would be constantly comparing, or trying to do things the same, or trying to do things differently. That's not

even part of how I plan, so I'm kind of glad for that. My brother was in Boy Scouts, and I was old enough to remember the kinds of things that they did in Boy Scouts that girls could not do and being really peeved at that. My mom actually started to lead a Girl Scouts group with my baby sister, who was in Girl Scouts, and they quit after a couple of months because all they were doing was cooking, sewing, interior decorating or something, and they never got to go fishing, or start their own fire, or make their own tools. So they were like, forget it! This isn't the fun stuff.[35]

SpiralScouts in full uniform are unlikely to be mistaken for Boy Scouts or Girl Scouts, mostly due to S*SI's addition of the distinctive dark brown capuche. A hooded cloak that covers the head and shoulders, the capuche gives the formal SpiralScouts uniform a distinctly medieval feel (appealing to the significant numbers of contemporary Pagans who are members of the Society for Creative Anachronism or other reconstructionist groups).[36] Throughout the spring of 2006, SpiralScouts parents and staff spent weeks on the main SpiralScouts e-mail group debating public perceptions of the capuche and suggesting alternatives to its inclusion in the official uniform.

The controversy seems to have begun when the leader of a newly chartered circle, the First Church of Wicca's Sea Witches, e-mailed the list wondering if scouts could substitute a dark brown sash for the capuche. Rev. Kendra, the Sea Witches' leader, noted that all three families involved in their new circle were "adamant that they do not want their children wearing the Capuche . . . because we live in the Plymouth area of Massachusetts it just looks too pilgrimish."[37] The S*SI new charters coordinator replied that while the capuche was currently part of the official uniform, a committee was at work on alternatives for those who did not like its appearance. Despite this seemingly straightforward response, an extended e-mail debate ensued regarding issues with and alternatives to the current uniform. Some parents argued in favor of the capuche because it "just shouts pagan" and the "Renaissance style . . . fits SpiralScouts." One parent wondered, "What *is* wrong with looking like a pilgrim? It's actually more Europe/Renaissance/Medieval." Others defended the capuches on principle, conceding that it might be true that they may be reminiscent of monks' robes but that it was "inappropriate to join an existing group and expect to make changes to it." At

A FireFly in uniform. Photo by Jess Gerrior.

one point during the e-mail exchange, a leader mentioned that some of the parents in her circle were complaining that "with the pointed hood they look like KKK robes," and the conversation picked up considerably more steam. A SpiralScouts staff member quickly attempted to curtail this line of discussion by noting that the capuche "is designed to be worn with the hood down, not up," but his attempt was in vain. E-mails flew back and forth among list members. One argued that the capuches were different colors than Ku Klux Klan robes; another suggested that other styles of Pagan clothing—for example, a sleeveless tunic of the sort "associated with Renaissance, Medieval, Pagan, Roman, Druid, and a variety of other non-christian [sic] groups"—might be more appropriate; and another proclaimed that the entire discussion was "making mountains out of molehills" and should take a backseat to more pressing issues like S*SI's finances and administration. The issue was finally addressed by Pete "Pathfinder" Davis, founder of S*SI, in a lengthy e-mail forwarded by the SpiralScouts coordinator:

> Anyone who thinks the capuche hood looks like a KKK hood has either never seen a picture of a Klu Klux Klansman [sic], or hasn't bothered to look at the capuche either, or perhaps both. . . . Seems to me that it is some mental image some folks are imagining enough to object to, rather than reality. The comparison to the KKK I find really offensive, but I'll get over it in time. Also seems to me to be much ado about nothing. It is the uniform. As others have mentioned, the kids seem to like it, too. If we wanted to look like Boy Scouts, we would be Boy Scouts.[38]

Davis's adamant resistance to SpiralScouts being mistaken for more mainstream scouts is apparent in his final comment here. Also apparent is the sense that his is ultimately the final word on the subject—solidified, in case this was unclear, by his e-mail signature: "Pete Pathfinder Davis, Archpriest, Aquarian Tabernacle Church, SpiralScouts founder, and resident curmudgeon."

This discussion echoed a similar exchange on the same e-mail list two months earlier, in which a circle leader suggested a cloak design as an alternative to the capuche. In a statement very similar to Davis's, the SpiralScouts program director effectively quashed this suggestion and further discussion with a terse explanation: "Uniform means the same—that's why we have a specific list of what constitutes a uniform—so that no matter where you go, you'll be able to recognize other SpiralScouts."[39] Inasmuch as contemporary Paganism ardently supports individual expression, it is interesting that the administrators of a Pagan family organization claim to welcome adaptations to S*SI at the local level and yet steadfastly resist suggestions for these adaptations. SpiralScouts is clear that it is fundamentally a hierarchical organization despite its "brown and serve" philosophy. At the same time, the organization seems to maintain a fundamental antipathy toward the traditional scouting organizations from which it draws its inspiration.

Unlike some SpiralScouts groups, Silverling Circle's activities reflect a creative reinterpretation of scouting activities rather than a consciously oppositional response to the BSA. For the families of Silverling Circle, S*SI provides the opportunity for community involvement and the normativity of a structured children's activity program. Girls and boys in SpiralScouts camp, build fires, earn badges, and perform community service. They clean up beaches and highways, pick up litter in parks, and—in an activity that is possibly more indicative of life in a small town than of a generally "Pagan" ethos—make cards to send to local soldiers stationed overseas. When I talked with Erin about her involvement in SpiralScouts, she told me that in the fall, the families of her local SpiralScouts hearth had performed community service at a retirement home. The children arrived in costumes and sang Halloween songs they had learned in school, but the SpiralScouts parents were unprepared for (and amused by) one of the residents attempting to lead them in the song "Jesus Loves Me." When she mentions SpiralScouts, Erin tells me, people frequently assume that she means Girl Scouts, and Erin rarely corrects them. Even at the Halloween community service, she says, one of the residents told Erin, "I used to be a Brownie leader, and you've got my support." Erin explains that she found this exchange "kind of sad . . . because we'd love to go caroling and things like that, but I don't think a retirement home—unless it's a Pagan retirement home—would be the right place to be singing different words to their favorite tunes."[40]

Amid the ambivalence and tension S*SI brings to its relationship with contemporary Paganism, SpiralScouts attempts to establish a moral framework for Pagan children. In many ways, though, this framework is less a coherent whole than it is a sketch of what Pagan children's moral education might look like. Some of the values SpiralScouts explicitly attempts to impart to its children are similar to those promoted by other scouting groups: responsibility, service, cooperation, courtesy, and respect. Others have a more decidedly Pagan slant: the "importance of the individual," "family participation," and "beauty of spirit and thought."[41] At the same time, many of these values seem to be challenged by practices within the organization itself. Another discussion among SpiralScouts leaders, parents, and administrators offered an example of the conflicting messages at play in S*SI's religious imagination. A question was posed to the main SpiralScouts e-mail group asking if the FireFly Promise, recited by SpiralScouts between the ages of three and eight, could be made "secular" by eliminating the first line, "I promise to serve the Wise Ones"—the line that had previously sparked debate on the e-mail group and in Silverling Circle concerning the enigmatic identity of the "Wise Ones." This time, the conversation focused specifically on parents' discomfort with the verb "to serve." One parent was adamant that her children not be asked to serve anyone or anything, human or divine, asserting, "If you serve someone, you are their servant." The official response from the program director of S*SI was, again, that the wording of the promise was "non-negotiable." Despite this mandate from SpiralScouts Headquarters, another lengthy e-mail exchange ensued about the nuances of the word "serve." List members compared the relative merits and difficulties involved in the different concepts of service to one's family, service to a superior, and service to humanity. S*SI's program coordinator argued that the line could already be construed as secular: "I wonder why you think the wise ones is necessarily religious? There are many wise people in our lives."[42] Her response suggested that S*SI's stance on this issue was that "serving" the "Wise Ones" did not inherently conflict with the deeply held and stalwartly defended values of self-sovereignty and personal freedom dear to many Pagans' hearts, nor did it conflict with the organization's claim to meet the needs of nonreligious families. Apparently unconvinced, the original poster ultimately decided that "[SpiralScouts] is just not for my family. . . . I'll just have to keep searching for a group that is just about doing nature stuff with no religious over- or under tones."[43] In the context of SpiralScouts International, it seems that Pagan adults, like Pagan children in many other situations, are expected to negotiate conflicting or dissonant moral messages. The organization promotes Wiccan values, but it assures parents that it is adaptable to any religion or to secular purposes; it encourages circles to adapt the program to meet the needs of specific families, but it asserts that much of the program is "non-negotiable." The dissonance present in these messages reflects the deep ambivalence within contemporary Paganism itself regarding the relationship of personal autonomy and individual will to community and social legitimacy.

Teaching Little Heathens

For many parents of very young children, modeling ritual etiquette and religious creativity is sufficient for their children's religious instruction. Pagan parents can include their children in seasonal rituals and daily spiritual practices and feel confident that the children are absorbing at least the fundamentals of their beliefs. As their children reach school age, however, parents often feel the need to offer children more explicit and systematized moral education, in much the same way that Christian or Jewish children may begin Sunday school or Hebrew school around this time. Children whose families have been closely involved with local Pagan communities may encounter their first non-Pagan teachers and peers upon entering school, often with resulting misunderstandings on both sides. One mother, a high priestess who led a teaching coven for several years and includes her children in many family rituals, related a memorable incident involving her five-year-old daughter. Selene, her husband, and their daughters are part of a small, tightly knit community of Pagan families in Austin, Texas, an "oasis in a desert" for politically and socially liberal families like theirs. Raised within this community since birth, Selene's oldest daughter, Raven, had little reason to believe that her family's spiritual beliefs were not shared by the larger (and far more conservative) local community. In a supermarket checkout line one day, Raven asked her mother, "Can I say hello to the other people in line?" Selene distractedly answered, "I suppose so." Raven continued, "And can I talk about how the Goddess loves me?" Selene relates the rest of this story:

> I said, "Well, you can if you want, honey, but you know there's a lot of people out there who don't really believe in the Goddess, and they may not really understand what it is that you're talking about." And she got this look on her face, like, "They don't believe in the *Goddess*?!" It was kind of an interesting concept to her, that there were people out there that didn't know about the Goddess and didn't believe that she was real and active in their daily lives.[44]

Other children raised in similar circumstances may find discussions of their families' religious beliefs met with apprehension, if not outright prejudice, from peers and educators. Conversely, solitary practitioners may understand all too well the potential social dangers of revealing their beliefs, often leaving them isolated and alienated—for example, when mainstream religious holidays are celebrated in their schools. One Pagan mother explained the difficulties inherent in raising her daughter as a Pagan:

> It's hard raising Pagan kids because you do meet [a lot] of opposition. Many people that your children are supposed to be able to trust and respect such as teachers and family members will tend to misunderstand the pagan life-style as being harmful to a child either spiritually or emotionally or whatever. . . . There have been times that my daughter's friends have turned around and screamed at her that we were going to hell. Sometimes a family member will take her aside and try to undo some of the basic morals or stories we've taught her with the mind that they are trying to "save" her. It's very confusing to children to have people she loves and trusts . . . undermining what their parents are teaching them.[45]

Starting school is often the first event that exposes Pagan children to unfamiliar situations and beliefs and frequently spurs parents to consider ways to provide their children with more explicit moral and spiritual instruction. Pagan parents sometimes choose alternative schooling arrangements for their children, partly as a way to minimize some of the difficulties faced by Pagan children in public schools and partly due to conflicts with the structure and ideology of public schools. Some Pagan parents find that the holistic, child-led curricula of Montessori schools and some public alternative and charter schools are appealing options for their families. Even a liberal outlook and progressive curriculum, however, does not guarantee that a Pagan child will not encounter intolerance and suspicion in these educational environments. Older children are generally aware of this possibility, and most prefer to keep their family's religious beliefs "in the broom closet." At several CMA festivals, I camped near the family of an articulate and animated eleven-year-old boy whose alternative public school offered classes in Greek mythology and recognized some Pagan holidays. When I asked him if there were other Pagan children at his school, he replied, "Probably, yes. But you don't exactly go around with a sign on your neck saying 'I'm Wiccan, I'm Wiccan!'"[46] Even if their children do not encounter overt prejudice in the classroom, most Pagan parents are aware that misunderstandings about their religious beliefs and practices are likely to occur. Depending on the local social and religious culture, these misunderstandings can range from mild annoyances to complicated legal issues. A Pagan mother responded to an open-ended question about raising children Pagan with the comment, "There is a fear of persecution should we be too open about our beliefs. Most people will tolerate other Judeo-Christian traditions and those very similar, but Paganism is not so well accepted and is often confused with Satan worship. I would not want my daughter hurt by the ignorant (nor my husband [hurt] for that matter) because of my spiritual beliefs."[47] More than one parent told me that Pagan parents in conservative parts of the country should "watch out for CPS [Child Protective Services]." Parents are aware of custody cases that pit a Pagan parent against a parent of a more common religion. In a study of contemporary Paganism as a "minority religion in a majoritarian America," the political science professor Carol Barner-Barry explains:

> Although it is currently not possible to get a definitive count of the number of child custody disputes that involve issues related to the religious convictions of one or both parents, it is clear this does happen with some frequency. . . . Even intact Pagan families may face custody challenges that are initiated by relatives, police, social workers, and adoption agencies.[48]

Most Pagans can relate stories of suspicion, intolerance, or overt persecution encountered by their own or friends' children in school. Pagan children have been sent home from school for wearing pentacles or other Pagan symbols on jewelry or clothing. The use of the word "witch" as a self-description by many Wiccans contributes to their self-positioning as "outsiders" and, often, to misunderstandings of the religion by non-Pagans—and sometimes by Pagans themselves. The First Church of Wicca's Rev. Kendra describes the resistance the church encountered when naming its SpiralScouts group, the Duxbury Sea Witches, noting that two former members of the church "left because they didn't like the name." She explains:

> [One of the ex-members] said, "I refuse to label my daughter as a witch." And so I said to her, "We are a church that practices witchcraft, and we are witches, and we are raising witches. If you don't like that because you're UU [Unitarian Universalist], by all means, go back to the UU church. But that's just the way it is." She said, "I feel Pagan, I identify with Paganism; I'm just not comfortable labeling myself or my child as a witch." And I said, "That's fine. Move on. You're not going to be able to stay here then." And even Pete "Pathfinder" Davis, who founded the SpiralScouts, he's hell-bent on not saying that we're witches. There's not another [SpiralScouts] circle out there that calls themselves witches. And I said, "No way. We are witches and we're using the name."[49]

Kendra's adamant opposition to a less provocative name for the children's religious education group reflects a common stance among many Pagans who not only choose to call themselves witches but also use the word as a means of establishing a careful and rigorously maintained distinction between Paganism and other religions. Although the need to maintain this distinction is a common feature of new religious movements, for some adult Pagans, this attempt to distinguish themselves from the religions they have (often quite deliberately) rejected seems to involve a provocative and reactionary rebellion against the religions of their birth families.

Not all adult Pagans adopt this confrontational stance toward larger American culture, of course, and many Pagans who call themselves witches do so because of a genuine affinity for the word and its connotations rather than as a reactionary position. Nevertheless, it is often difficult to reconcile self-identification as a "witch" with mainstream views of witches. Many Pagan families are dismayed by cartoonish representations of "witches" on young children's schoolroom Halloween decorations or by school projects and events that conflict with their beliefs. Jess remarked that her six-year-old son's class at school was decorating for Halloween and making witches "with the black pointy hats and the green warty faces and the whole bit." She explained to her son,

"There are two kinds of witches. There are the real ones, and there are the made-up, imaginary ones that they talk about on TV and in school. Real witches are people who practice Wicca, practice Earth magic." At this point, her son, Ryan, interrupted:

> RYAN: I want to say something. They do not have green faces. They don't have a black pointy hat.
> JESS: And do you remember when we were talking about why people think that witches have green warty faces and black pointy hats?
> RYAN: Because they don't understand.
> JESS: Right. And what do people do when they don't understand something?
> RYAN: Make a book about it?
> JESS: Make a book about it? Or they make up stories about it, and people listen to the stories. So if somebody says that a witch is a mean old lady with a green face and a black pointy hat, then people believe it, right? And then that's what they tell somebody else, and they tell somebody else, and they tell somebody else. Right?
> RYAN: Mmm-hmm.
> ZK: So, what do real witches do?
> RYAN: Um . . . turn bad witches into toads?
> JESS: Is that what *real* witches do? Or is that what storybook witches do?
> RYAN: Real ones.
> JESS: Who's a real witch that you know?
> RYAN: Hmm? [pointing at Jess]
> JESS: Do *I* turn people into toads?[50]

Jess's efforts to keep this conversation focused reflect the varying degrees of difficulty experienced by Pagan parents in explaining to their children why people may have negative reactions toward their religion. A Pagan mother of three describes her difficulties in explaining these types of situations to her children:

> It's hard to explain to a six-year-old why the other children at school don't understand when she sings songs about the Goddess, or why we can't always be open about our spirituality. My family is accepting, but my in-laws are hard-core Baptist, and my mother-in-law has actually

referred to me as "an agent of the devil"! It's difficult for children to understand why we don't see "other Grandma" very often . . . or why our bumper stickers are on magnets, for easy removal.[51]

This mother's experience points to an issue that complicates family and community interactions for many Pagan families: the vast majority of adult American Pagans come to the religion from more mainstream religions, and many maintain an abiding antipathy toward these traditions. This distaste for the religions of their childhoods, paired with the already thorny dynamics between many adult children and their parents, leads some adult Pagans to exaggerate perceptions of oppression or disapproval from family members. In some cases, of course, these perceptions may be accurate. Sitting in camp chairs in the sun at a CMA festival, Freya and Selene, both Wiccan priestesses in their forties, discussed their Methodist families—"those Methodist cultists," Freya jokes. She adds that her mother's side is "an entire family, ancestrally, of fundamentalists." As the adults compare their religious upbringings, the children play nearby, interrupting the conversation to request potato chips and to bring the adults into their conversations and jokes. Freya continues, "I think my aunt is—Selene, what did you say your dad was? Episcopalian? Yeah, I think my aunt is Episcopalian. Do they talk in tongues?" Selene says, "That sounds like Pentecostal," and her husband, Atashih, adds, "Dancing with snakes and all that." Freya laughs: "I don't think my aunt has ever danced with any snakes. Can you see my Aunt Beverly dancing with snakes? She is such a controlling person, she'd be telling the snakes what to do. She makes my mother look laid back."[52] At the next CMA festival, Freya relates another story about her mother. During a phone call with her mother, she mentioned that she would be attending this weekend campout for Beltane. Her mother replied, "Well, I just hope you're not worshipping." At the time, Freya was dumbfounded by this comment. As she recounts this exchange among friends, however, she laughs, and Freya's mother's comment becomes the source of jokes for the rest of the weekend, as the adults ask one another in mock horror, "You're not worshipping, are you?" (to which the others respond, "No! Maybe a little revering, or a bit of celebrating. Oh no—could I be inadvertently worshipping?").

Many parents make an effort to lessen these misunderstandings and misconceptions by educating their children's teachers, schoolmates, and grandparents about their beliefs, hoping to demystify their religion to others. Despite these efforts, however, Pagan parents remain wary of public reaction to their family's religious beliefs. Some parents refuse to allow photographs of their children to appear in local news articles about Pagan events for fear of (generally unspecified) "backlash" from the child's school, local community, or extended family. Because public school is often the source of Pagan children's earliest experiences of being religiously different from their peers, parents try to focus outreach attempts in these areas. An essay by the Pagan author Suzanne "Cecylyna Dewr" Egbert, titled "You Have a Pagan in Your Classroom," attempts to explain to educators the beliefs a Pagan child may hold.[53] This essay has been republished on numerous Pagan websites and widely circulated on Pagan parenting message boards. Still, Pagan parents are wary of public reaction to their family's religious beliefs. Many of these factors, combined with a general mistrust of the role of the "government" or the "state" in public education, contribute to the increasing popularity of homeschooling among American Pagan families.

For many parents, homeschooling or unschooling[54] offer ways to retain control over the information to which their children are exposed and allow parents to tailor a curriculum that is customized for their children and supportive of their beliefs. In a study of Christian homeschooling families, Colleen McDannell notes that of the nearly half a million homeschooled children in the United States, "the vast majority are being taught at home for religious reasons." She adds, "While the purported reason for home schooling is the education of children, what really happens is the religious education of the whole family. Christians who home school frequently are 'first generation' Christians."[55] Robert Kunzman's studies of homeschooling families support this observation; he finds that 83% of parents say they homeschool their children "to provide religious or moral instruction."[56] Kunzman notes that many homeschoolers are reluctant to participate in government surveys, such as the one conducted by the National Center for Education Statistics, and he suggests that the number of homeschooled children in the United States may be closer to two million. Pagan homeschooling families also express religious motivations for choosing to educate children at home. In fact, Pagan families often choose to homeschool for many of the same reasons offered by Christian families: dissatisfaction with the curriculum or social pressures of public schools; concern that public schools undermine or contradict their family's values; children's behavioral or learning problems, such as autism, ADHD, or Sensory Integration Dysfunction; mistrust of government influence on education; or simply the belief that parents are the most conscientious and committed educators of their own children. Some Pagan parents also see homeschooling as an extension of everyday spiritual practices with their children.

Beyond pragmatic attempts to reduce bullying, teasing, and potential legal or social service involvement in their children's lives, many Pagan parents choose alternative schooling due to a deep-seated distrust of public education. For some families, this distrust (some might say "paranoia") extends beyond the realm of schooling to include fundamental misgivings about public health as well. Some Pagan parents regard both public schools and "modern medicine" as institutions in league with Christian-centered, right-wing, conservative political and social agendas. The overlapping interest in and rationales for homeschooling among contemporary Pagans and conservative Christians as well as both groups' views on early childhood education and the role of the government (in health-related and educational matters) suggests an area deserving of future study.

Dawn is a homeschooling Pagan mother of two daughters who sees homeschooling as a way of reinforcing her family's religious and spiritual beliefs. Born and raised Catholic, Dawn considers her daughters Catholic and continues to attend Catholic services with them, although she now identifies as Wiccan:

> I homeschool so it's very easy to keep reinforcing my ideas toward nature, and life. I best communicate these ideals by simply acting as their role model. Whenever they catch a dragonfly or something I talk of how beautiful it is, and that it needs to be free. I teach them life is sacred . . . and it's all around them. It's not just a "sit and chat" discussion. It's living the way and teaching by example.[57]

At the same time, this casual approach to religious practice can prove frustrating, as Jess explains:

> [There is] a weakness in the Wiccan community. Some people may be just fine just practicing solitary and going for their walk in the woods

and communing with nature and things, but I think for kids, families—for young kids, especially—they need community. They need community as a basis for doing any of the other practice.[58]

Families who cannot or choose not to join SpiralScouts or similar organizations may address this need for religious community by attending services at Unitarian Universalist churches, where Pagan parents feel welcome and children can participate in religious education classes that stress a multi-faith approach attractive to many Pagan parents. Dozens of Pagan families with whom I spoke mentioned casual or regular attendance at UU services, often remarking, "That's where Pagans with kids go."[59] One midwestern mother, whose young children attend the local UU church's religious education classes every Sunday, explained to me that the UU church is where she and her husband can "meet with other parents of young children. It's where anybody can go and pretty much practice their faith in a safe place. . . . [It] helps with creating a sense of continuity in the religion."[60] (For his part, her four-year-old son told me that he liked attending the UU church because "church is a place where there's toys . . . and there's even a coffee room.") The Unitarian Universalist church tends to draw people of diverse theological and spiritual perspectives into its religious community; a 1997 survey of almost ten thousand UU members conducted by the Unitarian Universalist Association found theological perspectives from at least eight different religious traditions as well as many UUs who also considered themselves humanist (the most popular choice) or "other." In another 1997 UU study, James Casebolt noted the complexity of many UUs' theological outlooks, observing, "The typical [survey] respondent felt the need to circle three or four terms to describe his or her theological views."[61]

The Covenant of Unitarian Universalist Pagans (CUUPS), an interest group present in many UU churches, offers a particularly welcoming environment for Pagan families. Paganism officially came to Unitarian Universalism about ten years before the establishment of CUUPS through women's spirituality groups and religious education classes, such as Rev. Shirley Ranck's "Cakes for the Queen of Heaven" and Elisabeth Fisher's "Rise Up and Call Her Name."[62] The Women and Religion Resolution of 1977 was followed by the earliest organized UU Pagan worship at the UU Continental Feminist Theology Convocation in East Lansing, Michigan, in 1980. More Unitarian Universalists were introduced to Paganism at the 1987 General Assembly, where journalist and member of the Board of Advisors for CUUPS Margot Adler delivered the keynote speech, "A Pagan Spiritual View." In 1995, the inclusion of the "Sixth Source" in the UU Principles and Purposes affirmed as one of the sources of UU faith "spiritual teachings of Earth-centered traditions which celebrate the sacred circle of life and instruct us to live in harmony with the rhythms of nature."[63] Margot Adler explains that the two religious paths balance each other: Unitarian Universalism helps to ground Paganism, while Paganism "has brought to UUism the joy of ceremony . . . and a bit more juice and mystery."[64]

For many Pagan parents, the UU church offers a way to ground their families' individualized beliefs and practices within an established religious community. The UU acceptance of contemporary Paganism encompasses SpiralScouts International, as well, and UU churches frequently act as sponsors for local SpiralScouts circles, donating meeting space, hosting seasonal festivals and events, and often even paying local SpiralScouts circles' chartering fees. Like attendance at Unitarian Universalist churches, SpiralScouts offers an avenue through which Pagan families can attempt to systematize their values and practices within a like-minded community. Although UU churches offer Pagan families grounding and religious education within an established framework, SpiralScouts International seems to reflect the ambivalence with which Pagans and Pagan families approach community, organization, and the religious imaginations of children.

Like many new religious movements, contemporary American Paganism makes a deliberate effort to distinguish itself from mainstream religious traditions and organizations at the same time that it demands legitimacy and strives to institute organizations of its own. Sarah Pike has linked current Pagan practices, such as festivals and gatherings, to nineteenth-century camp meetings, revivals, and Spiritualist conventions, illustrating their similar "eclecticism and the challenge they represent to more orthodox and established religious practices."[65] Pike notes that these comparisons simultaneously illuminate aspects of these earlier religious idioms and raise questions about the future of contemporary Paganism:

Camp meetings and Spiritualist conventions seem to have been antinomian stages in emergent religious movements that later became more rigidly structured and institutionalized. If religious Americans assume they have inexhaustible religious options—an open spiritual frontier—then where will Neopagans go next, and what other religious movements will emerge from Neopaganism?[66]

Pike sees similar processes of boundary marking and identity construction in these movements, explaining that contemporary Pagans "follow a familiar American path of constructing spiritual space by rejecting the meanings and rituals proposed by culturally dominant Christian churches. Christianity becomes essential as that which is rejected—and which rejects—to establish Neopagans' own identity."[67] This emotionally and theologically fraught relationship with Christianity is evident in contemporary Paganism's rejection of institutions that the practitioners of the religion consider steeped in Christianity (such as organized scouting and, ironically, public schools) as well as in Pagans' daily reactions to mainstream religions.

Many Christians frequently misunderstand Paganism, but Pagan children often misunderstand Christianity as well. Second-generation Pagan children are raised in environments with a thoroughly Pagan religious imagination and ethos, often by parents who have varying degrees of animosity toward their own (often Christian) religious backgrounds. Pagan children's difficulties with Christianity may simply reflect confusion about its relationship to their own religious beliefs. Rev. Kendra of the First Church of Wicca related a story about her eight-year-old daughter's interaction with a Christian classmate when her daughter, Alana, attempted to explain a Yule ritual. The friend asked, "Do you drink wine and break bread?" When Alana said no, her friend asked, "Don't you think that Jesus was the son of God?" to which Alana replied, "I don't know if the God and Goddess ever had a son."[68] Parents clearly take pleasure in relating these stories of their children's confusion about or rejection of Christianity, and stories of this sort often receive enthusiastic receptions from other Pagan adults.

Pagan parents often encourage an oppositional approach to Christianity among their children, either explicitly or indirectly, and Pagan children demonstrate a variety of attitudes toward other religions.

Eleven-year-old Stephen made frequent references over the course of one Beltane festival weekend to Christianity as a "cult," remarking, "They think they have a religion like ours." When one of the adults brought out a craft kit that contained (to the adults' consternation) a coloring page with the words "Praise the Lord," Atashih, one of the adults, suggested that the children could add "and Lady" to the wording on the page. Atashih's five-year-old daughter, Deanna, asked what they meant by the "Lord," and Stephen laughed, "Atashih, success! Deanna doesn't know who Jesus is!" With thoroughly preadolescent self-confidence, he added, "I'm not saying [whether] Jesus existed . . . but he's very overrated. He said a lot of things that have been misinterpreted."[69]

The "Pagan carols" that Erin and Aisling were preparing to sing during the holiday season offer an example of Paganism's attempts to both subvert and appropriate aspects of Christianity:

> Hark, the neo-Pagans sing,
> Glory to the Holly King!
> Peace on Earth and mercy mild,
> God and Goddess reconciled.
> Hear us now as we proclaim,
> We have risen from the flames,
> Our ancient Craft now we reclaim,
> In the God and Goddess' names.[70]

Adult Pagans establish and maintain, with differing degrees of intentionality, a distinction between their chosen religion and the religions of their families and their childhoods. In doing so, they establish the religious worlds of their own children in opposition to the dominant religious culture. Erin, the creator of the ritual "toddler tools" for her daughter Aisling, explained her position in a way that reflects many Pagan parents' experiences with mainstream religious culture:

> If there's no "Pagan" [option on demographic forms] there, I just check "other" and don't mention anything. I took my daughter to the hospital last year about this time—she broke her arm—and they wanted to know religious affiliation, and I was like, why is that? . . . I just thought, that's none of your business. But there wasn't a "Pagan" box to check. . . . In our

family, especially when we talk about politics and all the stuff going on in the world, religion is a bad word, really. The idea that you believe like a bunch of other people . . . well, it's kind of cool to belong, but I'm not just going to believe a bunch of stuff because someone else does. We are not all going to agree to believe the same thing. I mean, that's just . . . I don't know, mind control or something.[71]

Through this complicated process of subversion, rejection, improvisation, and negotiation, contemporary Pagans position their religion, their daily lives, and the lives of their children in an ambivalent relationship with the culture that surrounds them.

6

My Dream Come True

"My Dream Come True": Erin's Blessing Ceremonies

Eoin laughs in a deep, full belly laugh that seems absurdly large coming from a three-month-old baby. The guests who have gathered at Erin's home this evening for Eoin's baby blessing ceremony find it impossible to resist tickling him and swinging him in the air, just for the reward of that unlikely sound. The adults admire the baby as the four older children—three daughters of guests and Erin's older daughter, Aisling—play a loud and elaborate game of tag in the dining room. A plaster cast of Erin's nine-month-pregnant belly is displayed in the living room near two large, framed portraits, one of Erin and Aisling and one of Erin pregnant with Eoin. In the middle of the coffee table, the altar is laid out for tonight's ritual. In addition to the standard candles, feathers, and food are elements that make it clear this is not an ordinary adult ritual. Piled in one corner are a handful of plastic baby rattles, and in the other corner of the table are two large, wooden cutouts of the sun and moon, one for Eoin and one for Aisling. This "baby blessing" will be a blessing ceremony for both of Erin's children. Because Erin was not yet Wiccan when six-year-old Aisling was born, Aisling did not receive a dedication or blessing ceremony when she was an infant. Throughout the evening, Erin repeatedly mentions that she wishes she had been able to raise Aisling Wiccan from birth, as Eoin will be. Because her husband, Joe, is not Wiccan—he is not, she admits, religious or spiritual at all—she had little support for her attempts to follow a spiritual path in Aisling's early years. She sighs: "Last time, I didn't get to do it the way I wanted, but this time I can."

As the guests gather around the coffee table, Erin exclaims, "Oh, where's the baby? I have to get him—this is his party!" She goes into the kitchen and retrieves Eoin from his father's arms. Joe has chosen not to participate in this ceremony, and he hands the baby to Erin and disappears into another part of the house. Erin has written tonight's ritual herself. She hands typed copies of the text to each guest with the lines each person is to read highlighted in yellow, and apologizes: "I feel bad asking you all here and then making you work." Erin holds Eoin in her arms and says, "Why don't the kids open the circle, since we have four adults and four children?" Aisling proudly exclaims, "I know how to do that!" As she reads the invocation to the Spirit of the East, Erin whispers to Lisa, "I can't remember. Which way do you start the invoking pentagram?" Lisa points clockwise, and Erin helps Aisling draw an invoking pentagram in the air with the wand, the magnolia twig with the rose quartz point. Aisling finishes her part of the invocation by shouting, "Hail and farewell!" Erin gently reminds her, "OK, but we're not saying good-bye yet." Aisling dramatically falls backward onto the couch behind her, covering her face in embarrassment: "Oh, I mean hail and welcome! Oh, why did I say that?" Erin reassures her that it's fine and nods for the next child to continue. Gail leans down next to her four-year-old daughter, Sky, and lines out the invocation to the Spirit of the South for her, and Sky repeats the words in a whisper. Gail's older daughter, Zara, reads the invocation to the West slowly but clearly, and then Lisa helps her daughter Casey read the final invocation to the North. Erin says, "The circle is cast. Naught but love shall enter in and naught but love shall emerge from within." She quickly reads the invocation to the God Apollo and the Goddess Artemis and then proceeds to seek blessings from the Four Quarters for each child. Gail reads the first line: "Hail East! Recognize Eoin and Aisling. Help them to soar in the limitless sky of thought and imagination. Send Eoin and Aisling gentle breezes to guide them on their paths. Bless Eoin and Aisling with all the airborne powers of the East." As she reads the last line, she smiles and gently touches Aisling's face and Eoin's blue sleeper-clad foot. The other guests read invocations to the remaining Quarters, calling on them to grant the children strength of will, empathy, clarity, and "rich soil to root in." The guests read similar requests for blessings from the God and Goddess, asking Lord Apollo to make them "valiant and wise" and Lady Artemis to make them as "strong, free, and independent as you are."

After all the blessings are completed, Erin explains, "Now I'll say my vows to the children and give them their Wiccan names, until they're old enough to choose their own." She smiles and adds, "I'm just going to read what I've written here. I'm not going to go into detail right now, because I'll start crying. I'll tell them the rest in private another time." She clears her throat and begins, "Eoin, my little blessing," then pauses to explain to the group, "I call Eoin 'my blessing' because I didn't think I'd have another baby and another chance to do all the things I wanted to do with a baby, like this kind of ceremony." She continues: "Thank you for choosing me as your mommy. I promise to love, respect, and protect you and to be the best mom I can be." She gives Eoin his magical Wiccan name, explaining that it means "blessing." Then she turns to Aisling and says, "Aisling has already had to deal with all my mistakes. Now here's where I make my vows to her. Aisling, my dream come true—I call her 'my dream come true' because all my life I wanted a little girl named Aisling, and I got her. Aisling, thank you for choosing me as your mommy." She repeats her promise to love, respect, and protect her, then says Aisling's magical name, explaining that it means "dream," "because Aisling is my dream come true." Aisling says quietly, "I think I like 'Aisling' a little better," and Erin assures her, "Well, Aisling is still your other name." Erin reads from the ritual text again: "Lord, Lady, Elements, and Friends, bear witness to the vows I have made to Eoin and Aisling. Let them be known by their Wiccan names by all who are present here. Welcome them. Greet them and give them your blessings." The rest of the children and adults present respond in unison, reading from their prompts: "We welcome them in perfect love and trust."

* * *

This chapter considers the formal inclusion of children into contemporary Paganism through adult-led rituals such as Wiccanings and coming-of-age rites.[1] As Pagan adults construct and conduct these rituals to formally welcome their children into their religion, they simultaneously reject the compulsory transmission of religious belief or practice. That is, Pagan children are welcomed into their parents' religion, but they are neither expected nor particularly encouraged to accept and practice these traditions themselves. Contemporary Paganism prioritizes religious choice, tolerance, and independence over familial or cultural homogeneity, potentially complicating both the growth of the religion and religious dynamics within families and communities. These rituals serve to reinforce adults' spiritual beliefs and relationships with the larger community. At the same time, these ceremonies offer Pagan adults, who are themselves converts to the religion, the opportunity to offer their children (and to vicariously experience) rites of passage for the Pagan childhoods they lacked. In the process of imagining, constructing, and performing these life-stage rituals, Pagan adults express deep ambivalence about childhood, adulthood, religious choice, and the fundamental values of their religious and moral imaginative worlds.

Wiccanings and Religious Choice

I think that if I were to demand that my children be Pagan,
I would be being the biggest schmuck I knew. Then my
mother would have the right to be pissed off at me.
—Freya, mother of two

Much like Christian baptisms, Wiccanings function as a way for a family to formally welcome new children into Paganism and into their spiritual and social community. Unlike their Christian counterparts, however, Wiccanings do not specifically dedicate or commit children to the Pagan religion. Rather, these ceremonies place Pagan children under the protection of the deities until the children are old enough to choose their own religious path. This distinction is crucial to understanding the role of Wiccanings within Pagan communities, and it reflects the deeply held (and nearly unanimous) belief among Pagan adults that religious practice must arise from personal volition and spiritual seeking rather than from "dedication" to one's parents' religious traditions. Erin's vows to her children reflect this emphasis on individual choice: their magical names are given until the children can choose their own, and each child is thanked for his or her voluntary choice to be born into this particular family.

Despite variations in setting and personal preferences in ritual structure and content, Wiccanings tend to follow a predictable outline. The Wiccaning ceremony performed by Erin and her guests contains the components present in most Wiccanings, albeit (in Erin's case) in a form modified for a solitary practitioner performing this ritual with an ad hoc "coven" of participants. The main participants at a Wiccaning are usually the parents' community—either the religious community of their coven or the social community of friends and family. The ritual leader (often, a high priestess; sometimes, the child's mother) sets up the altar, casts a circle, and invokes the Elements and the God and Goddess, from whom blessings are requested on the child's behalf. The child's magical name is bestowed, and the parents (and, often, additional adults who serve as God- and Goddess-parents) state vows of responsibility for the child's spiritual and moral education. The members of the community are given the opportunity to present blessings and gifts, both tangible and intangible, to the child. The baby is explicitly placed under the protection of the God/dess-parents and the deities, and then the circle is reopened and the participants share food and drink. Each element of this ritual functions as a way to welcome the child into the religious community, to express the blessings, abilities, and gifts that parents and participants find valuable enough to wish for the child's future, and to allow adult Pagans to shape Pagan childhood as they imagine it.

Most Wiccanings are performed for very young infants, and there is some debate about the appropriate time to hold these rituals. Typically, the ritual is held soon after a child's birth, either within the first year or when the child reaches "a year and a day." One worried mother of a ten-month-old baby submitted a question to a website that promised answers from "experts," wondering, "Is there any such thing as too old for a Wiccaning ceremony? I know they are like baptisms, as in they are usually done soon after the baby is born, but is it possible to do it later?" The Paganism expert (who included among his credentials that he had studied various forms of Paganism for "about 10 years now") responded:

> There really isn't a set age for a Wiccaning. . . . The reason that baptisms are done right away [is] because they are supposed to wash away original

sin.... Since a Wiccaning doesn't wash away original sin (Wiccans don't believe in it) nor is it intended to indoctrinate the child, a Wiccaning is essentially a baby blessing ceremony. Personally, I don't think that one is too young or too old for a blessing.[2]

Wiccanings held soon after a baby's birth also reflect the common Pagan belief in reincarnation and the accompanying belief that children's souls "choose" the family within which they incarnate.[3] Pagans tend to view life, death, and rebirth as a cyclical process, similar to the Wheel of the Year and the cycle of the sun's "death" and "rebirth" as the length of days fluctuates. This belief in reincarnation is reflected in many Pagan chants and songs, such as the popular "Hoof and Horn": "Hoof and horn, hoof and horn / all that dies shall be reborn / Corn and grain, corn and grain / All that falls shall rise again." Not surprisingly, reincarnation of the individual, personal soul is not unanimously accepted among contemporary Pagans, but the principle is common enough that one Pagan author could confidently call reincarnation the "most common eschatological belief held among Pagans."[4] The six-year-old who composed the lullaby for her mother about the cycle of life also explained to me that when people die, "they get reborn. They're reborn as—sometimes something else, and sometimes what they were before. But they don't look the same."[5]

The idea that the individual soul chooses the specifics of its life, such as its geographic location, socioeconomic status, historical time, and the specific parents to whom it will be born, is a way of extending the concept of religious choice both backward in time (to preconception and even earlier, to previous lifetimes) and forward through lifetimes (as souls choose the "lessons" to be learned in this lifetime, thus determining their future incarnations). Reincarnation also amplifies the concept of the "wise child" so that living, chronological children are not only more spiritually advanced than adults but are also active agents whose non-corporeal spirits chose their physical form.

Erin's ceremony, like many Wiccanings, also points to the belief that children's spirits voluntarily reincarnate in specific families based on lessons that soul needs to learn in this lifetime—that is, that children choose their parents and may also choose the time and place of their conception or birth. Many Pagans suggest that the Wiccaning ceremony is a "reminder that the child has *chosen* to be born to you" as well as a naming and community-building ceremony.[6] Holding the ceremony during the earliest part of a child's life is a way of welcoming back a newly reincarnated returning spirit. Some Wiccanings explicitly include this welcome in their ritual structure. In the Coven of the Fertile Earth's widely borrowed and adapted Wiccaning ceremony, the high priestess tells the gathered participants, "We gather together as a Circle of friends to welcome one of our own back to the community. In past lives we have lived, loved, and fought together. It is with great rejoicing that we greet one who has returned."[7] Raven's Wiccaning ceremony expressed a similar belief: baby Raven was welcomed into the community of Dragon Moon Coven as "a kindred spirit, who has chosen to sojourn with us, to learn from us and to teach us" and was encouraged to "learn the lessons that your Higher Self has assigned to you in this lifetime."[8] Some refer to these life lessons as karma, whereas others view these lessons in astrological terms, claiming that a child's natal astrological chart contains keys to the child's identity and necessary lessons in this lifetime.

This concept functions in a number of ways to shape Pagan childhood, adulthood, and family life. The idea that children choose their parents gives parents who believe they are raising Indigos (or otherwise "evolved" or exceptional children) additional validation for their own advanced spiritual capabilities—they are raising Indigos, for example, because they, too, possess spiritually advanced souls. This idea also effectively usurps children's agency, as adults become the interpreters of children's past lives, present karma, and future life lessons. More disturbingly, however, this concept potentially lays the groundwork for a less commonly expressed understanding of childhood, in which abuse and neglect are justified by the assertion of the child's conscious and deliberate reincarnation. If children choose their families because their souls need to learn certain lessons within this lifetime, difficult or abusive situations can be rationalized as valuable—and voluntary—karmic lessons. Responsibility for these situations can then be shared by children and adults or borne by children alone. Infant Wiccanings certainly serve their stated purpose of welcoming a child into the parents' community and granting him or her both earthly and divine blessings. Less explicitly, however, they can function as a blank slate on which a community of adults projects a child's past and future.

Wiccanings for older children are less common, but particular situations may warrant a later ritual. Unlike infants, who are usually Wiccaned alone in a ceremony timed to coincide with their birth or infancy, a group of older children might share a Wiccaning ceremony in situations where their families are joining an established coven or where a coven is forming with participation from families with older children. Erin's blessing ceremony included both her infant son and her school-age daughter because Aisling had not been given a Wiccaning ceremony as an infant—an omission Aisling may not have missed but that her mother sought to rectify. Older children have the advantage of being able to participate more fully in their own ceremonies: they can light candles on the altar, invoke deities and Quarters, and respond to questions or directions during the ritual.

I witnessed an unusually large group Wiccaning of six older children (between four and eleven years old) by Rev. Kendra in 2007. Like most services at the FCOW, this ceremony was highly structured and included significant participation by most of the children involved. Like most ceremonies featuring children, it also involved moments of uncertainty and ambivalence not generally present in adult rituals; one of the children, for instance, sat silently shaking his head in refusal when invited to line up before the gathered participants. At this Wiccaning, the older children's participation was highlighted in a number of ways. The minister's children collected the "freewill offering" from congregants, and the entire group sang two hymns written by the children. In addition to welcoming a group of older children, this ceremony was unusual in its use of the names of the Wiccaned children to raise energy for a cone of power. During this central part of the ritual, the entire group chanted the names of the children being welcomed to the tune of the Goddesses' names ("Isis, Astarte, Diana, Hecate, Demeter, Kali, Inanna") in the popular Wiccan chant. For this group Wiccaning, more than thirty people packed into the tiny basement of the home that housed the First Church of Wicca. As the group clapped and chanted their names in the stifling heat, the children initially seemed unsure how to respond, glancing at one another and staring at the floor. As the group continued chanting, most of the children joined in, and by the end of the chant, all six children were enjoying their moment in the spotlight, smiling and jostling one another every time their names were sung. The adults present seemed pleased with the level of energy raised during this chant, but it may have been altogether too much energy for some of the younger children, who giggled, nudged, poked, and whispered throughout the rest of the ceremony.

As in most Wiccaning ceremonies, Rev. Kendra reminded the group that a Wiccaning welcomes a child into the religion but "does not bind the child to the religion." This insistence on religious choice in a ceremony designed to welcome children into their parents' religion is one of the most obvious and unintended ironies of contemporary Pagan ritual. At Raven's Wiccaning, her God-father and Goddess-mother were asked, "Do you promise to educate her in the ways of the Craft of the Wise, as well as in other religions, so that when she reaches her Maidening she may choose her path with knowledge and wisdom?"[9] God/dess-parents may vow to instruct the child in their spiritual tradition, but they do not promise to ensure that the child lives a "Pagan life" in the same way that Christian godparents are expected to "help the newly baptized . . . on the road of Christian life."[10] Rather, God/dess-parents are more likely to promise to "be a friend" to the child and to guide, protect, and love her until she is ready to choose her own path. The vows of the God-father and Goddess-mother support and augment the parents' guidance and protection of the child and acknowledge the child's participation in the larger community beyond the nuclear family. Not all Wiccanings mention God/dess-parents; their inclusion in the ceremony is dependent on the availability of other adults within the community. Raven's Wiccaning ceremony included a God-father, a Goddess-mother, and an additional pair of legal guardians, who were not Wiccan (and who therefore promised to love and protect Raven, although not to help her on her spiritual path). Aisling and Eoin's ceremony, in contrast, included no mention of godparents—a reflection of their mother's solitary path.

Wiccanings often explicitly state that the purpose of the ritual is not to bind the child to the religion but to place her under the protection of the gods until she is old enough to choose her own path. The guests at Raven's Wiccaning were explicitly reminded of this: "Through this rite, we do not seek to bind her to any path or belief, for that is not the way of the Wicca; but with our loves we weave the protection of the gods about her, and give our promise to protect and to guide her to her own truth within." Raven's God/dess-parents were asked specifically to educate her in Wicca "as well as in other religions." The explicit right—the responsibility, some might say—of a child to choose his or her own spiritual path is a central part of nearly all Wiccaning ceremonies and is fundamental to Pagan religious lives.

Some Pagan parents take the affirmation of religious choice a step further, maintaining that they lack the authority to "indoctrinate" their children with their beliefs. While they may feel comfortable exposing their children to a variety of religious traditions, these parents insist that "it is not [our] place to push any religion onto [our] children but to guide them and show them the many paths to find inner peace."[11] Usually first-generation converts themselves, many Pagan parents are hesitant to impose their religion on their children in the way they feel their childhood religions were forced on them. Pagan parents have frequently rejected religious traditions they found oppressive or damaging, and they are adamant that their children's religious experiences will be more fulfilling—or, at least, voluntary. This adult rejection of childhood religion helps to explain the many structural and material similarities between Pagan Wiccanings and Christian baptisms. Pagan parents often construe Wiccanings as entirely novel ceremonies that both respond to and reject the ceremonies of their childhoods. In fact, Wiccanings and baptisms display a striking level of ritual symmetry that reveals Pagan adults' emergence from and participation in a religiously pluralist and predominantly Christian American culture. With childhoods rooted in Judeo-Christian tradition and ritual, the majority of Pagan adults possess at least enough familiarity with the sacrament of Christian baptism to use this rite as a foil for the Pagan alternative.

Pagans often compare baptisms to Wiccanings, usually unfavorably and with some disdain for the "indoctrination" aspect of infant baptism. Pagan parents' reluctance to "indoctrinate" children influences the type and extent of information these parents share with their children about their own spiritual paths, and this issue has (not surprisingly) sparked debate within some Pagan communities regarding the suitability of childhood rituals such as Wiccanings. While these ceremonies are usually explicit that they do not impose religion on children, some factions argue that these rituals do, in fact, effectively dedicate children to Pagan paths before they are old enough to accept this spiritual responsibility. One Pagan father explains, "I believe that forcing your children to believe the same as you do, spiritual or otherwise, is a form of proselytization," a practice Pagans do not support.[12] These parents frequently argue that a Wiccaning necessarily involves a parent choosing a child's faith for them, an act that is never appropriate. The opposing view contends that all parents have a responsibility to provide their offspring with a spiritual foundation and a religious education, neither of which precludes children's free choice as adults.

Many Pagan parents feel that exposure to multiple religious beliefs is a crucial part of one's psychological and spiritual development; as one mother reasons, "You can't make a truly informed decision without at least understanding what you aren't choosing."[13] Another highly eclectic parent (who feels that the label "Pagan" is "too limiting") explains that she encouraged her young children's interest in other religions by providing them with coloring books containing "various religious symbols from all religions" and telling them bedtime stories about the lives of Jesus, Siddhartha, and Muhammad. She says, "I have been asked, What is our religion? My answer is always, All religions."[14] As spiritual seekers themselves, these parents do more than accept their children's curiosity about other religions; they foster and encourage it. One mother reflected on her reluctance to provide her children with definitive, unquestioning theological answers: "You have situations where your five-year-old says, 'Who's God?' and you have no other answer than, 'People have been asking that for thousands of years, buddy.'"[15] The fundamental assumption among many of these parents seems to be that spiritual seeking is the "correct" trajectory for spiritual development and should be encouraged. But can very young children be considered spiritual seekers in the same way that adolescents or adults might be? When children seek philosophical or theological answers from parents, are they looking for open-ended responses that encourage further consideration or for answers to satisfy their immediate curiosity? One mother, a Druid married to a "Shaman," admits that her four-year-old occasionally has difficulty with the abundance of information she receives: "The only hard thing about teaching your children about all religions is they sometimes confuse the religions. . . . For instance, my daughter sometimes thinks the goddess is jesus' [sic] wife."[16] This type of religious confusion is not uncommon (and not altogether surprising) among young children raised with a superficial understanding of many world religions but lacking in-depth exposure to the theology of their own.

Because contemporary Paganism is quintessentially a "quest" religion (in the sense that sociologists such as Wade Clark Roof and Robert Wuthnow have described these traditions of personal seeking), it is not surprising that Pagan parents encourage religious flexibility and searching in favor of adherence to family tradition or religious authority. Roof called this shift from dogmatic religious adherence to the greater flexibility of an individual spiritual path "reflexive spirituality" and noted that it entails "a more deliberate, engaging effort on people's part for their own spiritual formation, both inside and outside religious communities."[17] When the people in question are children, however, how much responsibility do they bear for their own spiritual formation? The spiritual formation of children is inextricably bound to the religious life of the family, and Roof's analyses of religious life and family life in the United States support this connection as well. The two are interdependent and work together "to ensure the maintenance of beliefs and values in society through moral and religious socialization of the young. At stake is the transmission of the religious heritage itself."[18]

In its seeming disregard for the fate of its own religious heritage or demographic growth, contemporary Paganism diverges from most other established American religions. For the most part, contemporary Pagans seem considerably more concerned with Paganism's alignment with their own beliefs than with the religion's growth and continuation. Paganism's rapid growth rate thus far has been almost entirely the result of an influx of adult and adolescent converts, and adherents generally seem confident (or unconcerned) that this growth will continue to be supported by emigrants from other religions. This apparent lack of concern with the religion's viability and longevity is unusual for adherents of any religion. The socialization of successive generations is a priority for most religious traditions, but it is particularly crucial to the continuation of new religious movements. Many studies of children in new religious movements have focused on the effectiveness of a religion's socialization of children, with the understanding that this factor determines the relative success or failure of a movement.[19] For contemporary Pagans, however, this need to socialize the next generation to ensure the continuation of the religion is complicated by Paganism's emphasis on individual spiritual belief and religious choice. Eugene Gallagher's overview of common themes among new religious movements acknowledges "a quest for socialization that both effectively secures the full participation of children born into a movement and simultaneously respects their rights to make informed choices about their lives."[20] This situation presents a particularly puzzling dilemma for contemporary Paganism, where the focus on individual religious choice supersedes the desire for religious continuity.

Raymond Buckland has explained how some Pagan parents address this issue of religious choice. Given Buckland's reputation as the individual responsible for introducing Wicca to the United States, his view of this process is worth quoting at length:

> The child will be brought up to honor and respect the Old Religion and the Lord and Lady. But from here, there are two stages that may take place. At about the age of six, seven, or eight (much depends on the individual child), he may be brought into the coven in an actual Initiation ritual. At this time, he will take a new name that he has chosen himself. Then, probably around puberty, there will be a repeat of the Initiation as a confirmation that he is fully old enough to decide for himself. If at this time he has decided that the Craft is not for him after all, however, then he may leave the coven. This, in fact, applies to everyone. No one should be there under duress.[21]

Many Pagan parents concede that they would prefer that their children remain on some type of Pagan path. For example, Jessie, a Pagan mother of one daughter, acknowledges:

> It would be very nice if she stayed within our same religion because it makes celebrating holidays easier, but in the end it has to be up to her—and I'll just have to get used to whatever she goes with. Would it matter which one? Well, I hope that it will at least be something close, something we can all relate to, but if not then so be it. There are a couple of specific religions I might have a problem with, such as any religion that claimed they were the one truth and everyone else is damned, or any religion formed solely for the purpose of contradicting another (totally

immature), or any religion that is discriminating against race, creed, or gender. Basically, as long as she keeps to the core values that we've taught her, I'm good.[22]

Interestingly, like Jessie, many Pagan parents who are adamant about their children's right to choose their own religion as adults are clear that some religions are preferable to others. Many parents remarked that they would have difficulties if their adult children chose to practice "fundamentalist" religions. Although most parents were vague about what fundamentalism entailed, fundamentalist Christianity seemed to be the implication; very few parents seemed to worry about their children becoming Islamic or Hindu fundamentalists. Kendra and Tim, the leaders of the First Church of Wicca, discussed their expectations of their children with me one winter afternoon. I asked Kendra, "How important is it to you that [the children] practice something like the religion you've raised them?" She answered, "It's not important to me at all. It's important that they're good kids, that they have faith in a higher power, and that they practice their faith. That's what's important to me." Tim added, "It's the spirituality that's much more important than the religion, I think, when it comes down to it. In order for it to work, you've got to believe in it. So if we're going to tell them, 'You've got to believe in it this way,' and it doesn't work for them, then they're not going to be spiritual." Acknowledging that they had no idea what religion their two children would choose as adults, they continued the discussion:

> KENDRA: Maybe they'll come home and tell me they want to be Catholic. If they find spirituality in the Catholic church, more power to them.
> TIM: As long as they don't come home and say that they're Mormon. No, I'm kidding.

Most Pagan parents are quick to add that their desire for their children to share their religion reflects their own hopes but is not meant to constrain their offspring. In the second edition of the book *Family Wicca*, Ashleen O'Gaea discloses that her twenty-six-year-old son ultimately decided that he was no longer Wiccan. She admits that she continues to fantasize that her son will "marry a nice Wiccan girl and raise bouncing Wiccan babies," but she adds, in a telling statement, that she knows that it "has to be okay" that this is unlikely to happen.[23] O'Gaea's position here seems to be that her son's willingness to continue following the "precepts he learned as a Wiccan kid" is more important than his stated religion.[24] Within O'Gaea's comment is a fundamental belief shared by many contemporary Pagans: in terms of Pagan identity and the dynamics of Pagan families, the imaginative effectively trumps the religious, rendering the issue of generational transmission of religious belief moot—or, at least, leaving it a distant second behind the transmission of religious imagination, ritual fluency, and moral principles. Like O'Gaea, many Pagan parents see the values they impart to their children as essentially unconnected to (and, often, more important than) their religious teachings. These religious imaginations are ultimately the legacy Pagan parents bestow on their children.

Speculation about the implications of this emphasis on religious choice and the articulated valuation of the imaginative over the religious for Pagan children's spiritual paths is likely to be unproductive. My fieldwork seems to suggest that significant numbers of Pagan children do choose to leave the religion. Of the relatively small number of teenage and young adult second-generation (and a few third-generation) Pagans I met through this study, approximately equal numbers have remained in and left the religion.[25] Parents frequently responded to my requests to interview their older adolescent and adult children by explaining that the child was currently practicing another (or no) religion. Several parents expressed uncertainty regarding their children's current religious beliefs and were unsure whether their older children were still Pagan. Others told me that their teenage and adult sons and daughters considered themselves Buddhist, Episcopalian, Unitarian Universalist, or agnostic. Adult children seem more likely to diverge from their parents' religious beliefs, but some parents remarked that their younger children had taken advantage of the opportunity to choose their own religious paths. A homeschooling Pagan mother of six children under the age of thirteen told me that she and her husband emphasize "individual spiritual growth and self enlightenment" for their children. She writes, "I have at least one child that will probably grow up to be a christain [sic], another who is seriously [studying] Buddhism and a third who isn't sure there is anything out there at all."[26] An eighteen-year-old second-generation Wiccan—now a practicing Methodist—remarks that she plans to teach her children many of the values taught to her by her Wiccan parents:

> To love everyone, and to be able to find both the faults in yourself and the good in others. Not to let yourself fall prey to the temptation to hate those who fear or misunderstand you, and to help those that do. . . . It's also important to note that explaining my beliefs, not forcing others to believe them, was my goal. I've always been taught that understanding was far more important than agreeing.[27]

Despite the strong moral foundation that this young adult feels she received from her Wiccan parents, she is careful to add that she intends to raise her own children in an explicitly Christian framework: "I want my children to grow and live with the Lord truly in their lives—I want them to be good Christians, the kind of Christians I searched for all my life."[28]

In some ways, this encouragement of religious choice in second- and third-generation Pagans seems counterproductive. The sociologist Rodney Stark's examination of the factors contributing to the success of new religions notes the importance of the socialization of younger generations, pointing to Mormonism's expectation of missionary service from its youth as an example of a new religion's socialization practice that helps to ensure young people's continued adherence. Noting that this expectation of service increases religious loyalty among Mormon youth, Stark observes, "Indeed, it appears to me that people rate the value of religion not only on the basis of what it gives them, but on how much it costs them—that people place little value on religion that is cheap and prefer religions that are relatively costly. . . . [People] prefer costs of time and money as opposed to costs in terms of stigma."[29] Contemporary Paganism, for the most part, demands relatively little of its adherents in terms of time, money, or belief. Rather than attempting to inculcate religious tradition, nearly all Pagan parents opt to encourage the religious imagination and the spiritual quest:

> I would be fine if they chose another religion and I would be fine if they choose no religion as long as they grow up to be responsible adults.[30]

It is not important at all that they follow my path. It is of utmost importance that they find and follow one of their choosing, even if that is a choice of nothing.[31]

As far as I am concerned my children are free to choose any path that calls to them. I wouldn't be upset if that included no religion in particular. I want them to understand that there is a supreme source of life, which I see as pure love, from which I understand the Goddess and God. I want them to respect all life and the Earth. Beyond that it is not my decision how they find the Divine.[32]

It is not important for me for my children to practice the exact same path that I have chosen. A spiritual path is very much an individual choice. I would hope that they would practice any religion with the understanding that it is what is right for them, but not necessarily the same path that someone else might choose.[33]

The widespread support for religious choice among Pagan children is a fascinating and complicated issue because of the particular importance to new religious movements of religious transmission from parents to children and children's continued religious adherence.

Despite years of formal and informal interactions and conversations with Pagan parents, I have yet to meet a single Pagan parent who admitted to feelings of anxiety, disappointment, or anger at the prospect (or reality) of their children choosing another religion. This tendency is certainly due in part to Paganism's emphasis on the importance of finding a spiritual path that is a good personal fit (as evidenced by the overwhelming numbers of eclectic Pagans and those who practice highly individualized fabrications of spiritual practices, such as "Becktarianism"). Beyond this, though, this tendency may suggest doubts about the religion itself. Does Paganism's lack of historical grounding—as demonstrated by its ability to reflect and convey multiple historical and ideological perspectives—weaken its position as a religious "tradition" deserving of multigenerational continuity? When Pagan adults consider religious tradition insignificant and suggest to their children that, for example, all religions "are equally important and 'right,'"[34] one of the messages these children receive may be that there is nothing particularly special, true, or necessary about their parents' religion. It remains to be seen whether this focus on religious tolerance and religious choice necessarily leads to a phenomenon in which contemporary Paganism is composed entirely of adolescent and adult converts who lack historical, cultural, or familial ties to the religion.

In contrast to many parents' reluctance to provide religious boundaries or guidelines for their children, some parents offer at least a modicum of guidance by defining their moral and social (if not theological) expectations for their children:

> As long as my daughter can reason why a particular faith moves her and as long as the "religion" doesn't include violence and sexism, then I won't have a problem. Should [she] choose modern day christianity [sic], I wouldn't like it, but would try to understand and respect her. (Gnostic religions don't bother me in the least and don't seem to carry the cultural baggage that modern religions do such as subjugating women.)[35]

> [Choosing a religion] is entirely up to him. I would just hope that he wouldn't wind up joining a cult, or starting one.[36]

> I would like to think they would grow up and realize that Paganism fits them, but I would never force my beliefs on my children. I would only object to their identifying with or joining another religion if it was one that insisted they denounce us or our beliefs.[37]

> I definitely think that some kind of spirituality is helpful, but I wouldn't bully or push her into it. Some people just aren't wired that way. I wouldn't mind if she joined another religion as long as she didn't proselytize, and she respected other paths. I would be happier with her choosing to be Jewish or Buddhist over her choosing to be Christian or Muslim, probably because of my cultural baggage around those two religions, and the fact that they tend to be "one true way" sort of paths. Of course it would make me happiest if she stayed both Jewish and Pagan![38]

> It's important to me that my kids think critically, listen to their own feelings, and make their own decisions. Whether that includes religion is completely up to them. I would have no problem with them joining any

religion they felt was appropriate for them (except for the dangerous kinds of cults that brainwash people, of course).[39]

Whether or not they choose a pagan path or another path or no path is their choice, and they have to make it for themselves. Now, if they become the type of evangelical or fundamentalist Christian that is going to continual[l]y try to "save" their parents, I would have an issue with that action. Then again, my response could always be, "You've done your job and witnessed to us, if anything else is to happen, it's not up to you, it's up to the Holy Spirit."[40]

It is not very important to me that he share my beliefs. He already does not.[41]

Raven's Wiccaning concluded with the high priestess blessing the child with "love, light and laughter" and announcing, "On behalf of the Wicca and of the Lord and Lady, I welcome you into this circle of love, into this family, and into this world. May you always be aware of the mysteries that surround and permeate you." This awareness of "mystery" is a quality that adults strive to recall and reconstruct in their own lives, and it reinforces the Pagan understanding of children's enhanced spiritual capabilities. Encouraging children to pursue their own spiritual paths and to strive to maintain contact with the "mysteries" of the universe is a way for Pagan adults to reshape their own difficult or unsatisfying childhood religious experiences and to offer their children the religious freedom they lacked. Whether children are capable of maintaining the spiritual connection adults have lost is a moot point to Pagan parents. Pagan children are tasked with the responsibility of maintaining—and instructing the adults around them in—this connection to the universe.

Coming-of-Age Ceremonies

If Wiccanings serve as the Pagan counterparts to Christian baptism and reflect Pagan adults' rejection of their own religious childhood indoctrination, adolescent coming-of-age ceremonies reveal Pagan adults' understandings of sexuality and the transition from youth to (relative) maturity. Some Pagans (although far fewer than those who perform Wiccanings) construct and perform rituals to honor and celebrate their children's entrance into adolescence, often held around a boy's thirteenth birthday or a girl's menarche. Ideas and texts for these rituals abound on the Internet, in books, and in conversations among Pagan adults, but the actual execution of these rituals is relatively rare. Despite the dozens of adolescent rites of passage I have seen planned in elaborate prose and meticulous detail, I have yet to encounter a Pagan child who has actually experienced one. This is not to say, of course, that these rituals never occur, but their planning seems to significantly outweigh their practice.

The popularity of the concept stems, in part, from what these rituals demonstrate about adult Pagans' values: that they are sex-positive, comfortable with the maturity and physicality of their adolescent children, and cognizant of the need for rites of passage for adolescents. They allow parents to demonstrate that they are liberal, progressive, well-read (many reference Victor Turner's work on rites of passage and liminality), and unflinching in the face of their children's inevitable transition to adulthood. Further, they allow parents to commemorate their own adolescence in the way they believe—as adults, with the benefit of decades of hindsight—they would have liked it to be commemorated in their childhood. Perhaps more than most rituals, the planning of coming-of-age ceremonies is a clear indicator of adult Pagans' attempts to refashion and relive their own childhoods from the perspective of their adult selves. (When a ritual text suggests, for example, that Kool-Aid should be used instead of cakes and ale as a "pleasant reminder of youth,"[42] is it the child's or the parent's youth that is being recalled?) In fact, this is often the way that discussions and essays on the topic begin: with the adult speaker or writer's regret at their own lack of an adolescent rite of passage.

Despite adults' enthusiasm for these ceremonies, their rarity in practice may reflect the dismay with which many early adolescents greet the suggestion that their entrance to puberty be publicly observed. Pagan parents affiliated with Unitarian Universalist churches often choose to involve their children in the UU Coming of Age program, a relatively innocuous way to assist children in the transition to adolescence. A yearlong program for seventh graders, the COA curriculum includes education about UU history and world religions, retreats, a mentorship program, a service project, and weekly learning and discussion sessions.[43] In contrast, many of the rituals written by Pagan adults for children may understandably meet with greater resistance on the part of the child involved. It is difficult to imagine, for example, that a thirteen-year-old boy would appreciate a ritual in which he is "abducted from the encampment where he is staying" amid a theatrical "skirmish" between the older women and men, stripped and dressed in a "deerhide loincloth," and marched, blindfolded, along a five-mile journey to encounter a medley of multicultural "archetypes."[44] Likewise, it is likely that many pubescent girls—no matter how liberal and progressive their parents are—would be horrified at being asked to crawl through a symbolic "birth canal" consisting of the legs of the older women in the community while the girl is "lightly spanked . . . and the women moan as if in childbirth."[45] One ceremony including this "passage" concludes with a comment by the author requiring little interpretation: "I always wished I had had something this positive when I first started my period."[46] Another Pagan author offers a similar adult perspective on these ceremonies, acknowledging, "For girls, Coming of Age can be an embarrassing time." This author goes on to assure (presumably adult) readers, however, that "during the old days, this was a celebration of life. Many pagan mothers are trying to bring back some of the old customs which celebrate this coming into womanhood."[47] The historical and cultural specifics of these "old days" remain unspecified; reference to the "old customs" serves to legitimize current rituals rather than to connect these rituals to genuine historical precedents.

In both theory and practice, coming-of-age ceremonies can be understood as a way for adult Pagans to self-consciously and deliberately foreground their own understandings of the boundaries and character of both childhood and adulthood and to instruct Pagan children in culturally appropriate behavior (as perceived by individual adults). One ritual text concludes with this instruction for the adult coordinator of a girl's coming-of-age ritual: "It is also important to really emphasize that womanhood does not mean leaving one's childhood in the dust! Be playful so that the maiden will have visual notice that adults can and DO play silly!" This ritual's author notes this "important" aspect of the ritual without further discussion, assuming that her readers share her understanding of the value of "silly" behavior among adults. The ritual text itself addresses the common Pagan ambivalence about adulthood and childhood as well; at the end of the ceremony, the "maiden" is told (again, in faux-archaic style), "Thou art Goddess. Never let childhood be so far behind that you cannot turn easily to regain a laugh or play a silly game."[48] Regardless of whether coming-of-age rituals accomplish the goal of transitioning children into adulthood, they function as another way for adults to welcome the next generation into a religious community and provide a springboard for issues of sexuality and sexual ethics. The same ritual text that advises "silly" adult behavior also explicitly connects this ritual to the need to address sexual ethics with adolescents: "[A] pre-circle chat with [the girl's] mother and or HPS [high priestess] should include sexual awareness, sexual identity, safe sex, abuse issues, body awareness."[49] One would assume (or hope) that the conversation on this occasion would function as a recap of these themes rather than the preliminary discussion of these topics, although the author is unfortunately unspecific on this point.

Regardless of whether Pagan families choose to participate in coming-of-age ceremonies, discussions of sexuality and sexual ethics are generally an ongoing process rather than a one-time event. Most adult Pagans tend to hold and proudly proclaim relatively positive, progressive, and liberal views on sexuality, alternative sexual lifestyles, and sexual ethics. One of the most significant issues within contemporary Paganism involves children's participation in and exposure to clothing-optional rituals and festivals. The issue of clothing-optional (sometimes called "skyclad") events actually encompasses two separate concerns for most parents: the appropriateness of casual, nonsexual nudity in environments that include both adults and children and the issue of children's presence at sexually suggestive or adult-themed rituals, events, or discussions. Critics of contemporary Paganism often use the subject of skyclad rituals to illustrate and exaggerate the amoral, hedonistic, and child-endangering aspects of the religion. It is certainly the case that some adult Pagans take seriously the words of the Goddess in Doreen Valiente's "Charge of the Goddess": "As a sign that ye are really free, ye shall be naked in your rites."[50] In ritual settings involving adults and children, however, nudity is much less common.

In the interest of protecting children as well as preventing lawsuits, SpiralScouts International understandably maintains a strict policy against nudity at its events. Despite this policy, however, an extended discussion on this subject arose on the main SpiralScouts e-mail group when a list member, noting that SpiralScouts was a group for Pagan children and that Pagans performed "skyclad nude rituals," wondered whether SpiralScouts held "nudist activities."[51] Nearly a dozen quick responses to this inquiry offered variations on the same answer: "I would say that is a big no."[52] One poster added a reasonable level of suspicion to her response, acknowledging that the original poster may have had positive intentions but that these intentions should have been clarified.[53] Several respondents pointed out that not all SpiralScouts are Pagan and that not all Pagans perform skyclad rituals; on the contrary, one poster observed, "My experience with nearly 20 years of paganism is the vast majority of pagans do not perform skyclad rituals, and are beyond tired of the stereotype."[54] Regardless of individual adult Pagans' clothing decisions, the SpiralScouts administrators (and other respondents) were quick to advise the original poster that official SpiralScouts policy prohibits nudity at any SpiralScouts function, with "no leeway on this issue."[55] Commenting on this policy, one list member reflected, "I think of this as less being naked is bad, and more being naked is not something that it's SpiralScouts' job to teach the kids."[56] The consensus among these list members and among many Pagan families seems to be that ritual nudity is a matter of choice for adults but is inappropriate for children.

Public nudity in the more casual environment of a festival, however, tends to be a common occurrence that is deserving of discretion and discussion but not necessarily avoidance. The children at CMA festivals seemed thoroughly unconcerned about the presence of adult nudity. Pagan parents sometimes remark that their children have been raised to be "comfortable in their own skin" and that they tend to be nonchalant about the nudity of adults in public settings. One mother, responding to the inquiry about SpiralScouts and skyclad rituals, explained that her children had no difficulty distinguishing between a person who was "sacredly" skyclad for ritual and a person who was seeking sexual attention, and she was confident that her children would inform her if someone was behaving "inappropriately."[57] The CMA festival is entirely clothing-optional inside the check-in gates, and most festival-goers take full advantage of the opportunity to shed their clothing (and liberally apply sunscreen) in the hot Texas sun. In a play on the traditional Pagan parting blessing, a painted sign at the exit from the festival grounds reminds attendees that they are re-entering the world of conventional social mores by proclaiming "Dressed Be!" Even among adults, of course, enthusiasm for "clothing-optional" events varies. Some adults relish the opportunity to spend a weekend naked in the "temporary autonomous zone"[58] of festival space, whereas for others, body image issues and cultural norms make the clothing-optional aspect of events challenging. Several adults at CMA festivals recounted for me their first forays into public nudity at festivals, often experiences of embarrassment mixed with exhilaration. Often, they described the simultaneously liberating and disappointing realization that in large groups of costumed or naked Pagans, no one was really looking at them anyway. Of course, even those who choose to remain clothed throughout the festival weekend encounter hundreds of other bodies in various states of undress and are expected to approach interactions with naked strangers with a certain level of aplomb. At one CMA festival, Lady Freya remarked that she had discussed the etiquette of clothing-optional festivals with her children prior to their arrival at the festival and presented them with hypothetical situations in an effort to maximize the children's safety and comfort.[59]

The CMA offers hot running water for showers (a luxury on the otherwise undeveloped land), and the festival has two large shower rooms. Each shower area contains about half a dozen showerheads in a large, communal room in which the only semblance of privacy is one small, curtained showerhead in a corner. Both rooms are used by people of all genders, except for certain designated hours each day when the two shower rooms are gender-segregated. The children at my campsite—boys and girls between the ages of five and eleven—seemed nonchalant about showering with family and strangers, and their families seemed to see the single-gender shower times as somewhat of a nuisance (because each parent could chaperone only children of his or her own gender). Children generally act indifferent about adult nudity at festivals, but this does not mean they fail to notice. One of the eight-year-olds camping near me related a moment of surprise at seeing naked dancers at the evening bonfire, the Revel Fire: "I saw these people and I thought, can you be naked here? And then I remembered—oh yeah, you can!"[60]

Exit signs at the Council of Magickal Arts festival. Photo by Lisa H. Dugger.

For the most part, public nudity at festivals is nonsexual. In some cases, however, specific events or areas may convey a sexually charged atmosphere that some parents consider inappropriate for children. On one occasion, I entered the showers with the adults and children of my campsite to find several adults showering together more enthusiastically than necessary, prompting the parents in my group to immediately usher the children into the next shower room. Likewise, events such as workshops and discussions on polyamory and some fertility-themed festivities for Beltane are often considered too "adult" for children; walking through the woods at one Beltane festival, I followed a path into a clearing and found a pair of adults engaging in what I can only assume was part of a private fertility ritual. Much of the dancing that occurs at the Revel Fire, a bonfire and drum circle that goes on through most of the night, is also considered too "adult" for younger children. Children often attend the Revel Fire with parents early in the evening, but most are tucked into sleeping bags at their own campsites before the nudity and intoxication around the fire reaches more mature levels. Early in the evening, there may be as many as twenty children at the fire—younger children dancing with parents, older teenagers huddled into small, giggling groups on the outskirts of the circle. Some of the smaller children fall asleep on blankets on the ground, covered by parents' cloaks, seemingly oblivious to the revelry around them.

In much the same way that children's spirituality serves as the vehicle for adult Pagans' projections of virtue and wisdom, children's bodies function as the locus for anxieties and ambivalence around innocence and sexuality. The amount and type of clothing children are required to wear at festivals is the subject of extensive negotiations between children and adults at the campsite. Children's bodies are the source of considerably more discussion (and anxiety) than are the bodies of adults; a naked stranger helping to push a car out of a muddy ditch elicited no reaction from the children or parents at my campsite, but long conversations determine the level of acceptable clothing for children at different times of day. The children at my campsite were eager to take advantage of the festival's clothing-optional policy, at least to the extent determined by their parents. Negotiations began as soon as they arrived at the campsite: Could they take their shirts off? What about pants and shoes? Their mothers set the minimum clothing requirement for the weekend: underwear and shoes. To these basics, the girls add the long, hooded cloaks their mothers made for them, as protection from the sun and because these are their "witchy" cloaks. The three girls—two eight-year-olds and a five-year-old—go through this clothing negotiation at the beginning of every festival weekend, and every time, their mothers' minimum requirement remains the same: underwear and shoes. At one Beltane festival, Cricket argued with her mother; she saw adults wandering through the festival grounds with no clothes at all, and she wanted to take hers off as well, insisting, "I don't like clothes!" Her mother empathized, but stood her ground, saying, "I can see that you don't understand why I'm saying this, but I want you to be safe—from the sun, and from everything." The "everything" at the end of her explanation is a word fraught with dangers the parents seem reluctant to spell out, and Cricket eventually conceded to her mother's directive without pushing for clarification, keeping shoes and underwear on underneath her cloak. Her older brother's guidelines were somewhat different. Eleven-year-old Stephen's request to take his clothes off was met with a moment of discomfort by the adults at the campsite until the father of the other children joked, "If you do, then everyone will want to"—a meaningless comment in the clothing-optional context of the festival, but one that adequately conveyed the adults' awkwardness. Either Stephen understood that his age made nudity (or partial nudity) less acceptable or the conversation with his parents continued out of earshot, but, in any case, he remained clothed all weekend.

The standards for children's clothing at festivals reflect Pagan adults' deep ambivalence about the intersections of sexuality, spirituality, and societal expectations. Adults maintain a complicated tension between the desire for sexual freedom and the need to preserve children's innocence, freedom of expression and physical safety. In many ways, sexuality is an important part of Pagan spirituality, as evidenced by texts like Valiente's "Charge of the Goddess," ritual activities like the Great Rite or the Fivefold Kiss, and some Pagans' propensity, for example, to strip down to nothing but leggings and horns and "embody" the God at the Revel Fire. Expressions of "sacred sexuality" are generally acceptable among groups of forewarned and consenting adults. When children and teenagers are added to the mix, however, issues of personal expression become muddier. Adults often seem to want to both acknowledge and ignore children's sexuality, to be alert and cautious at the same time that they insist that the festival is a "safe" space. Fears for children's safety are, understandably, one of the reasons that child-centered ethnography is especially difficult; if the fact of children itself complicates ethnographic fieldwork, negotiating interactions with children and adults in a clothing-optional setting adds an entirely new level of complication. Even among families I knew well, I frequently found myself at festivals puzzling over how to respond to veiled anxieties in the form of "jokes" about my interest in children's activities. For example, in a "joke" that clearly conveyed anxieties about my non-parental status as a volunteer at Fairy Mound, the children's day-care area of the festival, a parent commented, "It's okay; *I* know you're not a stalker." In the same way that these anxieties shape children's and parents' experiences at CMA festivals, they shape the way these experiences are remembered, described, and understood by Pagan families.

Pagan adults construct and perform rites of passage for children that reflect their own revisionist histories of their own childhoods. These rituals mark the adults as freethinking progressives comfortable with children's religious choices, independence, and sexuality. At the same time, these rituals link Pagan adults to an imagined tradition of childhood rites of passage and a romanticized view of premodern cultures. The explicit assertions of religious choice in these rituals seem almost to undermine their power as rites of passage; if a child can choose to leave the religion at any time, a Wiccaning does not dedicate a child to the religion, nor does a religious ritual at puberty welcome the child into Pagan adulthood. Instead, these ceremonies reinforce the bonds between parents and other adults in their religious and social community, offer adults a way to think about and understand the Pagan childhoods they lacked, and strengthen other adults' sense of responsibility and affection for the children involved. Certainly, the effect of these rituals on the social, psychological, and religious well-being of Pagan families is significant; their effect on Pagan children, however—purportedly the subjects of these rituals—remains difficult to ascertain. Adults shape the religious worlds of Pagan children into the worlds they wanted as children themselves—worlds they can inhabit, within the spontaneous, childlike realm of rituals and festivals, as adults.

Conclusion

Building Fairy Houses

At a summer solstice campout for the SpiralScouts of Silverling Circle, one of the craft activities in a very full weekend called on the scouts to make "fairy houses." These houses were intended to provide the local fairies with shelter, but the craft needed very little explanation; scouts and parents alike seemed immediately to understand both the purpose and the need for these structures. Working with moss, bark, grass, and twigs they collected from the campgrounds, the adults and children set to work creating suitable lodgings for the fairy folk. While the children spread thick layers of glue on bark and pipe cleaners, the adult leaders and parents constructed elaborate structures with rounded walls and dozens of twigs painstakingly tied together with twine, and some of the adults worked on their houses long after the children had moved on to other activities. A six-year-old boy wondered aloud if they should go into the woods to find the fairy houses that were already there and copy them. Another six-year-old scoffed, "There aren't any fairy houses in the woods. Only animals live there, and they can't make them." One of the leaders told the scouts that if they concentrated, they would be able to hear the fairies tell them what they wanted their houses to houses to look like. They should listen to the fairies, she reminded them, because "these houses aren't for you—they're for the fairies."

A SpiralScout places her fairy house in the woods. Photo by Zohreh Kermani.

* * *

This book contends that the study of Pagan parenting and childhood illuminates important features of American parenting and childhood as well as religious communities and imaginations in the twenty-first century. Religion can be understood not only as a chain of memory, as Danièle Hervieu-Léger proposes, but also as a process of undoing certain kinds of religious, historical, and personal memory.[1] Moreover, as some American parents reshape conceptions of idealized childhood, they pave the way for experiences of parenting and families that recall Romantic ideals of childhood innocence and wonder. At the same time, they emphasize the precocious wisdom and spiritual gravity of these expectations of children. Pagans are not representative of all Americans, but both their specificity and their similarity can illuminate aspects of the American religious imagination.

Adults construct the architecture of Pagan childhood on a complicated framework of ambivalence, nostalgia, anxiety, and hope. Pagan children contribute to this project, and the relationships and interactions between Pagan adults and children provide the context for the formation of Pagan religious and imaginative worlds based on magic, fantasy, and complicated relationships between adults and children. In much the same way that Pagan adults construct religious and spiritual worlds that value childlike attitudes and behaviors and legitimize their refusal to "grow up," the religious and imaginative worlds of Pagan children are very often an adult endeavor. Adults shape the religious, moral, communal, and imaginative worlds of Pagan children to serve the needs of chronological children as well as their own ideals of children and childhood. Pagan religious childhood—much like Pagan identity and Pagan religious life—is shaped both in opposition to conventional societal expectations and in hopes of normalizing and legitimizing Paganism within the context of larger society. Pagan childhood and the Pagan religious imaginary are constructed in a way that sets them both in conflict and in conformity with broader American culture. Pagans fashion themselves as exceptional Americans producing a new kind of American childhood—one rich with fantasy, imagination, supernatural presence, and the (possibly overemphasized) spiritual capabilities of children.

In many ways, Pagan parents seem to be engaged in shaping new ways of being religious in the United States. At the same time, Pagan understandings of childhood, adulthood, and moral and religious communities reveal a longing to participate in organizations and communities not unlike those of more mainstream religious traditions. This ambivalence is a recurrent theme in contemporary Pagan interactions with larger American culture. In *Imagining Religion*, Jonathan Z. Smith contends that apologetic, historical, and demographic reasons are not sufficient for a scholar of religion's interest in data. Smith explains what he considers a legitimate basis for comparison (in this case, of Judaism):

> Rather, it is because of the peculiar position of Judaism within the larger framework of the imagining of western religion: close, yet distant; similar, yet strange; "occidental," yet "oriental"; commonplace, yet exotic. This tension between the familiar and the unfamiliar ... has enormous cognitive power. It invites, it requires comparison. Judaism is foreign enough for comparison and interpretation to be necessary; it is close enough for comparison and interpretation to be possible.[2]

Smith's discussion of the study of Judaism is relevant to the study of contemporary Paganism as well. Paganism presents itself to Western religion as "similar, yet strange . . . commonplace, yet exotic," and the difference between contemporary American Paganism and more familiar Western religions is both slight and significant. Pagan ideals of parenting, childhood, imagination, and religious choice illuminate fundamental aspects of Pagan religious worlds.

Contemporary Paganism's focus on individual belief and religious choice at the expense of religious continuity distinguishes it from religions that demand continuing religious adherence from practitioners. It also leads some observers of the religion to charge that its adherents are superficial, insincere, or shortsighted at best, and, at worst, that contemporary Paganism is not "really" a religion at all. It is simple enough to contend that contemporary Paganism is a religion because the First Amendment Free Exercise Clause legally protects it and because its practitioners consider it a religion.[3] The charges of superficiality, however, are answered less easily. Catherine Albanese notes that religions like contemporary Paganism do not necessarily lack depth; in fact, "religious combination is hardly *ipso facto* a sign of superficiality or shallowness. By contrast . . . it signals the constitution of a common American religious culture that at last takes seriously the non-Anglo Protestants and non-Europeans in our midst."[4] The philosopher Charles Taylor sees the push toward highly personalized religious belief and practice as a sign of a post-Durkheimian society characterized by moral and spiritual individualism and lacking a connection to a larger framework.[5] Rather than being fundamentally personal, "personal religion" is a product of this post-Durkheimian society.[6] He contends that this individualized religious experience runs the risk of degenerating into "trivialized and self-indulgent forms," of which "exotic spirituality" is an example. Despite this risk of superficiality, however, Taylor argues that this "individualism of self-fulfillment" can nonetheless support an ethic that extends beyond the individual. Personal authenticity, Taylor suggests, "is not the enemy of demands that emanate from beyond the self; it supposes such demands."[7] The search for personal authenticity does not necessarily preclude the development of and participation in a collective moral world. Sarah Pike's ethnographic work with contemporary Pagans remarks on the tensions within the religion as postmodern impulses meet desires for tradition and interconnectedness, and the urge toward collective identity battles with ideals of personal autonomy. Pike observes:

> Pagans constantly negotiate between the authority of the self and requirements for community life. The assumption that governs writing about contemporary moral life, namely that personalized religion necessarily means that each self is in its "own moral universe," neglects to consider the importance of relational factors to contemporary moral agents.[8]

This tension between a personal spirituality and a collective morality is a central issue for contemporary Paganism. Is there a Pagan way of being in the world that extends beyond the individual, or is the Pagan religious imaginary so personalized as to be meaningless to the formation of religious community, religious tradition, or religious heritage? In many ways, this tension is central to understanding the moral worlds of contemporary Pagan families. Pagan parents do attempt to instill in their children a set of values—not entirely cohesive, unique, or different from those of their neighbors—at the same time that they prioritize personal religious choice and the right to refuse the responsibilities of adulthood. Pagan parents pass along Pagan family values to their children, such as ecology, gender equality, independence, ethical sexuality, and appreciation for religious and cultural diversity. At the same time, they deliberately and continually stress the message that children, like adults, are free to construct their own authentic spirituality, even if this spirituality rejects the religious teachings of their parents. Whether this radically inclusive approach to religious "tradition" benefits contemporary Paganism in the long term (by encouraging Pagan children to integrate Pagan values of religious tolerance) or ultimately contributes to the religion's difficulties with legitimacy remains to be seen.

This study of contemporary American Paganism has implications for the study of new religious movements through its ethnographic examination of the religious lives and spiritual imaginations of Pagan families in the United States. More generally, this study suggests a movement in American parenting toward radically different ideals of adulthood and childhood. Childhood and parenting among American Pagans are areas fraught with the tensions, inconsistencies, desires, hopes, and fears familiar to many contemporary American families. Although American Pagans are certainly not representative of all Americans, the study of American Pagan families illuminates patterns and fault lines in American childhood and parenting. In a reflection of larger trends, Pagan adults' constructions of adulthood and childhood as realms that are simultaneously conflicted and parallel reflect attempts to unravel and reconfigure adults' own childhoods and their children's adulthoods. Pagans consistently and repeatedly historicize and reconstruct the foundations of their religion in ways that reinforce specific understandings of their beliefs and their ideals. In the same way, adult Pagans dismantle and reconstruct their own childhoods to reflect religious childhoods that support their adult religious experiences. Paganism maintains a tension between the religion's emphasis on identifying (or creating) legitimizing traditions and genealogies and the need to reject and negate inappropriate or unhelpful pasts.

Despite Hervieu-Léger's suggestion that the focus of religion is memory, Paganism is as much about forgetting as it is about memory. I argue that religion, for contemporary Pagans, as for many religious Americans, functions as both a form of memory and a type of intentional amnesia that allows adherents to construct the religious worlds they prefer and to reject conflicting alternatives by revising their personal, cultural, and religious histories. In many ways, this historical reconstruction is also an important part of American parenting in general. Pagan parents—like many contemporary American parents—orient their understandings (and their children's experiences) of childhood toward religious, magical, and imaginative idioms that allow adults to resolve their own ambivalent childhood memories at the same time that they endow children with a complex and vivid religious imaginary. For Pagans, this process often occurs at the expense of intergenerational religious homogeneity and theological consistency, the repercussions of which may require generations to manifest and may affect the ultimate growth and persistence of this new religious movement. Pagan parents frequently produce dissonant expectations of childhood and adulthood while they insist on their children's radical intellectual and spiritual freedom. At the same time, these parents work assiduously, both formally and informally, to bring their children into their moral and imaginative worlds in ways that reveal tensions and ambivalences in contemporary American Paganism and in American parenting in the twenty-first century. Robert Orsi observes that "prominent religious theorists"—and here we can effectively substitute "contemporary adult Pagans"—"claim that children have greater spiritual insight than adults and that children speak with prophetic voices. In such fantasies of childhood spirituality, maturation can only be seen as a fall from grace; holy children cannot really grow up (because then they cease to be holy)."[9] Adult Pagans construct childhoods—their children's and their own—to satisfy the needs of adult religious imaginations, and they expand the world of childhood to include both (imagined) children and adults.

Appendix A

"American Pagan Families and Family Values" Online Survey

Thank you for agreeing to participate in this online survey about Pagan families. This survey is part of the research for a study that will explore the ways that Pagan parents pass their religious and moral values to their children as well as the ways that second-generation Pagan children understand their religious practices and beliefs. Your participation in this study is voluntary. You should feel free to withdraw from this study at any time and/or to withdraw any information that you have provided. Research data will be stored in a locked file cabinet or on a password-protected hard drive until the study's completion and publication, at which point the research data will be destroyed. The results of this research study, including excerpts from this interview, may be quoted and published in future papers, journal articles, and books. Information obtained during the course of the study will remain confidential. Pseudonyms will be used in all publications, and factual details that might identify individuals will be withheld or changed. If you have any questions concerning this research study, please contact me at [phone number] or [e-mail address].

Feel free to write as much or as little as you would like for each question.

1. The nature and purpose of this research have been satisfactorily explained to me, and I give my consent to participate in the above study. I understand that I am free to discontinue participation at any time if I so choose and that the investigator will gladly answer any questions that arise during the course of the research. (Answer yes/no.)
2. What religion do you consider yourself? Any particular path/tradition (e.g., Wiccan, Pagan, Druid, etc.)? How, specifically, do you refer to yourself? What religion do you consider your children?
3. What is the history of contemporary Paganism, as you understand it? For example, how old is the religion? How did it start? How did it spread in America? (Feel free to write as much or as little as you would like. There is no "right answer" to this question—I'm interested in your understanding of the history of the religion.)
4. Is magic(k) part of your religious/spiritual beliefs? Do you practice magic? Do you talk with your children about magic? Can you give me an example of how you might talk about this or how your children understand and/or use magic?
5. What was your religious upbringing? What were your experiences of religion in childhood like? How and when did you get involved with Paganism?
6. How do you practice your religion? (e.g., Rituals, meditation, other activities)? Alone or with others? Daily practices or mostly on holidays?
7. Can you describe your family for me (e.g., How many parents? How many children? Number and ages of children? Do they live with you)?
8. What kinds of activities do you do with your children to help them understand their religion or spirituality? How do you explain your religious beliefs/practices to your child/ren?
9. How important is it to you that your children practice some form of your religious beliefs when they are adults? How would you respond if your child/ren decided to join another religion? Would it matter which religion they chose?
10. How has having children changed your experiences of religious practice/belief? Do you practice more or less often than before you had children? Do your children participate in rituals? In all, or only in some? Have you altered rituals to include children? How?
11. Can you describe a ritual or event you have performed with your children recently?

12. What values do you think are important to communicate to your children? How do you communicate these values? Can you give me an example of a conversation or activity between you and your child/ren in which you tried to teach them your religious and moral values?
13. Do you have an altar or other sacred space in your home? Can you describe it? Do your children have their own altars/sacred spaces? Can you describe these?
14. Do your children have toys, books, clothing, or decorations (posters, pictures, etc.) that are specifically "Pagan"? Can you describe these?
15. Do you read child-rearing advice books? (These might include Dr. Spock books, books like Starhawk's *Circle Round*, or any books about child behavior or development.) Which ones have you read? Which have you found useful, and why?
16. Are you familiar with SpiralScouts International, a scouting group for children of earth-centered and other minority religions? If so, how did you learn about SpiralScouts? Have you ever attended a SpiralScouts meeting or activity—and if so, can you describe the most recent SpiralScouts activity you and your child attended? What are your thoughts, impressions, or opinions about SpiralScouts?
17. Is there anything else you think I should know about what it is like to be a Pagan family and to raise your child/ren in a Pagan tradition?

If you would be willing to discuss your answers further, either over e-mail, chat/IM, or telephone, please provide your name (a pseudonym or public magical name is fine) and contact information below. If you live in the New England area and would be willing to participate in a thirty- to sixty-minute in-person interview, please give your name, e-mail address, city, and state.

This information is optional and voluntary—you do not need to give any personal information.

Appendix B

"Second-Generation Pagans: Experiences and Opinions" Online Survey

Thank you for agreeing to participate in this online interview about Pagan families. This survey asks for your experiences as a second-generation Pagan. This interview is part of a study that will explore the ways that second-generation Pagan children understand their religious practices and beliefs and the ways that Pagan parents pass their religious and moral values to their children. Your participation in this study is voluntary. You should feel free to withdraw from this study at any time and/or to withdraw any information that you have provided. Research data will be stored in a locked file cabinet or on a password-protected hard drive until the completion and publication of the study, at which point the research data will be destroyed. The results of this research study, including excerpts from this interview, may be quoted and published in future papers, journal articles, and books. Information obtained during the course of the study will remain confidential. Pseudonyms will be used in all publications, and factual details that might identify individuals will be withheld or changed. If you have any questions concerning this research study, please contact me at [phone number] or [e-mail address]. Feel free to write as much or as little as you like for each question. Please note that you can save the survey at any time and come back later to finish by clicking the "submit later" button at the bottom of the page.

1. The nature and purpose of this research have been satisfactorily explained to me, and I give my consent to participate in the above study. I understand that I am free to discontinue participation at any time if I so choose and that the investigator will gladly answer any questions that arise during the course of the research. (Answer yes/no.)
2. If you would like, you can choose a pseudonym (a fake name or public magical name) to be used in this project. This is optional; if you do not choose a name, one will be chosen for you. Your real name (if provided) will not be used.
3. What is your age (Note: if you are under eighteen years of age, your parent or guardian must give consent for your participation by contacting me)?
4. What religion do you consider yourself? Any particular path/tradition (e.g., Wiccan, Pagan, Druid, etc.)? How, specifically, do you refer to yourself religiously or spiritually?
5. How important are your religious/spiritual beliefs to your daily life?
6. Were you raised in the religious/spiritual tradition you practice now? If not, what religion were/are your parents, and what religion were you taught as a child?
7. How have your religious beliefs changed since your childhood?
8. If you were raised Pagan (any type—Wiccan, Druid, etc.), how did your parent(s) explain the beliefs and practices of your religion to you as a child?
9. Did you attend rituals or circles as a child (or do you, if you currently live with your parents)? If so, can you remember the first (or one of the earliest) rituals you attended and/or participated in? Can you describe this experience?
10. Can you give examples (anecdotes, stories, etc.) of how your religious/spiritual beliefs have changed since childhood?
11. How do you understand magic(k)? Is the concept of magic(k) important to your spiritual beliefs and/or practices?
12. What values were particularly emphasized in your household when you were a child?
13. What values do you think are most important to teach your own children? Would you (or do you) raise your own children Pagan? What religion (or spiritual path) would you/do you teach your children?

14. Can you give examples of some people (famous or not, living or dead) whose values and morals you respect—people you might think of as moral exemplars?
15. Have you ever experienced persecution (of any kind) as a result of your religious beliefs?
16. What kinds of books do you like to read? What were your favorite books as a child?
17. Is there anything else you would like to tell me about what it's like to be a second-generation Pagan?

Thank you for your help! If you would be willing to discuss your answers further, either over e-mail, chat/IM, or telephone, please provide your name (a pseudonym or public magical name is fine) and contact information below. If you live in the New England area and would be willing to participate in a thirty- to sixty-minute in-person interview, please give your name, e-mail address, city, and state. This information is optional and voluntary—you do not need to give any personal information.

Notes

NOTES TO THE INTRODUCTION

1. ARIS records a phenomenal growth rate for Wicca (not including other Pagan traditions) of 1,575% between 1990 and 2001, or a doubling of adherents every two years. Of course, these numbers may indicate increasingly higher levels of self-reporting among American Pagans or greater familiarity with the religion based on television and movies during this time. The 2008 version of ARIS included Pagans in the category of "other religions," making it more difficult to determine an accurate estimate or growth rate among Pagans. See the Pluralism Project, "Statistics by Tradition," n.d., http://pluralism.org/resources/statistics/tradition.php#Paganism (accessed February 26, 2009). See also Barry A. Kosmin, Egon Mayer, and Ariela Keysar, "American Religious Identification Survey (ARIS)" (The Graduate Center of the City University of New York, 2001); B. A. Robinson, "How Many Wiccans Are There in the U.S.?" Ontario Consultants on Religious Tolerance, May 20, 2003, http://www.religioustolerance.org/wic_nbr.htm (accessed December 1, 2007).
2. Helen A. Berger, *A Community of Witches: Contemporary Neo-Paganism and Witchcraft in the United States* (Columbia: University of South Carolina Press, 1999), xiv; Helen A. Berger, Evan A. Leach, and Leigh S. Shaffer, *Voices from the Pagan Census: A National Survey of Witches and Neo-Pagans in the United States* (Columbia: University of South Carolina Press, 2003), 34, 50.
3. Helen A. Berger, "The Routinization of Spontaneity," *Sociology of Religion* 56, no. 1 (1995): 50.
4. Émile Durkheim, *The Elementary Forms of the Religious Life* (London: G. Allen & Unwin, 1915), 44.
5. For comprehensive accounts of the history of contemporary Paganism, see Margot Adler, *Drawing Down the Moon: Witches, Druids, Goddess-Worshippers, and Other Pagans in America Today* (Boston: Beacon Press, 1986); Ronald Hutton, "Paganism and Polemic: The Debate over the Origins of Modern Pagan Witchcraft," *Folklore* 111, no. 1 (2000): 103–117; Ronald Hutton, *The Triumph of the Moon: A History of Modern Pagan Witchcraft* (Oxford: Oxford University Press, 1999).

6. Gardner's "findings" were first published in *Witchcraft Today* (1954). See Hutton, *Triumph of the Moon*, chap. 11; Charles G. Leland and Elizabeth Robins Pennell Collection (Library of Congress), *Aradia; or, The Gospel of the Witches* (London: David Nutt, 1899); Margaret A. Murray, *The Witch-Cult in Western Europe: A Study in Anthropology* (Oxford: Clarendon Press, 1921).
7. Hutton, "Paganism and Polemic," 114. For an extensive analysis of Gardner and the other early founders of contemporary Paganism, see Hutton, *Triumph of the Moon*, 171–252.
8. Dea M., e-mail communication, June 11, 2006; Carol, American Pagan Families and Family Values (APF&FV) survey, June 11, 2006; S.T., APF&FV survey, December 30, 2006.
9. Hutton, *Triumph of the Moon*, 390–91.
10. Ibid., 404.
11. Sarah M. Pike, *Earthly Bodies, Magical Selves: Contemporary Pagans and the Search for Community* (Berkeley: University of California Press, 2001), 14–19.
12. R. Laurence Moore, *Religious Outsiders and the Making of Americans* (New York: Oxford University Press, 1986), xi.
13. Susan J. Palmer and Charlotte E. Hardman, "Introduction," in *Children in New Religions*, ed. S. J. Palmer and C. E. Hardman (New Brunswick: Rutgers University Press, 1999), 7–8.
14. Robert A. Orsi, *Between Heaven and Earth: The Religious Worlds People Make and the Scholars Who Study Them* (Princeton: Princeton University Press, 2004), 77.
15. Lord Uthur, APF&FV survey, August 9, 2006.
16. Generally understood as a lifestyle involving sexual and emotional relationships of varying levels of commitment with multiple partners, polyamory tends to be more common (or more commonly discussed in public) among contemporary Pagans than among the general population, for reasons that probably stem from Pagans' tendencies toward more liberal and alternative lifestyles. A Pagan mother in Texas referred to polyamory as "pretty much the default relationship" among many Pagans, an observation that was supported by a number of my conversations with other Pagan adults. People who participate in polyamorous relationships generally establish extensive moral guidelines with their partners to ensure ethical behavior.
17. Willowhawk, APF&FV survey, June 12, 2006.
18. Some documents that are useful for examining practitioners' understandings of the rede include John J. Coughlin, "The Evolution of Wiccan Ethics," 2002, http://www.waningmoon.com/ethics/index.shtml (accessed May 3, 2004); Judy Harrow, "Exegesis on the Wiccan Rede," *Harvest* 5, no. 3 (1985), http://www.sacred-texts.com/bos/bos082.htm (accessed November 10, 2012); Shea Thomas, "The Wiccan Rede Project," n.d., http://www.draknetfree.com/sheathomas (accessed May 18, 2004).
19. Quoted in Stewart Farrar, *What Witches Do: The Modern Coven Revealed* (New York: Coward, 1971).

20. A Pagan author observes of these two moral codes, "The first is law, the second law enforcement." See Cory Ellen Gatrall, "Conscience and Consciousness," *Public Square: The Meaning of Existence*, May 25, 2009, http://www.patheos.com/Explore/Additional-Resources/Conscience-and-Consciousness.html (accessed July 1, 2009).

21. For more on sources of and opposition to some of the more controversial practices of contemporary Paganism, see Joy Dixon, "Sexology and the Occult: Sexuality and Subjectivity in Theosophy's New Age," in *Women, Gender, Religion: A Reader*, ed. Elizabeth A. Castelli (New York: Palgrave, 1997), 288–309; Mary Jo Neitz, "Defining and Sanctioning Sexual Deviance in Contemporary Witchcraft," in *Sex, Lies, and Sanctity*, ed. Mary Jo Neitz and David G. Bromley (Greenwich, CT: JAI Press, 1995), 223–235; Joanne Pearson, "Inappropriate Sexuality? Sex Magic, S/M, and Wicca (or 'Whipping Harry Potter's Arse!')," *Theology and Sexuality: The Journal of the Institute for the Study of Christianity and Sexuality* 11, no. 2 (2005): 31–42.

22. Susan Ridgely Bales, *When I Was a Child: Children's Interpretations of First Communion* (Chapel Hill: University of North Carolina Press, 2005), 58–59.

23. Douglas E. Cowan, *Cyberhenge: Modern Pagans on the Internet* (New York: Routledge, 2004), x.

24. Jess, e-mail communication, January 17, 2007.

25. Like many large Pagan events, the CMA holds festivals twice a year, at Beltane (in April or May) and at Samhain (in October), two of the major points on the Pagan Wheel of the Year.

NOTES TO CHAPTER 1

1. For more on the nature religion aspects of contemporary Paganism, see Catherine Albanese, *Nature Religion in America: From the Algonkian Indians to the New Age* (Chicago: University of Chicago Press, 1990); Dennis D. Carpenter, "Emergent Nature Spirituality: An Examination of the Major Spiritual Contours of the Contemporary Pagan Worldview," in *Magical Religion and Modern Witchcraft*, ed. James R. Lewis (Albany: State University of New York Press, 1996), 35–72; Chas S. Clifton, *Her Hidden Children: The Rise of Wicca and Paganism in America* (Lanham, MD: AltaMira Press, 2006); Chas Clifton and Graham Harvey, eds., *The Paganism Reader* (London New York: Routledge, 2004); Joanne Pearson, Richard H. Roberts, and Geoffrey Samuel, *Nature Religion Today: Paganism in the Modern World* (Edinburgh: Edinburgh University Press, 1998); Michael York, *Pagan Theology: Paganism as a World Religion* (New York: New York University Press, 2003).

2. A small (but vocal) number of my informants explained the origins of contemporary Wicca to me this way—for example, as a mystery religion "rooted in Etruscan civilization [and] not meant to be mainstreamed" (Atashih, personal communication, October 18, 2006).

3. Proponents of this view include Riane T. Eisler, *The Chalice and the Blade* (San Francisco: Harper, 1987); Marija Gimbutas, *The Civilization of the Goddess* (San

Francisco: Harper, 1991); Starhawk, *The Spiral Dance* (San Francisco: Harper, 1979); and Merlin Stone, *When God Was a Woman* (San Diego: Harcourt Brace and Company, 1976).
4. For a variety of approaches to these perspectives, see Catherine Albanese, *A Republic of Mind and Spirit: A Cultural History of American Metaphysical Religion* (New Haven: Yale University Press, 2006); Jon Butler, "Magic, Astrology, and the Early American Religious Heritage, 1600–1760," *American Historical Review* 84, no. 2 (1979): 317; Glenn Wm. Shuck, "The Myth of the Burning Times and the Politics of Resistance in Contemporary American Wicca," *Journal of Religion and Society* 2 (2000): 1–9; Hugh Urban, *Magia Sexualis: Sex, Magic, and Liberation in Modern Western Esotericism* (Berkeley: University of California Press, 2006).
5. SpiralScouts has since added another age group, RainDrops, and changed the ages within each level: RainDrops are 3–5 years old, FireFlies are 6–9, SpiralScouts are 10–13 years old, and PathFinders are 14–18 years old.
6. Albanese, *Nature Religion in America*.
7. Clifton, *Her Hidden Children*, 41–66.
8. Otter G'Zell, "Theagenesis: The Birth of the Goddess," first published in *Green Egg* 5, no. 40 (July 1, 1971): 1. Updated version available at http://caw.org/content/?q=theagenesis (accessed November 11, 2012).
9. Clifton, *Her Hidden Children*, 55.
10. Graham Harvey, *Contemporary Paganism: Listening People, Speaking Earth* (New York: New York University Press, 1997), 17.
11. Starhawk, *Dreaming the Dark: Magic, Sex, and Politics*, 15th anniversary ed. (Boston: Beacon Press, 1997). See also http://www.earthactivisttraining.org/ and http://www.starhawk.org/activism/activism.html (accessed November 11, 2012).
12. See Bron Taylor, "Resacralizing Earth: Pagan Environmentalism and the Restoration of Turtle Island," in *American Sacred Space*, ed. David Chidester and Edward Tabor Linenthal (Bloomington: Indiana University Press, 1995), 97–151.
13. Personal communication, May 23, 2006.
14. Anna Moura (Aoumiel), *Green Witchcraft* (St. Paul: Llewellyn, 2002).
15. This comment is a reference to "humanure," a form of "extreme composting" that uses composted human excrement for agricultural purposes. This is not a mainstream concept even among earth-based Pagans, but it is certainly more familiar than it might be to other segments of the American population.
16. H.M., personal interview, July 26, 2006, Ohio.
17. Alyson, APF&FV survey, June 12, 2006.
18. Janet, APF&FV survey, August 9, 2006.
19. Death, APF&FV survey, August 8, 2006.
20. Katness, APF&FV survey, June 30, 2006.
21. The understanding of these early societies as matriarchal, matrilineal, and pacifistic emerges primarily from the work of Marija Gimbutas, Riane Eisler, and Zsuzsanna Budapest. Adler notes that prominent Pagan author Isaac Bonewits refers to this as the "myth of the Unitarian, Universalist, White Witchcult of

Western Theosophical Britany ... much to the anger of many Witches." For more examples of the "Myth of Wicca," see Adler, *Drawing Down the Moon*, 45–47; Raymond Buckland, *Witchcraft from the Inside* (St. Paul: Llewellyn, 1971); Gimbutas, *Civilization of the Goddess*; Starhawk, *Spiral Dance*; Zsuzsanna E. Budapest, *The Holy Book of Women's Mysteries* (San Francisco: Wingbow Press, 1989).
22. Callisto, APF&FV survey, June 6, 2006.
23. Ronald Hutton provides an excellent discussion of this aspect of contemporary Paganism's history in *Triumph of the Moon*, 360–361.
24. Jessie, APF&FV survey, November 8, 2006.
25. The founding "elder high priestess and metaphysician" of the First Church of Wicca, Rev. Dr. Kendra (as she prefers to be called) holds a doctor of ministry degree in pastoral counseling from the University of Sedona's home study program and a doctoral degree in holistic ministry from the American Institute of Holistic Theology's distance learning program. She is ordained by the International Metaphysical Ministry and her own First Church of Wicca. The use of the title "reverend" is not common among Pagan clergy, and Rev. Kendra's attire and title have been the source of some debate on Pagan blogs. In January 2009, Rev. Kendra converted to Christianity and began serving as an ordained Christian pastor for her new church, Living Waters Community of Hope.
26. B.B., personal interview, September 23, 2006. In January 2009, visitors to the FCOW's website were directed, in a similarly abrupt fashion, to the website of the church's newest incarnation, Living Waters Community of Hope. The website for Living Waters described it as "a holistic Christian ministry devoted to helping people heal from their experiences of inequity from past religions and religious institutions, by using both the Old and New Testaments of the Holy Bible as our foundation in faith and moral conduct." Living Waters was subsequently closed, and its websites were removed.
27. Tim Hovey, personal interview, September 23, 2006.
28. Kendra Vaughan Hovey, "Magick and Metaphysics," sermon delivered at Metaphysical Service, First Church of Wicca, November 5, 2006.
29. "Our Tradition," First Church of Wicca website (accessed February 1, 2008). The websites of both Living Waters Community of Hope and the First Church of Wicca have been removed.
30. There are many excellent and comprehensive histories of the alternative, harmonial, and metaphysical religions of the late nineteenth and early twentieth centuries. These include Albanese, *Republic of Mind and Spirit*; James A. Herrick, *The Making of the New Spirituality: The Eclipse of the Western Religious Tradition* (Downers Grove, IL: InterVarsity Press, 2003); Sarah M. Pike, *New Age and Neopagan Religions in America* (New York: Columbia University Press, 2004); Beryl Satter, *Each Mind a Kingdom: American Women, Sexual Purity, and the New Thought Movement, 1875–1920* (Berkeley: University of California Press, 1999); Leigh Eric Schmidt, *Restless Souls: The Making of American Spirituality* (San Francisco: Harper, 2005); Ruth Tucker, *Another Gospel: Alternative*

Religions and the New Age Movement (Grand Rapids, MI: Zondervan, 1989); Catherine Tumber, *American Feminism and the Birth of New Age Spirituality: Searching for the Higher Self, 1875–1915* (Lanham, MD: Rowman & Littlefield, 2002).
31. Pike, *New Age and Neopagan Religions in America*, 39–40.
32. Ibid.
33. Ann Braude, *Radical Spirits: Spiritualism and Women's Rights in Nineteenth-Century America*, 2nd ed. (Bloomington: Indiana University Press, 2001), 6; Tumber, *American Feminism and the Birth of New Age Spirituality*, 10.
34. Tumber, *American Feminism and the Birth of New Age Spirituality*, 12.
35. Kendra Hovey, personal interview, January 24, 2007.
36. These classes were initially offered for a cost of a "freewill offering" but were later changed to set prices.
37. Kendra Hovey, personal interview, January 24, 2007.
38. Ibid.
39. Kendra Vaughan Hovey, "Church vs. Coven," lecture delivered for Pagan Pride Day 2008 (Connecticut).
40. Kendra Vaughan Hovey, "Closing of First Church of Wicca," e-mail communication, January 18, 2009.
41. Living Waters Community of Hope website (accessed March 1, 2009). This website has been removed.
42. Rev. Dr. Kendra Vaughan Hovey, *Handfasting: A Pagan Guide to Commitment Rituals* (Avon, MA: Provenance Press, 2007); Arin Murphy-Hiscock, ed., *Out of the Broom Closet: 50 True Stories of Witches Who Found and Embraced the Craft* (Avon, MA: Provenance Press, 2009).
43. "The Witches Next Door," *My Unique Family*, prod. Rishika Advani et al., TLC (originally aired February 19, 2007).
44. Kendra Vaughan Hovey, "Closing of the First Church of Wicca," e-mail communication, January 18, 2006.
45. The "Great Rite," an uncommon practice among most American Pagans, involves ritual sexual intercourse (sometimes real, though more often simulated with a chalice and athame) between a high priest and high priestess of a coven, in which the participants metaphorically embody the God and Goddess.
46. Hovey's speech led the coordinators of the Pagan Pride Day events to post a message on their website distancing themselves from and apologizing for Hovey's change of topic: "The SMPPD Board would like to assure the workshop attendees that we do not condone or endorse the actions of the Reverend Dr. Kendra Vaughan Hovey, DMin. We are greatly saddened that people were misled into believing the workshop was about something other than what was presented and would like to extend our sincere apologies to those who attended the workshop." Southern Maine Pagan Pride Day, "Index: Special Note," August 16, 2008, http://www.mainepaganprideday.org/ (accessed March 1, 2009).

47. "Reality Television Witch Converts," *The Wild Hunt*, January 19, 2009, http://wildhunt.org/blog/2009/01/reality-television-witch-converts.html (accessed March 1, 2009).
48. Hovey's new website explained, "My husband, Tim, is currently assisting in leading worship (music) at Journey Community of Faith and is leading worship in Living Waters Community of Hope. He is a sincere follower of Christ's teachings, and was baptized on September 7, 2009, but still has a difficult time with misunderstood labels. My son . . . is learning in Journeys Sunday school and enjoys it very much, but has not made any decision to become a Christian and also does not participate in communion. My daughter . . . is also in Sunday school at Journey. She has asked Jesus into her heart, participates in communion, and was baptized on September 7, 2009." Living Waters Community of Hope, "Questions and Answers," n.d., http://livingwatersch.org/QandA.html (accessed October 10, 2009, now defunct).
49. Tchipakkan, APF&FV survey, October 10, 2006.
50. Moonivy, APF&FV survey, December 30, 2006.
51. Jessie, APF&FV survey, October 13, 2006.
52. Atashih, personal communication, April 2006.
53. Danielle, APF&FV survey, June 13, 2006.
54. Kaida, APF&FV survey, June 13, 2006.
55. Celtic Wolf, APF&FV survey, September 15, 2006.
56. Willowhawk, APF&FV survey, June 12, 2006.
57. Anonymous, APF&FV survey, December 31, 2006.
58. Carol, APF&FV survey, June 11, 2006
59. Erin, APF&FV survey, October 20, 2006.
60. Katness, APF&FV survey, June 30, 2006.
61. GreyElf, APF&FV survey, June 16, 2006.
62. Lady Kelien, APF&FV survey, December 5, 2006.
63. "I can't remember the last time I went to church. My faith has carried me a long way. It's Sheilaism. Just my own little voice. . . . It's just try to love yourself and be gentle with yourself. You know, I guess, take care of each other. I think God would want us to take care of each other." Sheila Larson, quoted in Robert Neelly Bellah, *Habits of the Heart: Individualism and Commitment in American Life*, 1st Perennial Library ed. (New York: Harper & Row, 1985), 221.
64. Rebecca, APF&FV survey, January 2, 2007.
65. Ibid.
66. Callisto, APF&FV survey, June 17, 2006.
67. Sonas, APF&FV survey, August 8, 2006.
68. See, for example, Joe Harris, "Discordianism: A Religion Disguised as a Joke Disguised as a Religion," December 28, 2000, http://www.disinfo.com/archive/pages/dossier/id342/pg1/index.html (accessed November 11, 2012).
69. Shelley Rabinovitch and James Lewis, *The Encyclopedia of Modern Witchcraft and Neo-Paganism* (New York: Citadel Press, 2002), 75.

70. Eris (also known as Discordia) is the Greek goddess of discord and chaos and the central goddess of Discordianism.
71. Malaclypse the Younger, *Principia Discordia; or, How I Found the Goddess and What I Did to Her When I Found Her*, 4th and 5th ed. (1965; Port Townsend, WA: Loompanics Unlimited, 1979), 32.
72. J. Gordon Melton, *The Encyclopedia of American Religions* (Wilmington, NC: McGrath, 1978), 299–300. Melton notes that because Discordianism asserts that everyone is a Discordian pope, he chooses to wield this power to excommunicate all other Discordian popes, who then (being popes themselves) will certainly de-excommunicate themselves.
73. See, for example, Mark Bahnisch, "Sociology of Religion in Postmodernity: Wicca, Witches, and the Neo-Pagan Myth of Foundations," in *Proceedings of the Australian Sociological Association* (Sydney: University of Sydney, 2001), 3.
74. The postmodern aspects of contemporary Paganism have been noted by numerous scholars, including Lorne L. Dawson, "Anti-Modernism, Modernism, and Postmodernism: Struggling with the Cultural Significance of New Religious Movements," *Sociology of Religion* 59, no. 2 (1998): 131–156; Howard Eilberg-Schwartz, "Witches of the West: Neopaganism and Goddess Worship as Enlightenment Religions," *Journal of Feminist Studies in Religion* 5 (Spring 1989): 77–95; Adrian Ivakhiv, "The Resurgence of Magical Religion as a Response to the Crisis of Modernity: A Postmodern Depth Psychological Perspective," in *Magical Religion and Modern Witchcraft*, ed. James R. Lewis (Albany: State University of New York Press, 1996), 237–268; David Waldron, "Post-Modernism and Witchcraft Histories," *The Pomegranate: The International Journal of Pagan Studies* 15 (February 2001): 36–44.
75. The ahistorical tendencies of contemporary Paganism also align it with postmodernism; see, for example, Fredric Jameson, *Postmodernism; or, The Cultural Logic of Late Capitalism* (Durham: Duke University Press, 1991), ix.
76. A.D., APF&FV survey, June 9, 2006.
77. Sonas, APF&FV survey, August 9, 2006.
78. Pagan history-making seems to exemplify Constantin Fasolt's assertion that "history is one of the most important forms religion has taken in the modern world." Fasolt's analysis of the religious capacity of history seems particularly relevant to an understanding of Pagan historicizing as religious practice. See "History and Religion in the Modern Age," *History and Theory* 45, no. 4 (2006): 11.
79. The self-historicizing of Mormonism has a number of interesting correlations to the same practice among contemporary Pagans. See Jan Shipps, *Mormonism: The Story of a New Religious Tradition* (Urbana: University of Illinois Press, 1985), 54.
80. Clifton and Harvey, *Paganism Reader*, 80.
81. Charlie Murphy, "The Burning Times," in *Catch the Fire* (Good Fairy Productions, 1981).
82. Hutton, *Triumph of the Moon*, 380.

83. Diane Purkiss, *The Witch in History: Early Modern and Twentieth-Century Representations* (London: Routledge, 1996), 7–29.
84. Ibid., 8.
85. Shuck, "Myth of the Burning Times and the Politics of Resistance in Contemporary American Wicca," 1. See also Sarah Pike's discussion of the importance of psychological impact over historical authenticity in *New Age and Neopagan Religions in America*, 124–125.
86. CMA Samhain festival, October 2006.
87. Hutton, "Paganism and Polemic," 114.
88. Shuck, "Myth of the Burning Times and the Politics of Resistance in Contemporary American Wicca," 1.
89. Danièle Hervieu-Léger, *Religion as a Chain of Memory* (New Brunswick: Rutgers University Press, 2000).
90. Ibid., 96.
91. Ibid., 167. Helen Berger has discussed Wicca specifically as a community of memory based on its self-conscious, utopian continuation of (or return to) a pre-Christian religious past. See *Community of Witches*, 125.

NOTES TO CHAPTER 2

1. Hutton, *Triumph of the Moon*, viii.
2. Anne Higonnet, *Pictures of Innocence: The History and Crisis of Ideal Childhood* (New York: Thames and Hudson, 1998), 38.
3. Henry Jenkins, "Introduction: Childhood Innocence and Other Modern Myths," in *The Children's Culture Reader*, ed. Henry Jenkins (New York: New York University Press, 1998), 3.
4. James R. Kincaid, *Child-Loving: The Erotic Child and Victorian Culture* (New York: Routledge, 1994), 11–12.
5. Ridgely Bales, *When I Was a Child*, 9.
6. E. Burke Rochford's study of children in the International Society for Krishna Consciousness (ISKCON) described a similar view of the spiritually advanced state of childhood in the religion. Rochford explains, "Until the early 1980s, children born in ISKCON were commonly portrayed as being spiritually pure, as their souls were believed to have progressed spiritually to the point that they had had the good fortune of being born into a devotee family. But by the mid-1980s this view had changed, with some leaders complaining that ISKCON's children were turning out to be little more than 'karmies' (nonreligious outsiders) and therefore that the gurukala had failed in its mission to produce spiritually advanced children." *Hare Krishna Transformed* (New York: New York University Press, 2007), 80. Unsurprisingly, contemporary Paganism's view of the spiritual wisdom of childhood seems to be less structured and institutionalized than the view held by ISKCON adherents, but it is nonetheless similar. It will be interesting to observe whether understandings of children's spiritual precocity and spiritual

wisdom change if these children leave Paganism as adults, particularly if they leave for less "enlightened" spiritual paths.
7. Erin, personal interview, October 31, 2006.
8. Helen A. Berger, "Witches: The Next Generation," in *Children in New Religions*, ed. Susan J. Palmer and Charlotte E. Hardman (New Brunswick: Rutgers University Press, 1999), 15.
9. CMA Beltane festival, April 2007.
10. Katherine Clark, "Ten Steps to Encourage Magical Children," *The Blessed Bee: A Pagan Family Newsletter* 19 (Winter 2003): 17–18.
11. Connie Briggs, "The Lesson," *The Blessed Bee: A Pagan Family Newsletter* 1 (Summer 1999): 16. Some Pagans spell the word "magic" with a final *k* in an effort to distinguish "real" magic from the illusion of stage magic. This spelling was popularized by British occultist Aleister Crowley in the early twentieth century. Crowley defined magick as "the science and art of causing change to occur in conformity with Will." Aleister Crowley, *Magick in Theory and Practice* (1929; Eastford, CT: Martino Fine Books, 2011), xii. Crowley's understanding of magick remains highly influential for many contemporary American Pagans.
12. The accuracy of this skill, of course, is difficult to substantiate. See Margie McArthur, *WiccaCraft for Families: The Path of the Hearthfire* (Custer, WA: Phoenix, 1994), 21, 27.
13. Jennifer Carrington, "The Enchantment of Youth," *The Blessed Bee: A Pagan Family Newsletter* 26 (Autumn 2005): 25.
14. Sarah Pike discusses the disenchantment felt by many Pagans, who blame this on Christianity's salvific focus. See *Earthly Bodies, Magical Selves*, 160.
15. Kristen Madden, *Pagan Parenting: Spiritual, Magical, and Emotional Development of the Child* (Niceville, FL: Spilled Candy Publications, 2004).
16. Lady Galadriel, *A New Wiccan Book of the Law* (Atlanta: Moonstone Publications, 1985). The author's website (http://www.unicorntrad.org/info/BOTL.html) notes that the book's sources include *The Book of the Law* (Aleister Crowley's Thelemic text, written—some say "received"—in 1904), *The Old Laws for the Old Religion*, *The Great Book of the Law*, and *The Dragon Law*. Wiccan groups consider all of these texts "traditional" Wiccan texts, although their origins are uncertain, and it is unclear what criteria make a text a "traditional" source of contemporary Paganism. The faux-archaic language of the text is common among such "traditional" Wiccan sources. The First Church of Wicca specified as part of its credo, "We believe in the codes of conduct set forth in *A New Wiccan Book of the Law* by Lady Galadriel." This information was included on the (defunct) website of the First Church of Wicca and is available at http://www.wikinfo.org/Multilingual/index.php/First_Church_of_Wicca (accessed November 11, 2012).
17. Christina Aubin, "Children and the Wheel of the Year," Witches' Voice, March 19, 2000, http://www.witchvox.com/va/dt_article.html?a=usma&id=2729 (accessed May 23, 2012).

18. Katness, APF&FV survey, June 30, 2006.
19. New Age spirituality and Paganism differ in a number of ways. Most significantly, as Sarah Pike has noted, New Age locates its utopian vision in an ideal future, whereas Paganism envisions the reconstruction of an idealized past. The two share a number of common ideologies, however, and there is often considerable overlap between these groups. Pike's *New Age and Neopagan Religions in America* provides an excellent analysis of the similarities and differences between these groups.
20. Pike, *Earthly Bodies, Magical Selves*, 160.
21. Lee Carroll and Jan Tober, *The Indigo Children: The New Kids Have Arrived* (Carlsbad, CA: Hay House, 1999), 1.
22. Ibid., 1–2.
23. The *Diagnostic and Statistical Manual of Medical Disorders* (DSM) first included reference to an ADHD-like disorder (then called "hyperkinetic reaction of childhood") in the DSM-II (1968). The next edition (DSM-III, 1980) identified this disorder as Attention Deficit Disorder (ADD), and the revised version (DSM-IIIR, 1987) renamed it Attention Deficit Hyperactivity Disorder (ADHD). The current version of the manual (DSM-IV, 1994) lists two categories and three subtypes of ADHD. See American Psychiatric Association, Committee on Nomenclature and Statistics, *Diagnostic and Statistical Manual of Mental Disorders* (Washington, DC: American Psychiatric Association, 1952); American Psychiatric Association, Committee on Nomenclature and Statistics, *Diagnostic and Statistical Manual of Mental Disorders: DSM-II*, 2nd ed. (Washington, DC: American Psychiatric Association, 1968); American Psychiatric Association, Task Force on Nomenclature and Statistics, *Diagnostic and Statistical Manual of Mental Disorders: DSM-III*, 3rd ed. (Washington, DC: American Psychiatric Association, 1980); American Psychiatric Association and Work Group to Revise DSM-III, *Diagnostic and Statistical Manual of Mental Disorders: DSM-III-R*, 3rd ed. (Washington, DC: American Psychiatric Association, 1987); American Psychiatric Association and Task Force on DSM-IV, *Diagnostic and Statistical Manual of Mental Disorders: DSM-IV*, 4th ed. (Washington, DC: American Psychiatric Association, 1994).
24. Nancy Ann Tappe, "Introduction to the Indigos: Interviewed by Jan Tober (Part I)," in Carroll and Tober, *Indigo Children*, 9.
25. Anni Sennov, *Crystal Children, Indigo Children, and Adults of the Future* (Greve, Denmark: Good Adventures, 2006), 19.
26. John D. Spalding, "Brood Indigo," Beliefnet, n.d., http://www.beliefnet.com/story/122/story_12252_1.html (accessed December 10, 2007).
27. Ibid.
28. Jennifer Sue Kamish, *12 Ways to Cope with a Challenging Child: A Guide to Indigo/ADD/ADHD Children* (Bloomington, IN: AuthorHouse, 2007), 15.
29. Ibid.
30. LaraDee, "Re: What Do You Believe?" Beliefnet, September 17, 2003, http://www.beliefnet.com/story/122/story_12252_1.html (accessed December 11, 2007).

31. Laurel Chaisson, "Parenting the Indigo Children, from the Indigos' Point of View," May 15, 2005, http://laurelchaisson.proboards.com/index.cgi?board=published&action=print&thread=618 (accessed November 11, 2012).
32. Lorna Tedder, *Third Degree of Freedom* (Niceville, FL: Spilled Candy, 2006). Excerpt available at http://www.thespiritualeclectic.com/2008/04/07/indigo-children-when-i-give-birth-to-the-messiah/ (accessed May 27, 2012).
33. Kabir Jaffe, *Indigo Adults: Forerunners of the New Civilization*, trans. Ritama Davidson (New York: iUniverse, 2005).
34. In a paper presented at the Center for the Study of New Religions international conference, Sarah Whedon notes, "The New Age broadly, and believers in Indigo Children more specifically, tend not to be made of traditional communities of local proximity. What holds Indigo believers together as a movement is a commonality of ideas that are shared primarily through textual modes of communication." Much of the discussion and community building within New Age groups (and Pagan groups, as well) occurs on the Internet. Sarah W. Whedon, "The Wisdom of Indigo Children: An Emphatic Restatement of the Value of American Children," paper presented at the CESNUR 2004 International Conference, Baylor University, Waco, TX, June 18–20, 2004. For more on contemporary Paganism's propensity for online community building, see Alyssa Beall, "There's No Place Like Home.html: Neopaganism on the Internet," in *Religious Innovation in a Global Age: Essays on the Construction of Spirituality*, ed. George N. Lundskow (Jefferson, NC: McFarland, 2005), 199–227; Cowan, *Cyberhenge*.
35. Adarian, "Re: Indigo Children," April 18, 2006, http://www.magickaschool.com/boards/ (accessed December 11, 2007). Another parent enthusiastically agreed, noting that she was an Indigo adult and all three of her children, "especially" her youngest, were Indigos.
36. Felicity, "Re: Indigo Children," August 21, 2006, http://www.magickaschool.com/boards/ (accessed December 11, 2007).
37. Dylan Otto Krider, "Alien-ated Youth," *Houston Press*, December 19, 2002, http://www.houstonpress.com/2002-12-19/news/alien-ated-youth/www.texascrawfishfestival.com/ (accessed May 27, 2012).
38. Dr. Russell Barkley, quoted in John Leland, "Are They Here to Save the World?" *New York Times*, January 12, 2006.
39. Nick Colangelo, quoted in Jesse Hyde, "Little Boy Blue," *Dallas Observer*, March 9, 2006, http://www.dallasobserver.com/2006-03-09/news/little-boy-blue/ (accessed May 27, 2012).
40. Krider, "Alien-ated Youth," December 19, 2002, http://www.houstonpress.com/2002-12-19/news/alien-ated-youth/www.texascrawfishfestival.com/ (accessed May 27, 2012).
41. Douglas Cowan, sociologist of religion and Pagan studies scholar, sees this quality in the "more authentic self" Pagans construct through magical names and invented identities. Cowan remarks, "Identity in modern Paganism is an almost ludic process, a playful sloughing of mundane reality in favor of a magickal

recognition of those elements by which the modern Pagan self is more authentically characterized." See *Cyberhenge*, 154.
42. Lorne L. Dawson, "The Mediation of Religious Experience in Cyberspace," in *Religion and Cyberspace*, ed. Morten T. Højsgaard and Margit Warburg (New York: Routledge, 2005), 21.

NOTES TO CHAPTER 3
1. Madden, *Pagan Parenting*, 45.
2. Kimberly Upton, "Do You Believe in Faeries?" *The Blessed Bee: A Pagan Family Newsletter* 5 (Summer 2000): 17.
3. Pike, *Earthly Bodies, Magical Selves*, 155.
4. Ibid., 178.
5. Ibid., 180.
6. Katness, APF&FV survey, June 30, 2006.
7. D.B., APF&FV survey, June 13, 2006.
8. Carol, APF&FV survey, June 11, 2006.
9. Lady Kelien, APF&FV survey, December 5, 2006.
10. M. Skye, APF&FV survey, October 12, 2006.
11. Death, APF&FV survey, August 9, 2006.
12. Shawnya, APF&FV survey, June 13, 2006.
13. Moonivy, APF&FV survey, December 31, 2006.
14. Celtic Wolf, APF&FV survey, August 6, 2006.
15. Jennifer M., APF&FV survey, August 11, 2006.
16. Janet, APF&FV survey, August 10, 2006.
17. Anonymous, APF&FV survey, June 10, 2006; Anonymous, APF&FV survey, June 8, 2006.
18. Callisto, APF&FV survey, June 17, 2006; Anonymous, APF&FV survey, October 10, 2006.
19. Willowhawk, APF&FV survey, June 12, 2006.
20. Katness, APF&FV survey, June 30, 2006.
21. Lady Silverhorn, APF&FV survey, August 9, 2006
22. Jess, personal interview, May 23, 2006.
23. Pike, *Earthly Bodies, Magical Selves*, 167–168.
24. Sonas, APF&FV survey, August 9, 2006.
25. Daniel, interview, July 2006.
26. Carol, APF&FV survey, June 11, 2006.
27. Lord Uthur, APF&FV survey, August 9, 2006.
28. Kimberly, APF&FV survey, August 10, 2006.
29. Pike, *Earthly Bodies, Magical Selves*, 167.
30. Judith Warner, *Perfect Madness: Motherhood in the Age of Anxiety* (New York: Riverhead Books, 2005), 96.
31. Bruce G. Charlton, "The Rise of the Boy-Genius: Psychological Neoteny, Science, and Modern Life," *Medical Hypotheses* 67 (2006): 679–681.

32. Sonas, APF&FV survey, August 9, 2006.
33. Lady Silverhorn, APF&FV survey, August 9, 2006.
34. Atashih and Raven, CMA festival, April 2006.
35. Patricia C., APF&FV survey, August 9, 2006.
36. Bruce, interview, January 21, 2007.
37. Dea, APF&FV survey, June 11, 2006.
38. Ibid.
39. Lady Willow, APF&FV survey, August 9, 2006.
40. Jessie, APF&FV survey, October 13, 2006.
41. Jennifer H., APF&FV survey, October 15, 2006.
42. As noted in the "Fluffy Bunny" ritual scheduled at one CMA festival, Beltane, 2007.

NOTES TO CHAPTER 4

1. E-mail communication, October 20, 2006.
2. *The Ox-Cart Man* describes the daily life of a mid-nineteenth-century family through the changing seasons. Likewise, *When the Root Children Wake Up* (first published in 1906) follows the Root Children's activities through the seasons. Helen Dean Fish and Sibylle Olfers, *When the Root Children Wake Up* (New York: Frederick A. Stokes, 1930); Donald Hall and Barbara Cooney, *The Ox-Cart Man* (New York: Viking Press, 1979).
3. As discussed in a prior chapter, the "Great Rite" involves ritual sexual intercourse (sometimes real, though often simulated with a chalice and athame) between the high priest and high priestess of a coven, in which the participants "embody" the God and Goddess. Scourging is part of the initiation ceremony in some Wiccan traditions that involves the initiate being whipped lightly with a leather crop or cat o' nine tails. Both practices are far more common among traditional and Gardnerian groups than among American eclectic or Goddess-centered Pagans. In my fieldwork with a variety of both adult- and family-oriented Pagan groups, I have never encountered a group that practiced scourging, although the concept seems familiar to most practitioners; the priestess of one New England Wiccan coven assured me several times that their rituals were child-friendly because they "don't practice scourging."
4. Atashih, personal interview, October 17, 2006.
5. Michael Sontag, "Children, Magick, and Realism," *Mezlim: Practical Magick for Today* 5, no. 4 (1994): 13, quoted in Berger, *Community of Witches*, 84.
6. Kendra Vaughan Hovey, quoted in Andria Farrell, "The First Church of Wicca Celebrates with the Spirits," *Wicked Local Duxbury*, 2007, http://www.wickedlocal.com/duxbury/homepage/x1375672905 (accessed November 29, 2007).
7. Rev. Morninghawk Apollo, "Children Attending Pagan Rituals," Witches' Voice, May 7, 2004, http://www.witchvox.com/va/dt_va.html?a=usmn&c=words&id=8453 (accessed May 25, 2012).
8. Anonymous, APF&FV survey, June 9, 2006.
9. G.R., APF&FV survey, June 23, 2006.

10. Ashleen O'Gaea, *Raising Witches: Teaching the Wiccan Faith to Children* (Franklin Lakes, NJ: New Page Books, 2002), 21.
11. Ibid., 15.
12. Rev. Morninghawk Apollo, "Children Attending Pagan Rituals."
13. Madden, *Pagan Parenting*, 128.
14. Jess, personal interview, May 23, 2006.
15. Berger, "Witches," 17.
16. Kendra Hovey, personal interview, January 2007.
17. Ibid.
18. This Yule ritual was written by Jess Gerrior and performed by Silverling Circle at the "Yule Festival in the Ancient Tradition," Milford, New Hampshire, December 9, 2006.
19. Starhawk, Diane Baker, and Anne Hill, *Circle Round: Raising Children in Goddess Traditions* (New York: Bantam Books, 1998). Other useful and popular sources for creating and adapting child-friendly rituals include Cait Johnson and Maura D. Shaw, *Celebrating the Great Mother: A Handbook of Earth-Honoring Activities for Parents and Children* (Rochester, VT: Destiny Books, 1995); McArthur, *Wicca-Craft for Families*; Ashleen O'Gaea, *Family Wicca: Practical Paganism for Parents and Children*, rev. and exp. ed. (Franklin Lakes, NJ: New Page Books, 2006); and the (now defunct) print newsletter *The Blessed Bee: A Pagan Family Newsletter*, published by Blessed Bee Inc. and edited by Lauren Foster-MacLeod.
20. Jess, personal interview, May 23, 2006.
21. A.A., APF&FV survey, June 12, 2006.
22. Carol, APF&FV survey, June 11, 2006.
23. Tchippakan, APF&FV survey, October 10, 2006.
24. The version they sing is the popular combination of "We All Come from the Goddess" (usually credited to Zsuzsanna Budapest) and "Hoof and Horn" (credited to Ian Corrigan): "We all come from the Goddess / and to Her we shall return / Like a drop of rain / flowing to the ocean. / We all come from the Sun God / and to Him we shall return / like a spark of flame / rising to the heavens. / Hoof and horn, hoof and horn / all that dies shall be reborn / corn and grain, corn and grain / all that falls shall rise again."

NOTES TO CHAPTER 5

1. Moore, *Religious Outsiders and the Making of Americans*, 46.
2. Ibid., 29–31.
3. Ibid., xi.
4. Hutton, *Triumph of the Moon*, 96–97.
5. Raymond Buckland, *The Tree: The Complete Book of Saxon Witchcraft* (New York: S. Weiser, 1974); Clifton, *Her Hidden Children*, 26.
6. Ronald Hutton, "The Discovery of the Modern Goddess," in *Nature Religion Today: Paganism in the Modern World*, ed. Joanne Pearson, Richard H. Roberts, and Geoffrey Samuel (Edinburgh: Edinburgh University Press, 1998), 98.

7. Hutton, *Triumph of the Moon*, 360.
8. E-mailed press release for the 2006 Celebrate Samhain event, October 4, 2006.
9. Nancy McGee, "The FireFly Promise," in SpiralScouts International, *Circle Leader, Hearth Keeper: The SpiralScouts Leader Handbook*, ver. 2.0, draft ed. (Asheville, NC: SpiralScouts International Inc., 2004), 17.
10. Jennifer, "The Wise Ones," e-mail message to the New Hampshire SpiralScouts Yahoo! Group, November 4, 2006.
11. Aquarian Tabernacle Church, "The History of the Aquarian Tabernacle Church," n.d., http://www.aquatabch.org/branches-of-the-pagan-tree (accessed June 2, 2009).
12. Aquarian Tabernacle Church, "The ATC Tradition," n.d., http://www.aquariantabernaclechurch.org/the-atc-tradition (accessed June 2, 2009).
13. Aquarian Tabernacle Church, "The History of the Aquarian Tabernacle Church."
14. Ibid. Unfortunately, the identity of the "WebCrafter" and his or her relationship to Davis is unclear from the information on the website.
15. This phenomenon is not limited to the ATC. Other attempts at creating structured, large-scale Pagan organizations (e.g., the Covenant of the Goddess and the Church of All Worlds) have resulted in groups that are significant in terms of their contribution to the religion's history but are virtually unknown by the majority of American Pagans.
16. Mama Gaia, APF&FV survey, June 17, 2006.
17. Aquarian Tabernacle Church, "The History of the Aquarian Tabernacle Church."
18. SpiralScouts International, "Frequently Asked Questions: Religion," n.d., http://spiralscouts.org/node/29 (accessed November 11, 2012).
19. A circle is a group of SpiralScouts, usually led by one male and one female adult leader, who have completed the chartering process through SpiralScouts Headquarters. A hearth is a much smaller group of one or two families.
20. Janet C., "Re: Badges, badges . . . ," e-mail message to SpiralScouts Yahoo! Group, November 20, 2006.
21. Handfastings are Pagan wedding ceremonies. They do not necessarily follow a specific format, but they often incorporate many similar elements: jumping over a broom or small fire, ribbons to bind the couple's hands together, and the exchange of vows and rings. Contemporary Pagan handfastings reflect the creativity with which many Pagans approach romantic and sexual relationships. For example, handfastings may expressly unite a couple (or, sometimes, more than two people) for "a year and a day," a lifetime, all future lifetimes, or "as long as love shall last."
22. As noted in chapter 1, one of the hallmarks of contemporary American Paganism is its willingness to borrow from and adapt multiple religious and cultural traditions for its own purposes—a willingness that, depending on perspective, can be seen as either postmodern bricolage or cultural appropriation. The issue of cultural appropriation is a contentious topic in contemporary Paganism. The range

of opinions on the subject is addressed in nineteen essays collected in a recent edited volume, *Talking about the Elephant: An Anthology of Neopagan Perspectives on Cultural Appropriation*, ed. Lupa (Stafford, UK: Megalithica, 2008).
23. Organizational meeting, Silver Sapling Circle, November 12, 2006.
24. SpiralScouts International, *Circle Leader, Hearth Keeper*, 19–20.
25. SpiralScouts is only one indicator of this drive to provide Pagan communities with organizational opportunities that mirror those of mainstream, Christian-centered American culture. Other examples include Cherry Hill Seminary and Woolston-Steen Theological Seminary for the training of Pagan clergy, numerous failed attempts at "Pagan schools," the Covenant of the Goddess, Circle Sanctuary, the Church of All Worlds, and the First Church of Wicca.
26. Jess, "Re: Badges, badges . . . ," e-mail message to SpiralScouts Yahoo! Group, November 21, 2006.
27. These organizations maintain their own websites: see http://www.jewishscoutsforum.org/ (accessed November 11, 2012); and http://www.islamicscouting.org/ (accessed November 11, 2012). The Boy Scouts of America also includes Buddhist, Islamic, and Jewish scouting troops. However, the BSA does not approve atheistic or polytheistic troops.
28. SpiralScouts International, *Circle Leader, Hearth Keeper*, 13.
29. The Boy Scouts of America, "Religious Emblems Programs," 2009, http://www.scouting.org/scoutsource/Awards/ReligiousAwards.aspx (accessed November 11, 2012).
30. Melanie Crownover, "Scout's Admission of Being Wiccan Leads to Turmoil," *The Town Talk*, May 9, 2006.
31. See "Excerpts from the Supreme Court's Ruling on Gays and the Boy Scouts," *New York Times*, June 29, 2000; and Michael Alvear, "A Family Dilemma: To Scout or Not to Scout?" *Newsweek*, November 6, 2000. In his in-depth analysis of the Boy Scouts of America, Jay Mechling suggests that "the Boy Scouts in the first few years of the twenty-first century must be understood, at least in part, as a nineteenth-century solution to the cultural trauma experienced as a result of the twentieth century's assault on traditional understandings of what it means to be a boy and a man." *On My Honor: Boy Scouts and the Making of American Youth* (Chicago: University of Chicago Press, 2001), xvii.
32. Boy Scouts of America National Council, "Frequently Asked Questions," 2006, http://www.bsalegal.org/ (accessed November 11, 2012).
33. Public perception often conflates the BSA and the Girl Scouts of the United States, but the two are separate, independent organizations. In response to a 1993 religious discrimination lawsuit, the Girl Scouts of the United States modified its policies to allow individual Girl Scouts to replace the word "God" in the Girl Scout Promise with "whatever word your spiritual beliefs dictate." While this appeases some Pagan opposition, many parents nevertheless dislike the Girl Scouts' single-gender exclusivity. See Girl Scouts of the United States of America,

"Girl Scout Promise and Law," Girl Scout Central, 2008, http://www.girlscouts.org/program/gs_central/promise_law/ (accessed November 11, 2012).
34. Boy Scouts of America National Council, "Frequently Asked Questions."
35. Jess, personal interview, May 23, 2006.
36. The Society for Creative Anachronism is "an international organization dedicated to researching and re-creating the arts and skills of pre-17th-century Europe . . . with over 30,000 members residing in countries around the world. Members, dressed in clothing of the Middle Ages and Renaissance, attend events which feature tournaments, royal courts, feasts, dancing, various classes & workshops, and more." See Society for Creative Anachronism, 2009, http://www.sca.org/ (accessed November 11, 2012).
37. Kendra, "uniforms," e-mail message to SpiralScouts Yahoo! Group, May 29, 2006.
38. Pierre C. "Pete Pathfinder" Davis, "Re: [SpiralScouts] Digest Number 1458," e-mail message to SpiralScouts Yahoo! Group, May 30, 2006.
39. Janet C., "Re: Circle Uniform Idea," e-mail message to SpiralScouts Yahoo! Group, April 1, 2006.
40. Erin, personal interview, October 31, 2006.
41. SpiralScouts International, *Circle Leader, Hearth Keeper*, 22–23.
42. Janet C., "Re: Question about FireFly Promise," e-mail message to SpiralScouts Yahoo! Group, August 31, 2005.
43. R., "Re: Question about FireFly Promise," e-mail message to SpiralScouts Yahoo! Group, August 31, 2005.
44. Selene, group interview, February 11, 2006.
45. Jessie, APF&FV survey, October 12, 2006.
46. P.G., personal interview, CMA Samhain festival, October 21, 2006.
47. E.C., APF&FV survey, October 20, 2006.
48. Carol Barner-Barry, *Contemporary Paganism: Minority Religions in a Majoritarian America* (New York: Palgrave Macmillan, 2005), 116.
49. Kendra Hovey, personal interview, January 24, 2007.
50. Jess and Ryan, personal interview, May 23, 2006.
51. Willowhawk, APF&FV survey, June 12, 2006.
52. Freya, Selene, and Atashih, CMA Samhain festival, October 21, 2006.
53. Cecylyna Dewr, "You Have a Pagan Student in Your School: A Guide for Educators," 1998, http://www.paganpride.org/resources/paganstudent.html (accessed November 11, 2012).
54. "Homeschooling" generally refers to education conducted by parents outside a school setting, usually following one of a variety of established curricula. "Unschooling" (sometimes called "child-led learning" in an attempt to differentiate it from truancy or parental neglect) is a specific type of homeschooling that uses no set curriculum. Instead, children learn by following their own interests and learning styles; some parents "teach" children only what and when the child requests. State laws vary concerning mandatory levels of parental reporting of children's educational progress and activities.

55. Colleen McDannell, "Creating the Christian Home: Home Schooling in Contemporary America," in *American Sacred Space*, ed. David Chidester and Edward Tabor Linenthal (Bloomington: Indiana University Press, 1995), 189, 207.
56. Robert Kunzman, "Homeschooling FAQ," Homeschooling Research and Scholarship, February 13, 2009, http://www.indiana.edu/~homeeduc/ (accessed June 3, 2009).
57. Dawn, APF&FV survey, August 11, 2006.
58. Jess, personal interview, May 23, 2006.
59. Helen Berger also addresses the phenomenon of the UU church as a means of social legitimation for many Pagans and the development of the Covenant of Unitarian Universalist Pagans in *Community of Witches*, 114–20.
60. Crissy T., personal interview, July 10, 2006.
61. Unitarian Universalist Association, "The 1997 Unitarian Universalism Needs and Aspirations Survey," December 23, 1998, http://www.uua.org/directory/data/demographics/130035.shtml (accessed November 11, 2012); John Dart, "They Came from Other Churches," Beliefnet, 2001, http://www.beliefnet.com/story/95/story_9536.html (accessed November 11, 2012).
62. Covenant of Universalist Unitarian Pagans, "Women and Paganism," n.d., http://www.cuups.org/about/women.html (accessed May 27, 2012).
63. David Burwasser, "History of CUUPS," n.d., http://cuups.org/about/history.html (accessed November 11, 2012).
64. Margot Adler, "Vibrant, Juicy, Contemporary; or, Why I Am a UU Pagan," *UU World: The Magazine of the Unitarian Universalist Association*, November 13, 1996, http://moonpathcuups.org/margot.htm (accessed December 3, 2012).
65. Pike, *Earthly Bodies, Magical Selves*, 14–15.
66. Ibid., 18.
67. Ibid.
68. Kendra Hovey, personal interview, January 24, 2007.
69. CMA Beltane festival, 2007.
70. Like many Pagan songs, chants, and rituals, attribution for "Pagan carols" such as this one is difficult to determine. This song has been variously attributed on the Internet to "Sunblade" and to "Lady Morrigan."
71. Erin, personal interview, October 31, 2006.

NOTES TO CHAPTER 6

1. This ceremony is sometimes called a Paganing or (rarely, in a nod to the mythology of the unbroken indigenous European Pagan heritage) a Saining. Interestingly, the word "sain" literally means "to make the sign of the cross" over a person or thing as a form of blessing, including blessings "warding off the evil influences of witches." *Oxford English Dictionary*, 2nd ed., 1989, s.v. "sain."
2. Jason, "Wiccaning Ceremony," Pagan-Wiccan Religion, September 13, 2007, http://en.allexperts.com/q/Pagan-Wiccan-Religion-3207/Wiccaning-Ceremony.htm (accessed November 11, 2012).

3. Some Pagans supplement belief in reincarnation with the belief that the soul "rests" temporarily on an alternate plane, often called the "Summerland" or Valhalla, depending on the individual or group tradition.
4. Dewr, "You Have a Pagan Student in Your School."
5. E.S., personal interview, January 21, 2007.
6. Coven of the Fertile Earth, "A Wiccaning Ritual I," posted on The Cauldron: A Pagan Forum, n.d., http://www.ecauldron.net/wiccaning1.php (accessed November 11, 2012). This ritual has been widely reprinted and adapted on a number of Pagan websites and reflects many of the common elements of Wiccaning ceremonies.
7. Ibid.
8. Raven's Wiccaning, written and performed by Atashih and Selene of Dragon Moon Coven, March 28, 1999.
9. Ibid.
10. Catechism of the Catholic Church, "Faith and Baptism," #1255, n.d., http://www.christusrex.org/www1/CDHN/baptism.html#HOW (accessed November 11, 2012).
11. Lady Silverhorn, APF&FV survey, August 9, 2006.
12. G.R., APF&FV survey, June 23, 2006.
13. Dea, APF&FV survey, June 11, 2006.
14. Rebecca, APF&FV survey, January 2, 2007.
15. Crissy T., group interview, July 2006.
16. J.D., APF&FV survey, June 9, 2006.
17. Wade Clark Roof, *Spiritual Marketplace: Baby Boomers and the Remaking of American Religion* (Princeton: Princeton University Press, 1999), 75.
18. Ibid., 217.
19. See, for example, E. Burke Rochford, "Education and Collective Identity: Public Schooling of Hare Krishna Youths," 29–50; Judith Coney, "Growing Up As Mother's Children," 108–123; Massimo Introvigne, "Children of the Underground Temple: Growing Up in Damanhur," 138–152, in Susan J. Palmer and Charlotte Hardman, ed., *Children in New Religions* (New Brunswick: Rutgers University Press, 1999).
20. Eugene V. Gallagher, *The New Religious Movements Experience in America* (Westport, CT: Greenwood Press, 2004), 234–235.
21. Raymond Buckland, *Wicca for Life: The Way of the Craft—From Birth to Summerland* (New York: Citadel Press/Kensington, 2001), 84.
22. Jessie, APF&FV survey, October 13, 2006.
23. O'Gaea, *Family Wicca*, 64.
24. Ibid., 23.
25. Longitudinal studies of the religious beliefs and practices of second-generation Pagan children would provide a significant addition to the existing literature on contemporary Paganism and American Pagan families.
26. R.D., "Re: Request for assistance and/or interviews with Pagan Parents," e-mail communication, December 20, 2005.
27. Etoile, online survey, December 5, 2006.

28. Ibid.
29. Rodney Stark, "How New Religions Succeed: A Theoretical Model," in *The Future of New Religious Movements*, ed. David G. Bromley and Phillip E. Hammond (Macon: Mercer University Press, 1987), 25.
30. Anonymous, APF&FV survey, June 8, 2006.
31. Anonymous, APF&FV survey, January 2, 2007.
32. Carol, APF&FV survey, June 11, 2006.
33. Danielle, APF&FV survey, June 13, 2006.
34. Anonymous, APF&FV survey, June 15, 2006.
35. Erin, APF&FV survey, October 20, 2006.
36. Claddaugh, APF&FV survey, August 9, 2006.
37. Willowhawk, APF&FV survey, June 12, 2006.
38. Jennifer, APF&FV survey, October 15, 2006.
39. Moonivy, APF&FV survey, December 31, 2006.
40. Anonymous, APF&FV survey, October 10, 2006.
41. Jennifer M., APF&FV survey, August 11, 2006.
42. Arwen Nightstar, "Coming of Age for a Young Woman Pt 3/3," Lady of the Earth: Rituals, n.d., http://www.ladyoftheearth.com/rituals/age-3.txt (accessed June 27, 2009).
43. Margy Levine Young and Rev. Jone Johnson Lewis, "Coming of Age: Deepening Ties within the Congregation," UUA News and Events, General Assembly 2006, http://archive.uua.org/ga/ga06/4010.html (accessed June 27, 2009).
44. Malakus, "Coming of Age Ritual Notes," Lady of the Earth, n.d., http://www.ladyoftheearth.com/rituals/coming-age.txt (accessed June 27, 2009).
45. Lady Damorea, "Coming of Age," Merry Meet Temple: Wiccan/Pagan Rites of Passage, n.d., http://merrymeettemple.org/wrop.html (accessed June 27, 2009).
46. Otter, "Menarche Ritual (The Binghamton Pagan Community)," Pagan Homeschool Page, n.d., http://web.archive.org/web/20080221062016/http://barbooch.homestead.com/menarche.html (accessed November 18, 2012).
47. Lady SpringWolf (Rev. Vickie Carey), "Coming of Age as a Pagan," *The New Statesman*, April 29, 2008, http://www.newstatesman.com/blogs/the-faith-column/2008/04/young-age-children-coming (accessed June 27, 2009).
48. Nightstar, "Coming of Age for a Young Woman Pt 3/3."
49. Ibid.
50. The full line reads, "And ye shall be free from slavery; and as a sign that ye are really free, ye shall be naked in your rites; and ye shall dance, sing, feast, make music and love, all in my praise." Valiente's "Charge of the Goddess" is among the most popular pieces of contemporary Pagan literature. Written in the 1950s (near the time Valiente left Gardner's coven to form her own), the charge is considered a "traditional" inspirational text by many modern Wiccans. The text takes the form of instructions or guidelines for worshippers in the voice of the Goddess, and it draws heavily on earlier texts by Charles Leland, Aleister Crowley, and Gerald Gardner. See Doreen Valiente, "The Charge of the Goddess," n.d., © John

Belham-Payne, http://doreenvaliente.org/2009/06/poem-the-charge-of-the-goddess/ (accessed November 18, 2012).
51. J.L., "Nudity/Paganism/Spiral Scouts," e-mail message to SpiralScouts Yahoo! Group, June 28, 2007.
52. D.M., "Re: Nudity/Paganism/Spiral Scouts," e-mail message to SpiralScouts Yahoo! Group, June 28, 2007.
53. O.H., "Re: Nudity/Paganism/Spiral Scouts," e-mail message to SpiralScouts Yahoo! Group, June 28, 2007.
54. Z. McAtee, "Re: Nudity/Paganism/Spiral Scouts," e-mail message to SpiralScouts Yahoo! Group, June 28, 2007.
55. Anthony "TJ" Smith, "Re: Nudity/Paganism/Spiral Scouts," e-mail message to SpiralScouts Yahoo! Group, June 28, 2007.
56. S., "Re: Nudity/Paganism/Spiral Scouts," e-mail message to SpiralScouts Yahoo! Group, June 28, 2007.
57. B., "Re: Nudity/Paganism/Spiral Scouts," e-mail message to SpiralScouts Yahoo! Group, June 28, 2007.
58. A temporary autonomous zone (TAZ) can be understood (in part) as a liminal space beyond the structures of normal societal control. See Hakim Bey, *T.A.Z.: The Temporary Autonomous Zone, Ontological Anarchy, Poetic Terrorism* (Brooklyn: Autonomedia, 1991).
59. CMA Beltane Festival, April 27, 2007.
60. CMA Beltane Festival, April 26, 2007.

NOTES TO THE CONCLUSION
1. Hervieu-Léger, *Religion as a Chain of Memory*.
2. Jonathan Z. Smith, *Imagining Religion: From Babylon to Jonestown* (Chicago: University of Chicago Press, 1982), xii.
3. *Dettmer v. Landon*, 799 F.2d 929. (4th Cir. 1986).
4. Catherine L. Albanese, "The Culture of Religious Combining: Reflections for the New American Millennium," *Cross Currents*, Spring/Summer 2000, 21–22.
5. Charles Taylor, *Varieties of Religion Today: William James Revisited* (Cambridge: Harvard University Press, 2002), 101.
6. In his review of Taylor's book, Robert Bellah notes that his own *Habits of the Heart* found personal religion similarly shaped by societal trends "when questions about individuality triggered some of the most stereotypical language we encountered: it seems that were all unique; were all different in exactly the same way." Robert N. Bellah, "New-Time Religion," review of *Varieties of Religion Today: William James Revisited*, by Charles Taylor, *Christian Century*, May 22–29, 2002, 25.
7. Charles Taylor, *The Ethics of Authenticity* (Cambridge: Harvard University Press, 1992), 40–41.
8. Pike, *Earthly Bodies, Magical Selves*, 223.
9. Robert A. Orsi, "A Crisis about the Theology of Children," *Harvard Divinity Bulletin* 30, no. 4 (2002): 29.

Selected Bibliography

Adler, Margot. *Drawing Down the Moon: Witches, Druids, Goddess-Worshippers, and Other Pagans in America Today*. Boston: Beacon Press, 1986.

Albanese, Catherine L. *Nature Religion in America: From the Algonkian Indians to the New Age*. Chicago: University of Chicago Press, 1990.

———. *A Republic of Mind and Spirit: A Cultural History of American Metaphysical Religion*. New Haven: Yale University Press, 2006.

Barner-Barry, Carol. *Contemporary Paganism: Minority Religions in a Majoritarian America*. New York: Palgrave Macmillan, 2005.

Berger, Helen A. *A Community of Witches: Contemporary Neo-Paganism and Witchcraft in the United States*. Columbia: University of South Carolina Press, 1999.

———. "The Routinization of Spontaneity." *Sociology of Religion* 56, no. 1 (1995): 49–61.

———. "Witches: The Next Generation." In *Children in New Religions*, edited by Susan J. Palmer and Charlotte E. Hardman, 11–28. New Brunswick: Rutgers University Press, 1999.

Berger, Helen A., Evan A. Leach, and Leigh S. Shaffer. *Voices from the Pagan Census: A National Survey of Witches and Neo-Pagans in the United States*. Columbia: University of South Carolina Press, 2003.

Braude, Ann. *Radical Spirits: Spiritualism and Women's Rights in Nineteenth-Century America*. 2nd ed. Bloomington: Indiana University Press, 2001.

Buckland, Raymond. *Wicca for Life: The Way of the Craft—From Birth to Summerland*. New York: Citadel Press/Kensington, 2001.

———. *Witchcraft from the Inside*. St. Paul: Llewellyn, 1971.

Butler, Jon. "Magic, Astrology, and the Early American Religious Heritage, 1600–1760." *American Historical Review* 84, no. 2 (1979): 317–346.

Carpenter, Dennis D. "Emergent Nature Spirituality: An Examination of the Major Spiritual Contours of the Contemporary Pagan Worldview." In *Magical Religion and Modern Witchcraft*, edited by James R. Lewis, 35–72. Albany: State University of New York Press, 1996.

Carroll, Lee, and Jan Tober. *The Indigo Children: The New Kids Have Arrived*. Carlsbad, CA: Hay House, 1999.

Clifton, Chas S. *Her Hidden Children: The Rise of Wicca and Paganism in America*. Lanham, MD: AltaMira Press, 2006.
Clifton, Chas S., and Graham Harvey, eds. *The Paganism Reader*. London: Routledge, 2004.
Cowan, Douglas E. *Cyberhenge: Modern Pagans on the Internet*. New York: Routledge, 2004.
Durkheim, Émile. *The Elementary Forms of the Religious Life*. London: G. Allen & Unwin, 1915.
Gallagher, Eugene V. *The New Religious Movements Experience in America*. Westport, CT: Greenwood Press, 2004.
Harvey, Graham. *Contemporary Paganism: Listening People, Speaking Earth*. New York: New York University Press, 1997.
Hervieu-Léger, Danièle. *Religion as a Chain of Memory*. New Brunswick: Rutgers University Press, 2000.
Higonnet, Anne. *Pictures of Innocence: The History and Crisis of Ideal Childhood*. New York: Thames and Hudson, 1998.
Hutton, Ronald. "Paganism and Polemic: The Debate over the Origins of Modern Pagan Witchcraft." *Folklore* 111, no. 1 (2000): 103–117.
——. *The Triumph of the Moon: A History of Modern Pagan Witchcraft*. Oxford: Oxford University Press, 1999.
Jenkins, Henry, ed. *The Children's Culture Reader*. New York: New York University Press, 1998.
Kerr, Howard H., and Charles L. Crow, eds. *The Occult in America: New Historical Perspectives*. Urbana: University of Illinois Press, 1983.
Kincaid, James R. *Child-Loving: The Erotic Child and Victorian Culture*. New York: Routledge, 1994.
Madden, Kristen. *Pagan Parenting: Spiritual, Magical, and Emotional Development of the Child*. Niceville, FL: Spilled Candy Publications, 2004.
Melton, J. Gordon. *The Encyclopedia of American Religions*. Wilmington, NC: McGrath, 1978.
Moore, R. Laurence. *Religious Outsiders and the Making of Americans*. New York: Oxford University Press, 1986.
Orsi, Robert A. *Between Heaven and Earth: The Religious Worlds People Make and the Scholars Who Study Them*. Princeton: Princeton University Press, 2004.
——. "A Crisis about the Theology of Children." *Harvard Divinity Bulletin* 30, no. 4 (2002): 29.
Palmer, Susan J., and Charlotte Hardman, eds. *Children in New Religions*. New Brunswick: Rutgers University Press, 1999.
Pearson, Joanne, Richard H. Roberts, and Geoffrey Samuel, eds. *Nature Religion Today: Paganism in the Modern World*. Edinburgh: Edinburgh University Press, 1998.
Pike, Sarah M. *Earthly Bodies, Magical Selves: Contemporary Pagans and the Search for Community*. Berkeley: University of California Press, 2001.

———. *New Age and Neopagan Religions in America.* New York: Columbia University Press, 2004.
Purkiss, Diane. *The Witch in History: Early Modern and Twentieth-Century Representations.* London: Routledge, 1996.
Rabinovitch, Shelley, and James Lewis, eds. *The Encyclopedia of Modern Witchcraft and Neo-Paganism.* New York: Citadel Press, 2002.
Ridgely, Susan B. *When I Was a Child: Children's Interpretations of First Communion.* Chapel Hill: University of North Carolina Press, 2005.
Shuck, Glenn Wm. "The Myth of the Burning Times and the Politics of Resistance in Contemporary American Wicca." *Journal of Religion and Society* 2 (2000): 1–9.
Smith, Jonathan Z. *Imagining Religion: From Babylon to Jonestown.* Chicago: University of Chicago Press, 1982.
Taylor, Charles. *Varieties of Religion Today: William James Revisited.* Cambridge: Harvard University Press, 2002.
Tumber, Catherine. *American Feminism and the Birth of New Age Spirituality: Searching for the Higher Self, 1875–1915.* Lanham, MD: Rowman & Littlefield, 2002.
Urban, Hugh B. *Magia Sexualis: Sex, Magic, and Liberation in Modern Western Esotericism.* Berkeley: University of California Press, 2006.
Warner, Judith. *Perfect Madness: Motherhood in the Age of Anxiety.* New York: Riverhead Books, 2005.
York, Michael. *Pagan Theology: Paganism as a World Religion.* New York: New York University Press, 2003.

Index

activism. *See* politics
Adler, Margot, 33, 149, 200n21
adolescents: converting to Paganism, 33, 63, 164, 170; festivals and, 178, 179, 180; Indigo children, 65–66; leaving Paganism, 21, 28, 167; rites of passage and, 171–172, 174, 180; rituals and, 23, 171–172, 174; second-generation Pagan, 167; SpiralScouts and, 28; survey of, 19, 193–195. *See also* PathFinders; rituals
adulthood: expectations of, 3, 61, 71, 72, 173, 180, 183; Pagan constructions of, 185, 186; rejection of, 71, 72, 87, 185; religious community and, 156, 159; retaining childlike aspects in, 84, 87, 88, 174, 185. *See also* ambivalence
affirmations, positive, 36, 39, 40, 41, 106
agnosticism, 29, 49, 63, 133, 167, 169
Aisling: on Christians, 115–116; Pagan carols, 114–115, 151; "toddler tools" in ritual, 89–91, 93, 94; Wiccaning of, 153–155, 160, 161
Albanese, Catherine L., 30, 184
altars, 157; children and, 101, 153, 160; eclecticism of, 46, 47, 77
ambivalence: toward adulthood, 87–88, 183, 186; toward American culture, 8, 11, 23, 116, 129, 152, 183; toward childhood, 88, 94, 112, 113, 178, 182, 186; toward history, 26, 52; toward life-cycle rituals, 24, 174; toward magic, 4–5, 83; toward organization (*see* organization); toward religion, 22, 24, 156, 160
American Pagan Families & Family Values survey (APF&FV), 18–20, 189–191
American Religious Identification Survey (ARIS), 3–4, 197n1
amnesia. *See* memory
ancestors, 77, 93, 122, 124
animals, 13, 14, 17, 83, 109, 181; communication with, 60, 73, 83; spirituality of, 95, 122
antimodernism, 34. *See also* premodernism
anxiety: religious, 26, 53, 94, 97, 169, 182; sexual, 178
Apollo (god), 104, 154, 155
appropriation, 27, 49, 52, 86, 94, 212n22
Aquarian Tabernacle Church (ATC), 125–126, 129, 137
archaeomythology, 33. *See also* mythology
Artemis (goddess), 77, 154, 155
astrology, 46, 59, 159
Atashih, 8, 45–46, 145, 151; on parenting, 60, 85; on Wicca, 46, 47, 55, 94, 199n2
atheism, 29, 89, 128, 132, 133
Attention Deficit Hyperactivity Disorder (ADHD), 64–65, 147, 207n23
authenticity: of religion, 7, 34, 53, 99, 205n85; of the self, 74, 184, 185, 208n41

authority: opposition toward, 38, 64, 66, 85–88, 125; parental, 85, 86, 162; religious, 44, 62, 164; spiritual, 185. *See also* clergy, Pagan
autism, 65, 147
autonomy, 140, 185

baby blessing ceremonies. *See* rituals
Bahnisch, Mark, 204n73
baptism, Christian, 23, 43, 49, 156, 157, 162, 171
Baptist churches, 72, 76, 77, 121, 144. *See also* Christianity; Protestantism
Barner-Barry, Carol, 142
Barrie, J. M., 69, 81
Beall, Alyssa, 208n34
Becktarianism, 49, 169. *See also* Bellah, Robert
Beliefnet, xii, 18, 65
Bellah, Robert, 49–50, 203n63, 218n6
Beltane. *See* rituals
Berger, Helen, 4, 59, 94–95, 100, 105, 205n91, 215n59
Blessed Bee, The: A Pagan Family Newsletter, 211n19
blessings: ceremonies for children (*see* Wiccanings); everyday, 14, 16, 40, 106, 176. *See also* rituals
bodies: attitudes toward, 30, 37, 42, 174, 176; children's, 112, 178
Bonewits, Isaac, 200n21
books: introduction to Paganism through, 33, 52, 73, 75, 78–79, 80–81, 89; Pagans' love of, 21, 31, 79–81, 144; read by Pagan parents, 59, 79, 106; read to/by Pagan children, 31, 79, 91, 115
Boy Scouts of America: comparisons with SpiralScouts, 1, 29, 132, 134–135, 137; Paganism and, 132–133; values, 132–133, 213n27, 213n31, 213n33
Braude, Ann, 37–38
broom, 40, 41, 212n21

"broom closet," 21, 43, 141. *See also* persecution
Buckland, Raymond and Rosemary, 5, 33, 119, 165
Budapest, Zsuzsanna, 200n21, 211n24
Buddhism, 47, 48, 49, 74, 163, 167, 170, 213n27
Burning Times, The, 53–55, 205n85

Callahan, Janet, 127–128, 139
Calvin and Hobbes, 8, 79
camping: activities, 86, 109, 111, 181; campfires, 27, 46, 55, 59; campsites, 45, 178; children and, 18, 46, 85, 176, 179; festivals, 145, 176, 177; SpiralScouts and, 30, 41, 138
candles: alternatives to, 89, 90, 91; in ritual, 1, 28–29, 110, 153, 160
Carolyn, 1–2
Carr-Gomm, Philip, 48
Carroll, Lee, 63
cars, magic in, 83, 107
Casebolt, James, 148
Catholicism, 11, 17; acceptance of, 48, 77, 147, 166; rejection of, 74–75, 80. *See also* Christianity
Cauldron: A Pagan Forum (website), xii, 18
Celebrate Samhain, 120–121, 134, 212n8
Celestine Prophecy, The, 36
Census, Pagan, 4. *See also* Berger, Helen
chants, 36, 53, 54, 91, 100, 103, 215n70; "Goddess chant," 160–161; "Hoof and Horn," 109, 158, 211n24
Charge of the Goddess, 174, 179, 217n50
Cherry Hill Seminary, 213n25
child abuse, 159, 174
childhood: adults' disappointment with religion in, 45, 57, 73–77, 91, 96, 145, 171; construction of, 3, 57, 79, 81, 113, 157, 186, 187; idealization of, 22, 57, 71, 72, 81, 133, 182, 183; innocence (see innocence, childhood); memories

of, 61, 66, 73, 79, 129, 134, 180; Pagan children's experiences of, 9, 12, 26, 86, 87, 88, 92–93, 112–113, 124; Pagan understandings of, 9, 24, 88, 118, 120, 133, 159, 173–174; religion, 91, 97, 151, 156, 162, 171, 172, 187; spirituality in, 3, 60, 61, 69, 84, 113. *See also* narratives, spiritual; spirituality

childhood stories. *See* narratives, spiritual

childlike wonder, 3, 58, 62, 63, 72, 73, 81, 88, 182

children, 59–61, 87; leaving Paganism, 205n6; relationships with adults, 23, 32, 71, 72, 85–87, 88, 91, 113, 145, 183; second-generation Pagan, 4, 8, 45, 86–87, 116, 155–156, 193–195. *See also* spirituality of children

choice: children and, 28, 45, 49, 96, 118, 162, 170, 171, 180; reincarnation and, 158, 159; religious value of, 6, 13, 22, 97, 98, 162; spirituality and, 96, 97, 114–115, 118, 156–162, 166–171; tradition and, 180; Wiccanings and, 162. *See also* tradition

Christianity: children's understandings of, 150, 151; comparisons with Paganism, 115–116, 146–147, 156, 161, 162, 171, 213n25; family of origin and, 74, 75, 76, 78, 89, 151; interactions with Paganism, 68, 121, 128; Paganism combined with, 46, 83, 122, 201n26; Pagan conversion to, 42, 43, 44, 45, 128, 168, 201n25, 203n48; persecution by, 54, 55, 61, 73, 80, 116, 142; rejection of, 137, 150–151, 166, 170, 171, 206n14; resistance to, 33, 54, 132. *See also* Catholicism; conversion; narratives, spiritual; persecution; *Protestant denominations*

circle: as symbol, 105, 107, 149, 159; casting by adults and children together, 90–91, 92, 93, 101, 102–103–104, 154; casting by children, 90–91, 92, 93, 109, 111–112;

children and energy in, 91, 94, 95–96, 98–99, 103, 112. *See also* energy

clergy, Pagan: authority of, 42, 125, 137, 201n25; lack of paid, 51, 125, 126, 137; in ritual, 95, 157, 159, 171, 174

Clifton, Chas, 30

clothing, adults', 71, 112, 137, 175, 179, 214n36

clothing, children's: clothing-optional festivals, 176, 178, 179; costumes, 86, 110, 124, 138; in SpiralScouts, 134, 135, 137; Pagan, 142. *See also* nudity; uniforms

community service, 29, 70–71, 120, 138

continuity, religious. *See* tradition

conversion: from Paganism as adults, 42, 43, 44, 128, 165, 201n25; from Paganism as children, 45, 168, 203n48; resisting, 33; to Paganism, 63, 77, 128, 156, 162, 164, 170

costumes. *See* clothing, adults'; clothing, children's

Council of Magickal Arts (CMA), 70–71, 109–113, 175–177; as clothing-optional space (*see* nudity); children's area (*see* Fairy Mound); labyrinth (*see* labyrinth); Revel Fire (*see* fire)

counterculture, Paganism and, 7, 26, 119

Coven of the Fertile Earth, 159

Covenant of Unitarian Universalist Pagans (CUUPS), 148, 149. *See also* Unitarian Universalism

Cowan, Douglas, 19, 208n41

crafts (activities), 31, 35–36, 106, 121, 127, 151, 181

Cricket, 21, 46, 59–60, 110, 178–179

Crowley, Aleister, 12, 34, 60, 206n11, 206n16, 217n50

crystals, 36, 37, 39, 46, 47, 60; rose quartz, 109, 154

Crystal Children. *See* Indigo Children

cultural borrowing. *See* appropriation

custody, child, 142

Daniel T., 45, 57
Davis, Pierre C. "Pete Pathfinder," 125–126, 137, 143
Dawn, 147
Dawson, Lorne, 69
Deanna, 8, 21, 110–112, 151
death, 86, 113, 158, 216n3. *See also* reincarnation
decentralization, 9, 17, 21, 25, 51, 120
deities: belief in, 5, 6, 37, 40, 58, 140, 144, 150, 163, 217n50; invoking, 90, 104, 154–155, 157, 160; names of, 20, 160, 204n70; protection of, 83, 156, 157; representations of, 47, 90, 122, 151, 169, 174, 179, 202n45, 210n3; role of, 15, 41, 211n24. *See also names of specific gods and goddesses*
Derek, 2–3
Dettmer v. Landon, 38
Diagnostic and Statistical Manual of Medical Disorders (DSM), 207n23
Discordianism, 50–52, 69, 79, 204n70, 204n72
disenchantment, 50, 61, 206n14
divination, 46, 151
Dr. Phil, 36
dragons, 83, 102
Druids, 48
Dungeons & Dragons, 80
Durkheim, Emile, 5–6, 7, 118, 184

Earth First!, 30
Earth-based religion, 1, 6, 27, 29, 31–32, 128
eclecticism, 27–32; as appropriation, 27; as self-identification, 7, 14, 27, 29, 36, 41, 46–50, 59, 74, 75, 163; of religious belief, 37, 43, 125, 149; of religious practice, 45, 49, 52, 169, 210n3; as value, 42, 50, 51, 52, 118. *See also* syncretism
Egbert, Suzanne "Cecylyna Dewr," 146
Eisler, Riane T., 199n3, 200n21
elements, 28, 46, 90, 104, 155, 157
enchantment, 9, 33, 60, 61, 62, 82, 106, 108

Encyclopedia of American Religions, 51
energy: for change, 40, 83, 84, 89; in ritual, 61–62, 64–65, 95, 96, 99, 111, 112; raising, 91, 93, 94, 95, 103, 160–161. *See also* psychic abilities
entitlement, 64, 65
environmentalism, 6, 25, 29–30, 31
Eoin, 153–155, 161
Erin: and SpiralScouts, 17, 138; on children's spirituality, 59; on Paganism, 89, 92, 114–116, 151–152; "toddler tools" in ritual, 90–91, 93, 100; Wiccaning, 153–156, 157, 158, 160. *See also* toddler tools
Eris, 51, 204n70
ethnography: children and, 17, 21, 22, 179; Paganism and, 17, 18, 19, 21, 41, 73, 79, 185; virtual, 19
evolution, spiritual, 63, 64, 65, 66, 67, 68, 159

fairies: belief in, 83, 181; contact with, 70–71, 73; houses, 181, 182
Fairy Mound, 70–71, 85–87, 179. *See also* Council of Magickal Arts (CMA)
family: importance of, 88, 104–105, 122, 185, 186; interreligious, 48, 49, 63, 89, 142; of origin, 73, 74, 77, 78, 98, 141, 143, 145; religion and, 9, 45, 72–73, 108, 116, 124, 129, 141; rituals, 91–93, 95, 99, 106, 107, 111, 140; varieties of, 8, 11, 13, 47, 50, 127–128. *See also* tradition; values, Pagan
fantasy: childhood and, 3, 58, 59, 70, 83; literature, 79, 80; Paganism and, 9, 71, 73, 83, 88, 183
feminism, 6, 9, 12, 33, 78, 119, 148–149
festivals, 10, 18, 20–22, 179, 199n25, 211n18. *See also* Council of Magickal Arts
fire: campfire, 55, 135, 138; in ritual, 28, 90, 104, 212n21; Revel, 176, 178, 179. *See also* Council of Magickal Arts
First Amendment, 38, 184

First Church of Wicca (FCOW): children and, 39, 45, 95, 101–102, 166; conversion of, 41–45, 201n26, 201n29; New Thought and, 35–37, 38, 41; rituals, 40, 160–161. *See also* Hovey, Kendra Vaughan; Hovey, Timothy; Sea Witches
Fisher, Elisabeth, 148
freedom: ethic of, 6, 74, 82, 97, 125, 139, 186; religious, 7, 22, 26, 28, 38, 45, 96, 171; sexual, 179
Freya, 45, 55, 145, 176; on spirituality, 46, 59–60, 110, 156
fundamentalism, 68, 145, 166, 171

Gage, Matilda Joslyn, 33–34
Galadriel, Lady, 62, 206n16
Gallagher, Eugene V., 165
Gardner, Gerald, 5, 12, 34, 198n6, 198n7, 217n50. *See also* Wicca
Gardnerian Wicca. *See* Wicca, Gardnerian
Gatrall, Cory Ellen, 199n20
Gawain, 46
gender: equality in Paganism, 12–13, 37, 38, 166, 185; SpiralScouts and, 127, 132, 213n33
genealogies, 56, 186
Gerrior, Jess, 20; ritual and children, 30–31, 98–99, 106–107, 147–148; SpiralScouts, 17, 27–29, 102–105, 121–124, 131, 134–135; witches, 143–144. *See also* Silverling Circle
Gimbutas, Marija, 33, 199n3
Girl Scouts, 134, 135, 138, 213n33
God (Christian): Boy Scouts of America and, 133; conversion to Christianity and, 42, 168; Pagan conflicts with, 75, 77, 80; Paganism and, 104, 121, 150
Goddess-mother. *See* Goddess-parents
Goddess-parents, 157, 161, 162
God-father. *See* Goddess-parents
Godparents. *See* Goddess-parents

grandparents, 68, 75, 77, 78, 145, 146
Graves, Robert, 79
Great Rite, 44, 94, 179, 202n45, 210n3
Green Wicca, 6, 25, 27–30, 31, 32, 39
guardianship, 85, 87

handfasting. *See* rituals
Harvey, Graham, 30
Hermetic Order of the Golden Dawn, 34, 38
Hervieu-Léger, Danièle, 56, 182, 186
high priest. *See* clergy, Pagan
high priestess. *See* clergy, Pagan
Higonnet, Anne, 58
Hinduism, 46–47, 78, 166
historicizing: identity and, 26, 53–54, 186; legitimation and, *(see* legitimation); religion and, 33, 38, 52, 53–56, 204n78, 204n79
history: memory and, 56, 182, 186; multiple views of Pagan, 5, 25–27, 50; mythologized, 3, 33, 52, 54, 55–56, 204n75, 204n78; prehistoric religion and, 32, 33, 34, 35; roots of Paganism, 6, 25, 35, 37–38, 58, 119, 197n5, 201n23. *See also* historicizing; legitimation
homeschooling. *See* school
Hovey, Kendra Vaughan: on children's spirituality, 95, 101, 102, 166; conversion of, 41–43, 45, 201n26, 203n48; criticism of Wicca, 44, 202n46; philosophy, 39–41; public image, 36, 43, 201n25; religious services, 160–161; SpiralScouts and, 135, 142–143, 150. *See also* First Church of Wicca; metaphysics; Sea Witches; "Witches Next Door, The"
Hovey, Timothy, 36–41, 166, 203n48. *See also* First Church of Wicca; Hovey, Kendra Vaughan; Sea Witches
humanure, 31, 200
Hutton, Ronald, 6, 33, 54–55, 58, 119–120, 201n23

identity: adulthood and, 67, 78, 85, 174; children's, 159, 167; construction of, 150, 185, 208n41; oppositional, 7, 118, 142, 143, 151; religious, 26, 27, 54, 67, 88, 118, 167, 183

idioms, religious, 57, 149, 186

imagination, religious: constructed in relationship, 3, 8, 57, 87, 88, 91, 183; encouragement of, 83, 84, 107, 150, 154, 168; importance in Paganism, 9, 26, 56, 106, 107, 139, 156, 167, 182, 184, 185; literature and, 79; of adults, 72, 73, 90, 187; of children, 5, 9, 63, 71, 82, 84, 108, 113, 149, 168–169, 183. *See also* books

improvisation: by adults, 52, 89–91, 92, 93; by children, 29, 93, 106, 108, 109, 110–111, 112, 113; in Paganism, 4, 28, 51, 99, 100, 118, 152

incense, 90, 94, 100, 110

indigenous religion, Paganism as, 6, 7, 25–27, 46, 61, 125, 215n1. *See also* reconstruction

Indigo Children, 63–68, 159, 208n34, 208n35

individualism: ethics and, 8, 11, 44; Paganism and, 17, 43, 49–50, 118, 119, 129, 137, 149, 156, 165, 184, 185; religious belief and, 6, 8, 12, 14, 218n6; religious practice and, 4, 51, 52; spiritual quest and, 99, 164, 167, 169; value of, 13, 14, 38, 79, 131, 138, 140

indoctrination, fear of: by parents, 96–97, 162; by SpiralScouts, 127, 129; religion and, 158, 171

innocence, childhood, 22–23, 58, 59, 61, 62, 72, 84, 87, 178, 179, 182

insects, 86, 109–110

International Society for Krishna Consciousness (ISKCON), 205n6

Internet: as source of information on Paganism, 11, 52, 114, 125–126, 172, 216n6; community and, 36, 208n34;

ethnography and, 18–20; Pagan activity on, 42, 65, 98, 146, 157

irony, 2, 51, 52, 86, 150, 161

Islam, 132, 163, 166, 170, 213n27

Jenkins, Henry, 58

Jessie, 128–129, 165–166

Jesus, 42, 43, 78, 138, 203n48; and Paganism, 150, 151, 163

Judaism, 53, 78, 132, 183–184, 213n27; family of origin and, 48, 61, 74, 75; Paganism and, 48, 128, 170

Kabbalah, 46, 47, 75

karma, 113, 159

Kincaid, James R., 58

Kipling, Rudyard, 53

kitchen witch, 47, 78

Krider, Dylan Otto, 67–68

Kunzman, Robert, 146

labyrinth, 109–112. *See also* Council of Magickal Arts (CMA)

Law of Return. *See* Threefold Law

legitimation: conflicts regarding, 45, 51, 69, 118, 131, 149; desire for, 23, 126, 129, 140, 185, 215n59; historicizing and, 33, 34, 52, 53, 55, 173, 186, 206n16; successive generations and, 4, 99, 185

Leland, Charles, 5, 198n6, 217n50

Lewis, C. S., 70

liminality, 172, 218

Living Waters Community of Hope, 42, 201n26, 201n29, 202n41, 203n48

longitudinal studies of Pagan children, lack of, 4, 53, 87, 216

Lothlorien, 83

Lovecraft, H. P., 79

Madden, Kristen, 61–62, 98

Maggie, 16

magic: childhood and, 3, 22, 23, 59, 60, 61, 63, 71, 73, 81, 86, 186; children and, 1,

60, 61, 62, 82–84, 85, 98, 111; "Church of," 5, 7, 118; ethics of, 83; names (*see* names); Paganism and, 4–5, 23, 30, 33, 46, 73, 76, 82–84, 95, 107, 113, 144, 183, 208n41; prayer and, 39–40, 83; rituals and, 40, 114; spelled magick, 82, 206n11; traditions of, 25, 26, 34, 38, 77
Magic Chef, 2
manners, 65, 71
marginalization, 9, 19, 29, 55, 116, 117, 151
matriarchal prehistory, myth of, 25, 33–34, 200n21
McArthur, Margie, 60
McDannell, Colleen, 146
Mechling, Jay, 213n31
Melton, J. Gordon, 51, 204n72
memory: childhood and, 72, 73, 74–75, 79, 134–135, 186; children and, 2, 92, 105; forgetting and, 56, 186; of events, 89–90, 98–99, 140, 180; Pagan history and(*see* history); religion and, 90, 93, 205n91; religion as chain of, 56, 182, 186; spiritual history and, 56, 186. *See also* Hervieu-Leger, Daniele; history; childhood; narratives; spirituality
menarche. *See* rituals
metaphysics, 30, 82, 201n30; First Church of Wicca and, 27, 36–40, 41, 43, 44–45, 102, 201n25. *See also* First Church of Wicca
Mike, 71, 85, 86, 87
Mind Cure movement, 27, 36
ministry. *See* clergy, Pagan
Moore, R. Laurence, 7–8, 116–117. *See also* religious outsiderhood
morality: children and, 72, 82, 86, 129, 138, 141, 146, 157, 164, 168, 170, 183, 186; collective, 5, 7, 184; critiques of Pagan, 42, 44, 69, 174, 185; history and, 26, 55; metaphysics and, 37–38; Pagan, 8, 9, 44, 139, 156, 167, 185; religion and, 15, 117, 133, 201n26; systematized, 11–12, 140, 199n20

Mormonism, 77, 166; as new religious movement, 53, 116, 117–118, 168; compared with Paganism, 117, 204n79
Murray, Margaret A., 5, 198n6
mystery traditions: learning from, 47, 171; Paganism as, 25, 94, 149, 199n2
mythology: other cultures, 46, 77, 79, 128, 142; Pagan history and, 33, 34, 38, 54, 55, 200n21, 204n73, 205n85, 215n11; Pagan religion and, 3, 26, 27, 31, 85, 94, 118

names: magical, 20, 21, 46, 52, 155, 156, 157, 165, 208n41; methodology and, 20, 21, 189, 191, 193–195; power of, 20, 21, 49, 60, 62, 160
Narnia, 83
narratives, spiritual: books, importance of, 73, 75, 79, 80, 81; Paganism as culmination of quest, 76, 77, 78, 89; rejection of childhood religion, 73, 74, 75–76, 80, 89, 134, 145, 151; spiritual precocity, 76, 77, 78. *See also* childhood; conversion; family
Native American religions, 32, 46, 47, 78, 79, 128, 129
nature: alignment with, 12, 13, 31, 32, 48, 54, 84, 125, 139, 147, 148, 149; childhood and, 60, 69, 70, 73; sacredness of, 6, 30, 32, 33, 34, 37, 58, 91, 120, 122, 147, 148
nature religion, 25, 27, 30, 199n1
Neopaganism. *See* Paganism
New Age: relationship to Paganism, 22, 38, 125, 207n19; shared beliefs with Paganism, 36, 37, 63, 66, 81, 208n34
new religious movements: American religions and, 116, 118, 143, 149, 185; Paganism as, 4, 9, 17, 51, 186; role of children in, 169, 185, 205n6, 216n19; socialization of children in, 23, 53, 94, 164, 168
New Thought, 35–41, 43, 125, 201n30
New Wiccan Book of the Law, A. See Galadriel, Lady

nineteenth-century religious movements, 7, 36, 149–150, 201n30. *See also* Mind Cure movement; New Thought
Norse Paganism, 46, 47
nostalgia: for childhood, 61, 182; for premodern past, 34, 51, 58. *See also* premodernism
nudity: children and, 94, 174, 175, 179; festivals and, 175, 176–177, 178, 179; rituals and, 94, 174, 175, 217n50

O'Gaea, Ashleen, 97, 166–167
"Old Religion," 33, 34, 35, 129, 165, 205n91
"Oliver" (Spencer), 1–3
Oppositional Defiant Disorder (ODD), 64
oppositional identity. *See* identity
Ordo Templi Orientis, 38
organization: ambivalence toward, 120, 129, 130–132, 138, 149, 150; attempts at, 148, 212n15; SpiralScouts as, 102, 124–126, 127, 129. *See also* SpiralScouts
Orsi, Robert A., 9, 187
Ox-Cart Man, The, 91, 210n2

paedomorphism, 81–82
Pagan carols, 114–115, 138, 151, 215n70
Pagan family values. *See* values, Pagan
Paganing. *See* rituals
Paganism: as minority religion, 3, 9, 14, 29, 102, 127, 129, 130, 131, 132, 142; demographics 3–4, 51, 63, 197n1. *See also* history; rituals
Pagan Pride Day, 20, 44, 202n46
Palmer, Susan, 9, 198n13
parades, 38, 106
parenting: attachment, 11; ideals of, 184, 185; in the United States, 3, 118, 182, 186, 187; Pagan views of, 57, 61–62; religious practice and, 98, 99; religious values and, 26, 56, 67–68, 72–73, 82, 86, 97, 120
PathFinders, 28, 200n5

persecution: and child custody (*see* custody, child); by Christianity, 53–54, 55; by family of origin, 73, 74, 145; fears of, 21, 101, 141, 142; resistance to, 20, 55
Pike, Sarah M.: on childhood, 74, 79; on festivals, 7, 149–150; on New Age, 37, 207n19; on Paganism, 63, 73, 184–185, 205n85, 206n14
politics: activism, 30, 119; alignment with history, 56; conservative roots of American Paganism, 34, 119; distrust of government, 146, 147; "family values" and, 12; liberal views among Pagans, 7, 37, 118, 140
polyamory, 11, 198n16, 212n21
postmodernism, 50–53, 55, 184, 204n74, 204n75, 212n22
prayer, 39–40, 47, 83, 106,107
pregnancy, 61–62, 153
premodernism, 31, 32–35, 51, 58, 173, 180. *See also* nostalgia
Principia Discordia, 51, 79
proselytization, 73, 97, 163, 170
Protestantism, 89, 184; conversion from Paganism to, 44, 167, 168; family of origin and, 72, 76, 77, 144–145; interactions with Paganism, 49, 63, 121, 128. *See also* Christianity
pseudonyms, 20, 21. *See also* names
psychic abilities: among adults, 77; among children, 59, 60, 61–62, 206n12; Indigo Children and, 63, 64, 66, 67
public school. *See* school
Purkiss, Diane, 54–55

Quakers, 35, 128
quest religion, Paganism as, 22, 42, 45, 99, 164, 168

Ranck, Shirley, 148
Raven, 8, 21, 83, 109, 110, 140; Wiccaning of, 159–162, 171
Reclaiming Collective, 30, 48

reconstruction: of childhood, 3, 73, 171, 186; of indigenous religion, 6, 25, 26, 32–33, 125, 207n19
reconstructionist, 7, 128, 135
recycling, 13, 30, 32, 71, 107
reincarnation, 59, 86, 158, 159, 211n24, 216n3
re-enchantment. *See* enchantment
religious choice. *See* choice
religious instruction: ambivalence toward, 94, 164; by parents, 13–15, 35, 53, 141, 144, 146, 147, 163; lack of, 22, 52, 162, 163, 165, 169; modeling by adults, 71, 107, 140; SpiralScouts and, 31, 122–124, 138, 139, 143, 149; Unitarian Universalism and, 148, 149. *See also* ambivalence; indoctrination, fear of; rituals
religious outsiderhood, 7–8, 116–117, 142, 205n6
responsibility: adults and, 23, 71, 85, 87, 88, 97, 157, 159, 163, 180; children and, 17, 159, 162, 163, 164, 171; value of, 10, 11, 13, 15, 106, 138, 168
Ridgely, Susan, 17, 58
rites of passage. *See* rituals
ritual fluency, children's, 12, 87, 108, 109–113, 167
rituals, 89–113, 102–106, 212n21; Beltane, 59, 96, 145, 151, 177–178, 199n25; children's exclusion from, 23, 94–95, 96, 174; children's improvisation of, 112–113; children's participation debated, 23, 93–97; children's participation in, 40, 89–91, 92–93, 98, 99, 100–101, 102–106, 154–155, 160–161; coming-of-age, 155–156, 171–174; handfastings, 128, 212n21; nudity and (*see* nudity); purpose of, 174, 180; rites of passage, 180; Samhain, 20, 93, 96, 106, 120–121, 134, 199n25; tools, 84, 89, 90, 94, 95, 109, 114, 154, 202n45, 210n3; Yule, 102–105, 106, 114, 129, 134, 150, 211n18. *See also* toddler tools; Wiccanings

Rochford, E. Burke, 205n6, 216n19
Romanticism: childhood and, 22, 57–58, 180, 182; Paganism and, 26, 30, 34, 58, 119
Roof, Wade Clark, 164
routinization, 4, 8
Ryan, 17, 28, 29, 98–99, 105, 123, 124, 136, 144

sabbats, 6, 22, 101, 106, 120. *See also* rituals
Saining, 215n1. *See also* rituals
Samhain. *See* rituals
Satanism, accusations of. *See* persecution
school: homeschooling, 98, 116, 146–147, 167, 214n54; public, 11, 14, 23, 133, 141, 146–147, 150; unschooling, 116, 146, 214n54
science, relationship to Paganism, 31, 34, 49, 84, 206n11
scourging, 94, 210n3
Sea Witches, 11, 18, 35–36, 39, 41, 135, 142–143
Seacoast Dragon Riders, 18
Secret, The (book), 36
Selene, 46, 47, 140, 145
sexuality: adult, 58, 171, 175, 177, 179, 180; children and, 174, 178, 179; ethics and, 78, 118, 172, 174, 185, 198n16; ritual and, 96, 179, 199n21, 202n45, 210n3
shamanism, 128, 163
Sheilaism, 49, 203n63
Shipps, Jan, 53, 204n79
Shuck, Glenn W., 55, 56
silence, of children in ritual, 103, 104, 105, 123, 124, 160
Silver Sapling circle, 18, 128–129
Silverling Circle, 18, 22, 27–32, 98, 114, 138, 139; meetings, 16–17, 27–29, 122–123, 181; rituals, 102–106. *See also* Gerrior, Jess
skyclad. *See* nudity
Smith, Jonathan Z., 183–184
socialization, 164, 165, 168

Society for Creative Anachronism (SCA), 135, 214n36
solitary Paganism, 6; children and, 89, 141, 147–148, 161; rituals and, 100–101, 119, 157, 161
solstice, 6, 103–104, 106, 114, 181
songs: 54–55, 86, 91, 102, 103, 138, 144. *See also* chants; Pagan carols
Spiral Bear hearth, 11, 18
Spiral Winds coven, 18, 20, 22, 45–47, 55, 59, 85
SpiralScouts, 95–96, 120–140, 174; administration, 1, 126, 127, 135, 137, 175, 212n19; pledges, 1; 17, 121, 122, 139; policies, 127, 129, 131, 132, 135–137, 139, 174–175; structure, 28, 120, 200n5, 212n19. *See also* Sea Witches; Silverling Circle
spiritual narratives. *See* narratives, spiritual
Spiritualism, 7, 26, 37, 149–150
spirituality of children: innate, 59, 60, 61, 84, 87, 95, 100; purer than adults, 62, 63–68, 86, 133, 158, 187, 205n6; *See also* Indigo Children; "wise child" motif
Starhawk, 30, 119–120, 199n3
Stark, Rodney, 169
Stephen, 21, 46, 55, 60, 151, 179
superficiality, accusations of, 49, 69, 169, 184, 210n42
syncretism: by individual Pagans, 29, 43, 46, 47, 48, 49, 50, 74; in Paganism, 52, 128, 163, 212n22

tantrums, 1–2, 67
Tappe, Nancy Ann, 63, 64
Taylor, Charles, 184
Tedder, Lorna, 66
teenagers. *See* adolescents
temporary autonomous zone, 176, 218n58
Threefold Law, 7, 11–12
Tober, Jan, 63–64
toddler tools, 89–90, 91–92, 93, 100, 151
tolerance: as central value, 6, 13–14, 15, 120, 156, 185; of other religions, 1, 53, 128, 170. *See also* values, Pagan
tradition: in families, 10, 22, 74, 96, 99, 100, 156, 164, 167, 170; in Paganism, 6, 35, 45, 56, 164, 165, 168, 169, 180, 185, 186; synthesizing (*see* syncretism)
Tumber, Catherine, 38
Turner, Victor, 172

uniforms, 43, 124, 129, 132, 134–137
Unitarian Universalism, 80, 128, 172, 200n21, 215n59; and Paganism, 149; and SpiralScouts, 148–149
unschooling. *See* school
Utopia, 34, 205n91, 207n19

Valiente, Doreen, 33, 174, 179, 217n50
values, Pagan: central, 42, 96, 120, 156; childhood and, 69, 183; children and, 94, 99, 102, 106, 113, 164, 166, 168, 172; examples of, 13, 14, 15, 82; implications of, 88, 167, 185; "Pagan family values," 10, 12, 13, 14, 120, 127, 185; SpiralScouts and, 129, 138, 139, 149; "traditional" values and, 11, 12, 117–118, 146–147. *See also* choice; freedom; imagination, religious; individualism; tolerance
virtue, 117, 178
visualization, 36, 39, 41, 91. *See also* New Age; New Thought

Warner, Judith, 81
Weber, Max, 4–5
Whedon, Sarah, 208n34
Wheel of the Year, 6, 62, 120, 158, 199n25
When the Root Children Wake Up, 91, 210n2
Wicca: demographics, 4; distinct from Paganism, 6, 7, 11–12, 14, 48, 165, 197n1,

199n2, 200n21, 206n16; history and myth of, 5, 6, 33–34, 200n21
Wicca, Gardnerian, 5, 6, 7, 12, 36, 119, 210n3
Wiccan Rede, 7, 11, 131, 198n18
Wiccanings: debates about, 23–24, 180; examples of, 102, 153–155, 171–172, 216n6; purpose of, 23, 108, 156–163, 215n1
Willow, 11, 16
Wilson, Robert Anton, 79
"wise child" motif, 59, 62, 56–66, 68, 158, 159
Wise Ones, the, 54, 121–124, 139
witch hunts, 25, 53–54. *See also* Burning Times, The
witches: self-identification by adults, 48, 49, 74, 77, 80, 83, 142, 143–144; self-identification by children, 10, 45, 178; connection with premodern, 5, 25, 33–34, 50, 53–54, 78; rhetoric of victimization, 54–55
"Witches Next Door, The" (TV episode), 202n43
Witches' Voice, The (website), 18, 98
Woolston-Steen Theological Seminary, 213n25
Wuthnow, Robert, 164

Yeats, William Butler, 34

Zell-Ravenheart, Oberon (Tim), 30

About the Author

S. Zohreh Kermani received a PhD in American religions from Harvard University in 2010. Her research interests include the history of new and alternative religions in the United States and childhood and religion. She currently teaches religious studies part-time at Youngstown State University. She lives in Youngstown, Ohio, with her husband, Dev, and their son, Hank.